KAMET CONQUERED

KAMET CONQUERED

BY

F. S. SMYTHE

Author of
The Kangchenjunga Adventure

"The mystery and thrill of travel is always upon one in the Himalaya, but the mystery is awful and the thrill is sometimes a shudder."

—C. F. Meade

GYAN

Published by

Gyan Publishing House
5, Ansari Road
Daryaganj, New Delhi-110002
Phone: 011-47034999, 9811692060
E-mail: books@gyanbooks.com

Distribution Network
gyanbooks.com
India, USA, Canada, UK, Australia, France

ISBN : 978-81-212-2105-4 (HB)
First Published, 1932

2nd Impression 2021

Printed at: Gyan Press, Delhi.

Kamet Conquered
Author: F. S. Smythe

KAMET CONQUERED

by

F. S. SMYTHE

author of
The Kangchenjunga Adventure

"The mystery and thrill of travel is always upon one in the Himalaya, but the mystery is awful and the thrill is sometimes a shudder."
—C. F. Meade

LONDON
VICTOR GOLLANCZ LTD
14 Henrietta Street Covent Garden
1932

KAMET—THE LAST FEW FEET

To

MY COMPANIONS

CONTENTS

Preface *page* xi

Foreword by Sir Francis Younghusband xv

Chapter I The Himalaya 1

II Kamet 9

III The Conditions of Success 31

IV To Ranikhet 43

V The Foothills 49

VI The Kuari Pass 70

VII To Niti 86

VIII A Stalk after Bharhal 100

IX The Base Camp 105

X Camps One and Two 120

XI Camp Three : The Advanced Base Camp 134

XII Camp Four 147

XIII Camp Five 182

XIV Kamet Conquered 194

XV The Second Ascent 212

XVI The Descent 220

XVII To Gamsali 231

XVIII The Bhyundar Pass and the Valley of Flowers 242

XIX To Mana 254

Chapter XX The Arwa Valley *page* 270
XXI The 20,000 ft. Pass 281
XXII The Avalanche Peak 291
XXIII Sources of the Ganges 307
XXIV Down the Pilgrim Route 319
XXV The Medical Aspects of High Climbing, by Raymond Greene 333
XXVI The Flowers of the Kamet and Badrinath Ranges, by R. L. Holdsworth 348

Appendices

I Short Summary of Expedition 373
II Peaks climbed by the Expedition 378
III The Ascent of Kamet 379
IV Weather 381
V Food 386
VI Equipment 395
VII Photography and Cinematography 406
Index 412
Map *at end*

LIST OF ILLUSTRATIONS

Kamet—the last few feet	*Frontispiece*
Alaknanda River at Nandaprayag	*facing page* 10
Camp Fire	20
Hindu Temple	28
The Expedition at Ranikhet	34
Map—The Approaches to Kamet	43
Lewa	44
Nima Tendrup, the " Old Soldier "	44
Achung, the Cook	44
Nima Dorje	44
Dotial Porters and one of our Gurkha Soldiers	52
Trisul from Gwaldam	60
Between Wan and Kanaul	66
Sunset from Kanaul	68
Path near Ramni	74
The Kuari Pass	82
Dhaoli Valley	88
Niti Gorge	96
Yaks on March	102
Niti	108
Yak	108
Base Camp, 15,500 ft., on Raikana Glacier	114
Local High Camp Porters, Kesar Singh standing on right	114
Above Camp One	126
Sunset from Camp Two	132
Camp Two and East Kamet Glacier	136
The Route above Camp Two	138
Camp Three and Kamet	144
The Precipice between Camps Three and Four	150
The Ice Slope below Camp Four	164

Climbing to Camp Four *facing page* 164
Camp Four, 22,000 ft., and Meade's Col, 23,500 ft. 168
The Ice Wall between Camps Four and Five 182
Between Camps Four and Five 187
The Summit from Camp Five, showing Track of Party 188
View from 25,000 ft. on Kamet 196
The Summit Ridge 202
View from Summit, looking South-East 204
Holdsworth on Summit 204
Shipton on Summit 204
East Kamet Glacier from Summit of Kamet 206
Holdsworth returning from Meade's Col, 23,500 ft. 216
Below Camp Five 216
At Camp Five 216
How the Yaks crossed the Dhaoli River 222
Rope Bridge 234
Village School 238
Bhyundar Valley 250
The Valley of Flowers 252
Pilgrims at Hanuman Chatti 260
The Rawal of Badrinath 264
The Bridge at Badrinath 264
Map—Glaciers and Peaks: Arwa Valley and Tehri Garhwal Watershed 281
Fording the Arwa Torrent 284
Avalanche Peak 298
Where the Ganges falls 308
The Source of the Alaknanda 314
Temple Steps, Badrinath 324
Nilkanta—Moonlight 328
Snow Bridge over Alaknanda 330
Peaks climbed by Holdsworth and Shipton, north of 19,000 ft. Camp 376

PREFACE

IT WOULD be an impossible task to thank here all those whose kindly interest or practical help contributed to the pleasure and success of the Kamet expedition. I should like, however, to express the sincere thanks of the expedition to the Yorkshire Ramblers Club and the Ski Club of Great Britain, who generously contributed towards the expenses of the expedition. I must also express the gratitude of the expedition to the Government of India, who kindly allowed our equipment into India free of customs duty, and to the many officials, especially Mr. N. C. Stiffe, Commissioner for the Kumaun Division, who assisted the expedition in India.

Before leaving England we were the recipients of valuable advice from Mr. C. F. Meade, Mr. H. Ruttledge, Doctor T. G. Longstaff, and Brigadier-General the Hon. C. G. Bruce, all of whom were intimately acquainted with the Kamet district, whilst General Sir William Beynon was instrumental in securing for the expedition two Gurkha N.C.O.s, who were selected by Captain Bradford, Commandant of the Third Gurkha Regiment at Almora.

In India we owe much to the kind help and hospitality of Sir Malcolm Hailey, the Governor of the United Provinces, and to Lady Hailey. In Ranikhet we were entertained by Major and Mrs. Crowe, and elected honorary members of the club there, thanks to the courtesy of the hon. secretary, Major Brown. Transport arrangements were facilitated in Bombay by Mr. Golding and

Mr. Boreham, of the Army and Navy Co-operative Society Ltd., and by Mr. Osler; at Ranikhet by Captain J. Clarke; and at Calcutta by Mr. G. B. Gourlay; whilst Colonel H. W. Tobin selected and despatched porters from Darjeeling. Mr. Browne, Deputy Commissioner for Almora, and Mr. Smythies helped us *en route* to Kamet, and Mrs. Brown helped with arrangements for porterage by writing to the Rawal of Badrinath, who was most useful to the expedition.

It was arranged that the expedition's dispatches should be sent to *The Times*, the *Statesman* of Calcutta, the *New York Times*, the *Asahi* of Japan, and other newspapers.

Thanks to the courtesy of the Indian Posts and Telegraphs, communications between the expedition and England were greatly facilitated, and I should like to express here our gratitude to its officials, especially Mr. Wears Taylor and Mr. Martin.

I should like also to testify here to the efficient work of the two Indian Assistant Commissioners, Hukam Singh Sahib and Ram Singh Sahib, who accompanied and assisted the expedition, and also to the Indian surgeon at Joshimath.

Among a number of firms who helped the expedition the following must be gratefully mentioned:

The Lloyd Triestino Steamship Co., who generously assisted the expedition to and from India.

Messrs. Spencer Ltd. of Calcutta, who supplied a large quantity of foodstuffs to the expedition.

Messrs. Huntley & Palmer Ltd., who supplied a large quantity of biscuits.

Messrs. Wander Ltd., who supplied Ovaltine.

Messrs. the Horlick Malted Milk Co., Ltd., who supplied their products.

Messrs. Nestlé, the Anglo-Swiss Condensed Milk Co. Ltd., who supplied condensed milk and chocolate.

Messrs. Leitz Ltd. of Calcutta, who supplied a " Leica " camera.

Messrs. the Gramophone Co. Ltd. of Calcutta, who supplied a gramophone and records.

Messrs. Kodak Ltd., who supplied photographic materials.

Messrs. Ilford Ltd., who supplied photographic materials.

FOREWORD

THE STRUGGLE of man with the mountain continues apace. Man reels back again and again. But again and again he returns to the onslaught. What is it in the mountain that so allures him ? He knows full well that, in order to stand for a bare half-hour on the summit, he must endure incredible hardships, run most fearsome risks, hazard even his life. Yet nothing daunts him. It would almost seem as though the greater the danger the stronger was the attraction. What is the secret of it ?

Quite certainly it is the power the mountain has to force the best out of man. Man likes to be his best. But often nothing short of a Himalayan peak can extract it from him —can compel him to be his fittest in body, alertest in mind, and firmest in soul. So he is drawn to the mountain. And the mountain makes a man of him. And he is grateful. This is the true secret of the lure of the mountain.

Owing to the reluctance of the Tibetan Government to allow another Mount Everest expedition, the monarch of the mountains has a short reprieve from her inevitable doom. But the first of the seventy peaks of over 25,000 ft. in height has now been conquered by Mr. Smythe and his companions. Every year now, mountaineers from Europe— from Italy, Germany, and England—go forth to the attack of the Himalayan peaks. And we may be certain that giant after giant will be vanquished till the mightiest of them all has lain under the foot of man. We may be certain also that, in pitting himself against the mountain, man will himself have added to his stature and be better able for loftier living.

FRANCIS YOUNGHUSBAND.

CHAPTER I

THE HIMALAYA

TWO HUNDRED years ago mountains were regarded as useless and terrible masses of inert matter where dragons had their lairs and the spirits of the damned lay in wait to claim the unwary. But as man emerged from the superstitions and materialisms of the Middle Ages he began to realise that mountains were beautiful and their summits worthy of attainment. The nineteenth century saw the conquest of the Alps. Unknown difficulties and dangers had to be faced by the pioneers of mountaineering. Disasters occurred, lives were lost, and mountaineering thrown into disrepute. The mountaineer was not dismayed. He knew that beauty was his for the seeking ; he rejoiced in a new-found comradeship, and in the acquirement and exercise of a new craft.

The great Alpine summits fell one by one; traditions were established ; a technique was evolved ; a literature was born. The ripples of Alpine mountaineering radiated outwards, bearing with them mountaineers to other ranges : the Caucasus, the Rockies, the Andes, the New Zealand Alps. On their highest peaks the skill acquired in the Alps was sufficient to ensure success. But there remained one great range that defied invasion of its strongholds—the Himalaya. There, the technique acquired in the Alps was not sufficient. Height alone was a physical deterrent, and coupled to height was steepness and danger. Expeditions had to be organised to reach even the foot of the great peaks, time and money had to be found. Yet, despite these disadvantages, Himalayan mountaineering and exploration progressed steadily. Pioneers such as the Schlagintweit Brothers, Sir Joseph Hooker, The Duke of the Abruzzi, Mr. W. W. Graham, Lord Conway, Sir Francis Younghusband, Mr. D. W. Freshfield, Doctor T. G. Longstaff, Doctor A. M. Kellas, General Bruce, Mr. C. F. Meade, Doctor and Mrs. Bullock Workman, Messrs. Rubenson and Monrad Aas, and many other pre-war pioneers opened up a region unsurpassed for its beauty and grandeur, and by their experiences pointed the way to the highest summits.

Many people refer to the Himalaya as though their limitations in scenery and climate were similar to those of the Alps. The tourist who gazes upon Kangchenjunga, 28,226 ft.,[1] from Darjeeling returns home saying that he has seen the Himalaya. So he has, but how much of two thousand miles of mountains stretching from the Pamirs to the borders of Indo-China, and beyond these limits, in terms of mountains ? A lifetime might be spent wandering about the Himalaya, yet the knowledge acquired would embrace but an infinitesimal portion of that vast labyrinth of peaks, valleys and plateaux scrawled across the map of Asia.

In climate alone there is an extraordinary variety. From hot steamy tropical valleys, filled with luxuriant vegetation, it is but a few horizontal miles to zero temperatures and the highest snows in the world. Between these two extremes is an immense range of climate, the common despot of which is a fierce sun. Added to the complexities of climate

[1] Heights given are latest measurements. See also p. 4.

due to height alone is the added complexity of seasonal weather fluctuations, due directly or indirectly to the influence of the monsoons and weather conditions emanating from the plateaux of Central Asia.

Racial characteristics are as diversified as the climate. From the people of Hunza and Chitral to the Sherpas and Bhotias of Northern Nepal, the almost extinct Lepchas of Sikkim and the wild races of Bhutan, the Himalaya can show many different types, for they form a natural frontier between India and Tibet, and a pudding-bowl wherein is stirred a mixture of Mongolian and Indian blood.

Politically, only a comparatively small portion of the Himalaya is accessible to the mountaineer and explorer. Democracy is unknown in Tibet and Nepal, and both these countries have closed their frontiers to Europeans and resolutely set themselves against infiltration of European thought and ideas. Some of the finest peaks of the Himalaya lie within the borders of Nepal, including the southern side of Everest, 29,140 ft., Dhaulagiri, 26,795 ft., Gosainthan, 26,305 ft., and many other great peaks. In addition there are other districts where the mountaineer is not always welcomed, owing to political and other objections. The three most interesting districts accessible to mountaineers and explorers are the Karakorams, the Kumaun and Garhwal Himalaya and the Sikkim Himalaya, including the eastern side of Kangchenjunga, and it is in these three districts that the most notable mountaineering expeditions have been carried out, with the exception of Everest, which is now barred politically, and the northern side of Nanga Parbat, which is forbidden territory to expeditions at present. Each of these districts is magnificent in its own way. In the Karakoram there is no glacier to rival in grandeur the Baltoro, and no peaks surpassing in ferocity the terrific ice-armoured spires dominated by K2 (Mount Godwin Austin), 28,187 ft. From the Kumaun Himalaya rises Nanda Devi, the highest peak entirely within the confines of the British Empire, a mountain so difficult to approach that no one has yet succeeded in treading the glaciers at the foot of it, whilst Kamet, 25,447 ft., dominates the ranges of Northern Garhwal. In Sikkim, Kangchenjunga boasts the most wonderful snow and ice scenery in the Himalaya, owing to its exposure to the moisture-laden airs of the monsoon. It has defeated three determined attempts to climb it, in 1929, 1930 and 1931, by mountaineers well versed in the technique of high-altitude mountaineering. The highest point reached was 26,000 ft., by the gallant Bavarian expedition in 1931, and that only after incredible difficulty.[1]

Geologically, the Himalaya are a young mountain range, due to an uplift of the ancient sea-bed covering Central Asia. This uplift took place so slowly that rivers such as the Indus and the Brahmaputra, which have their sources to the north of the Himalaya, have been able to carve their way through the range as it rose. This is the only explanation that can account for the deep valleys cutting through from Tibet to India. According to geologists, the uplift is still proceeding, but whether or not it is taking place at a greater speed than the lowering of the peaks by weathering is a matter for conjecture. Owing to

[1] The former measurement of Kangchenjunga was 28,156 ft., and that of K2, 28,250 ft. The latest measurements of these mountains are Kangchenjunga, 28,006 ft., K2, 28,187 ft.; the difference is so negligible and so dependent on the perfect accuracy of instruments, and even upon fluctuating snowfall, that it is best to assume equality in height.

their geological youth, the Himalaya have not weathered as have the Alps. Their peaks are often wedge-like in form, wall-sided, and with incipient ridges and buttresses. This formation is unsatisfactory from the mountaineer's standpoint, for it too often means that a summit cannot be reached by following a continuous ridge. A ridge is always the safest way up a mountain, and the modern Alpine-trained mountaineer soon realises this triusm in the Himalaya. It is a humbling experience, after climbing steep and difficult Alpine mountain-sides, to be confronted with a Himalayan giant. Putting aside the peculiar difficulties of altitude, the mountaineer finds himself confronted by difficulties and dangers which can only be described as appalling in their frequency and magnitude.

The difficulties are due primarily to sheer length and steepness. In addition, ice-ridges are formed such as are never seen in the Alps, ridges so thin and steep that the sun may be seen gleaming through them many feet below their crests.

The principal dangers are avalanches and bad weather. Owing to an immense range of temperature,[1] Himalayan ice is more plastic in its consistency than Alpine ice, and it can adhere to mountain-sides at an extraordinary angle. This ice is the product of countless snowfalls which go to form hanging glaciers. These glaciers are frequently hundreds of feet thick, and on peaks such as Kangchenjunga may exceed 1,000 ft. Every hollow in the mountain-side is plastered with them ; gravity is ever dragging them downwards—a movement accelerated by snowfalls

[1] A temperature of 219° F. direct sun heat has been observed (*Alpine Journal*, vol. xxiv., p. 141), whilst at night it may fall to – 30° F. or lower—a range of about 250° F.

accumulating above them. When these hanging glaciers come to the edge of a precipice, they overhang it and then break away in masses of ice weighing tens of thousands of tons that crash with appalling force down the precipices and sweep the whole breadth of the main glaciers beneath. The mountaineer must discover a route, both in approaching the foot of the mountain and on the mountain itself, that is not exposed to this danger. In the Alps a chance is sometimes taken, even on standard routes, but in the Himalaya a chance should never be taken, for Himalayan ice avalanches are cataclysmic in their magnitude. It must be remembered, too, that where a portion of an Alpine route is exposed to falling ice the risk of traversing it is not taken more than once, or at the most twice, on an expedition. In the Himalaya, however, it might be necessary to take the risk every day for weeks on end. Unless a line of communication from the base camp to the high camps on the mountain can be found that is free of this danger, the route is unjustifiable.

And then, there is the weather—the incalculable factor in mountaineering. If Himalayan weather was as consistently treacherous and evil as Alpine weather, few parties would return alive from the great peaks. The Alpine mountaineer benighted in a storm and forced to bivouac has a chance of survival, but the Himalayan mountaineer knows that to bivouac without protection in bad weather at a great altitude can have but one ending. At mid-day the sun's rays at great altitudes are sometimes almost paralysing in their intensity, but when the sun has set a coldness akin to the coldness of space comes to the upper world. In the Alps, mountaineering is a sport. The mountaineer starts from a hotel and ascends to a hut. The following day he climbs his mountain, and returns to the hut or the hotel. In the Himalayas he may have to march weeks to get to the foot of his mountain ; then he may spend weeks in climbing his mountain. If it is a mountain such as Kangchenjunga, the chances are in favour of him returning defeated to Europe. It is not really fair to compare Alpine mountaineering with Himalayan mountaineering ; they are so different that comparison is liable to become odious, but it is the only possible and understandable comparison. Had it not been for the Alps, a great deal of what has been accomplished in the Himalaya would not have been accomplished. For, even though the mountaineer in the Himalaya must readjust his ideas if he would climb safely and successfully, the knowledge he has acquired on Alpine peaks will be invaluable to him. But let him beware of approaching the Himalaya with preconceived and bigoted notions, for not only will he find conditions that are unintelligible to him until he has learnt to understand them, but he is liable, on the strength of his Alpine knowledge, to under-estimate the dangers. An Alpine mountaineer walking up to the Concordia hut along the eastern bank of the Aletsch Glacier does not expect to be blotted out of existence by an ice avalanche falling from the cliffs of the Dreieckhorn, a mile away on the opposite side of the glacier, yet if the Aletsch Glacier was under the hanging glaciers of Kangchenjunga or Nanga Parbat, this is what he would have to expect. Such things are not to be learned by trial and error, they should be assumed beforehand, and heed taken of the experiences of others.

The Himalaya must be approached humbly. Respect their beauty, their majesty, and their power, and they will treat you as you deserve : approach them ignorantly or in a spirit of bravado, and they will destroy you. Other mountains forgive mistakes, but not the Himalaya.

CHAPTER II

KAMET

THE PRIMARY object of the Kamet Expedition, 1931, was the ascent of Kamet, 25,447 ft., the great peak in the Central Himalaya; and the secondary object, exploration in the Badrinath Himalaya to the west of Kamet, which form the watershed of the Gangotri and Alaknanda Rivers, the two parent tributaries of the Ganges.

Kamet has known various names. The Schlagintweit brothers, who in 1855 were the first to attempt its ascent, referred to it as the Central Ibi Gamin; it has been called Kangmen by surveyors, whilst it is known to the Tibetans as Kangmed (the "Lower Snows"), as distinct from the "Higher Snows" of Kailas, in Tibet, 110 miles east of Kamet, although this last range is lower than Kamet, the highest peak being Gurla Mandhata, 25,355 ft.

Strictly speaking, Kamet does not rise from the main Himalayan Chain, but is the culminating point of the Zaskar Range, which forms a northern bifurcation. It is situated in the extreme north of British Garhwal, on the watershed of the Upper Alaknanda and Dhaoli Rivers, and its summit is one mile south of the Tibetan border between the Mana and Niti Passes, which are traversed by trade routes between British India and Tibet.

Climatically, the mountain lies on the borderline between the dry westerly Tibetan winds and the area invaded by the Indian monsoon: it receives a heavy precipitation of snow during the winter months, but during the summer months, although subject to local bad weather, it is struck by an attenuated monsoon. Much of the monsoon moisture is precipitated on the intervening foothills, the Zaskar Range to the south of Kamet, and the main Himalayan chain; but the Upper Alaknanda Valley and the Dhaoli Valley form funnels for the warm moisture-charged airs that survive their passage of the foothills or penetrate the Lower Alaknanda Valley, and it is left to the dry Tibetan westerly winds to exercise a sheering effect on the clouds and evaporate their moisture.

Snowfalls during the summer months, comparable to those of Kangchenjunga, 570 miles south-east of Kamet, are unknown, whilst winds seldom persist for long or rival in remorseless ferocity those that assail Everest, 500 miles to the south-east. Even during the height of the monsoon season, fine spells, when the hot Tibetan sun blazes down from cloudless skies, are common.

Another reason for Kamet's equable weather, as compared to that of Everest or Kangchenjunga, is that deep, hot tropical valleys do not lie close to the mountain, and convection air currents are therefore less strong.

In scenery and climate Garhwal is comparable to Switzerland at its best, and no district in the Himalaya can show scenery combining such tender beauties and savage grandeurs. From valleys carpeted in Alpine flowers and lined with noble pine forests, the traveller passes through gorges of terrific aspect, where eagles wheel aloft, and the dark knees of the peaks bend down towards thundering glacier torrents. Then, in a few horizontal miles, he climbs up to the snows, where peaks unknown

ALAKNANDA RIVER AT NANDAPRAYAG

and unnamed stand watch and ward over untrodden glaciers.

A simple, friendly people inhabit the upper valleys of Garhwal, varying in race from the Hindu to the Mongolian, a mixture of blood due to the linking of Garhwal to Tibet by the Niti and Mana Passes. Fate, if not choice, has decreed their existence to be a nomadic one. In the winter months, when snow and avalanches render impassable the upper valleys, they are forced to descend to lower and warmer levels, but, when the snows melt, they return to their primitive villages and pastures with their flocks of yaks, sheep, and goats, bearing grain, wool, cloth, and other commodities, which they barter with the Tibetans for salt, borax, and ornaments, of which they are inordinately fond.

Kamet, as the crow flies, is some ninety miles from the Indian hill station of Ranikhet, and nearly as far from Ranikhet's sister station Almora. Seen from these hill stations, it appears as an insignificant point, just peeping over the intervening foothill ranges, and not to be compared in size or magnificence with the main Himalayan Chain, that culminates in the great peak of Nanda Devi, 25,645 ft., 198 ft. higher than Kamet, and the highest mountain entirely within the British Empire. Seen, however, from the Kuari Pass, other elevated points of the higher foothills, the valley of the Sutlej, and Tibet, its majestic pyramidal peak of reddish granitic schist forms a towering landmark.

Kamet is the highest of a group of four peaks which, ranged in order from north to south, are : the Western Ibi Gamin, 24,200 ft. ; the Eastern Ibi Gamin, 24,170 ft. ; Kamet, 25,447 ft. ; and the Mana Peak, 23,860 ft.

Owing to Kamet's apparent insignificance when viewed from the Indian side, it remained unmeasured until 1848, when Richard Strachey determined trigonometrically the height and position of its four peaks. The mountain was not again visited by Europeans until 1855. In the August of that year, however, a resolute attempt to climb it was made by the brothers Adolphe and Robert Schlagintweit, of the Magnetic Survey of India. Approaching from Tibet they ascended the Ibi Gamin Glacier. Their highest camp was at 19,325 ft., and from this they reached an altitude of no less than 22,239 ft., after bivouacking continuously for ten days at altitudes over 17,000 ft. Theirs was an amazing performance, especially if it be remembered that at that date many of the great Alpine peaks had not been climbed, and not for another nine years was this altitude surpassed. One thing, however, is certain ; the mountain the Schlagintweits attempted was not, strictly speaking, Kamet, but the Eastern Ibi Gamin, for to climb Kamet from the Tibetan side would be impossible without first traversing that mountain.

Three weeks later, Adolphe Schlagintweit made a panoramic drawing of the Kamet group from the Boko La, fifty-seven miles distant in Tibet, yet, although he correctly delineated the Eastern and Western Ibi Gamin, as well as Kamet itself, he apparently did not realise his original mistake. It was, however, a natural mistake, for the traveller approaching from Tibet cannot see Kamet, as it is hidden behind the Eastern Ibi Gamin.

No further expedition of importance to Kamet appears to have taken place until the survey of it under Mr. E. C. Ryall, of the Survey of India, in 1877. Kamet was then accurately fixed both for position and height, but the earlier trigonometrical observations relating to the Eastern and Western Ibi Gamin being considered doubtful, were rejected, and both those peaks remained unmeasured for some time.

During a topographical survey, Mr. I. S. Pocock, of the Survey of India, set up his plane table at 22,040 ft. As he approached from the Mana or western side of the group, his route must have lain up the slopes of the Eastern or Western Ibi Gamin. He reported that from the Mana side the illusion that the Eastern Ibi Gamin is merely an excrescence on the northern ridge of Kamet is extraordinarily strong.

No further attempt or reconnaissance of Kamet was made until 1907, when Doctor T. G. Longstaff, Major (now Brigadier-General) the Honourable C. G. Bruce, and Mr. A. L. Mumm, made a preliminary reconnaissance from both the Niti (east) and the Mana (west) sides. This expedition was fully reported in the *Alpine Journal*, vol. xxiv., page 125 *et seq.*, and the *Geographical Journal*, vol. xxxi., p. 379 *et seq.* After a preliminary excursion up the Raikana Glacier, Doctor Longstaff and General Bruce started to reconnoitre Kamet, taking with them the Italian guides Alexis and Henri Brocherel, six Gurkhas, and ten coolies.

Crossing the Raikana Glacier from their base camp, which they had pitched at 15,350 ft., they ascended the East Kamet Glacier and made a camp at 16,800 ft. on its north lateral moraine. A mile beyond this point the East Kamet Glacier narrows abruptly and becomes little more than an ice-filled gorge, less than half a mile wide. The glacier is bounded on its southern side by a steep wall of peaks, that culminates in the Mana Peak, 23,860 ft. Every hollow and shelf in this wall is filled with hanging glaciers hundreds of feet thick, which appear ready to discharge ice avalanches of appalling magnitude at any moment across the whole breadth of the East Kamet Glacier beneath.

As Doctor Longstaff considered the direct ascent of the glacier too dangerous, the party turned sharply to the north-west up steep moraine-clad slopes to the north of the glacier. This landed them on a glacier of a secondary order, which they followed upwards towards a snowy saddle at its head. They hoped that this saddle would prove the key to the situation, and lead them on to the slopes of Kamet. Mist enveloped them, but they pushed on up steep snow-slopes to the saddle, 20,180 ft. On their arrival, the mist cleared somewhat, and they saw below them the upper portion of the East Kamet Glacier, winding down from the foot of Kamet. But disappointment awaited them ; they found themselves completely cut off from the slopes of Kamet by impracticable precipices, and what they saw of the East Kamet Glacier confirmed their opinion that it is " horribly dangerous, lying in so narrow a gorge that it would be quite impossible to escape the ice avalanches which constantly fall on to it."

As the party considered it useless to attempt Kamet from the east, they decided to cross the Zaskar Range to the Alaknanda Valley. Utilising and re-opening the Bhyundar Kanta Pass, 16,700 ft., and the Khanta Khal Pass, 14,750 ft., they reached the Bhotia village of Mana, to the west of Kamet. Thence, they ascended the Khaiam Glacier for some little distance, and climbed to the summit of a peak of 17,550 ft. They experienced very bad weather, with high winds and frequent snowstorms, and their reconnaissance was cut short by the breaking of the monsoon rains on July 23.

One result of their reconnaissance was that they came to the conclusion that the Khaiam Glacier was the most likely approach to Kamet.

It is interesting to note that during the same summer, and prior to this reconnaissance, Doctor Longstaff made his memorable ascent of Trisul, 23,406 ft., which, until the ascent of the Jonsong Peak, 24,344 ft., in 1930 by Professor Dyhrenfurth's expedition, was the highest actual summit attained.

Unfortunately, no complete record exists of the determined attempts made to climb Kamet by the late Captain A. Morris Slingsby, of the 56th Frontier Force Rifles, who was killed in 1916 at the head of his regiment in Mesopotamia. He bid fair to be a great mountaineer, and, had he lived, would undoubtedly have achieved much in the Himalaya. As few will have read the account of his attempt in vol. iv. of the *Yorkshire Ramblers' Club Journal*, I make no excuse for quoting it.

With Captain (now Lieut.-Colonel) H. Ch. de Crespigny he set off from Ranikhet early in May 1911 with eighty coolies, carrying stores for two and a half months. It was an exceptionally late winter, and at Badrinath the party were delayed for two weeks owing to no Bhotia coolies being available.

Early in June, however, they set off up the Ghastoli Glacier with ten picked coolies, who were well provided for with warm clothing, sleeping-bags, and boots. They camped at 15,500 ft., and next day continued on up the

Glacier, having to toil knee deep through soft snow. They were overcome by mountain sickness, and had to halt and camp at a height of 18,000 ft. They gave up all idea of reaching the col below Kamet at which they were aiming, and returned to Ghastoli with their stores.

A day spent in a comfortable camp aided acclimatisation, and Slingsby set out again with six coolies and double-marched up to the 18,000 ft. camp in eight hours.

Next day he left the camp at 6 a.m. for the col between the Eastern and Western Ibi Gamin, confident that the former peak was merely a minor pinnacle on a continuous ridge leading to the summit of Kamet. He now felt very fit, and the coolies also were going well. After two hours' walking, the foot of steep slopes leading up to the col was reached. The party found themselves standing in a snow-field almost surrounded by an amphitheatre of ice, snow, and ice-covered rocks, cleft by gullies stretching up to the col some 1,500 ft. above them.

The slopes to the col were very steep, but a thin covering of frozen snow over the ice sufficed for footholds and saved them the exertion of step-cutting. At last, however, step-cutting became necessary.

A thick mist enshrouded them, and the Bhotia coolies became tired and dispirited : after three hours' climbing, all but one were weeping bitterly and declaring that they could go no farther. They did not, however, dare to retreat, as Slingsby had taken off the rope. By way of cheering them up, he let them sit down, and went on ahead by himself to cut steps. He got above the snow, and had to climb steep ice. The rocks also were sheeted with ice, and the whole burden of chipping this off and making footholds fell upon him. At intervals of a hundred feet he halted to fix the rope round an ice-axe or a rock and threw it down to the coolies, who, utilising it as a handrail, hauled themselves up one by one.

It was very slow work. Thick mist made it difficult to keep to the route that had been mapped out from below, and it was essential that this route should be adhered to owing to falling stones. As Slingsby wrote, " We went on slowly like this, until, after ascending about 1,000 ft., we came to more rocks and ice, where we had to cross over to the main gully, and, after getting across it, climbed up by its easterly side. I had hoped the abundance of rocks would have made it easier, but they only added to the labour, for they were all covered with ice so hard that even at noon it was only with difficulty that I could chip off enough to get a foothold. Each coolie had to be carefully watched, for there would have been little hope of saving anyone who slipped, as there was nothing over which to hitch the rope. They were now very tired, dread of the unknown adding to their physical weariness, and it was only with the greatest difficulty that with the help of Gulab Khan, after nine hours spent in climbing some 1,500 ft., we reached the top of the col (21,000 ft.) at 6.30 p.m., as the day was drawing to a close. The place was so steep that it was only with difficulty that I found a site for our Mummery tents. One coolie, overcome with weariness, sat down and, slipping his arms from the rope by which he held his load, stood up. Immediately, and without warning, the load slid away before he could stop it and went bumping down to the bottom of the gully, where we found it the next day."

In reaching this col, Slingsby had accomplished a

splendid piece of mountaineering. His account in the *Yorkshire Ramblers' Club Journal* continues :

" After settling down in camp, I went on to the top of the pass and got a glimpse of Kamet and the country to the north. The mists slid away, and the panorama before me was magnificent. Just below the corniced slope of the col, a very high glacier, starting from the north-west side of Kamet, stretched away at our feet and curved gradually north until it merged in the low grey hills of the distant Sutlej Valley. Beyond, the untrodden summits of the Kailas Mountains rose tier after tier up into the skies, girt here and there with long straight lines of hovering clouds, which seemed to add considerably to their height. Turning from this vast upland view of Tibet, I looked eastwards on Kamet. From the col, a long snow-slope swept up to a great rock tower, itself a minor peak, some 2,000 ft. above me, from which, if it were climbed, it would be necessary to drop down many hundreds of feet before again commencing to climb up the slopes of Kamet itself. By going more to the east, however, and avoiding it altogether, it would, I believe, be possible to get on to a long continuous snow-slope, and so to the top of Kamet. What manner of hidden crevasses lie between the col and this slope I cannot say, but the snow, of course, gets the full effect of the sun at the early dawn, and here undoubtedly would be the greatest difficulty. To the south and west were countless small peaks, and here and there a larger one that raised its head above its fellows, their eternal snows flushing pale yellow in the rays of the setting sun. As I gazed on this sea of peaks, as yet untrodden by man, the last parting rays of the sun lit up their upper slopes, the wind dropped, the peaks grew dim beneath the twinkling stars, the avalanches from Kamet ceased, and over all a great stillness reigned.

"Next morning, after a cold but windless night, I tried to get the coolies to come on, but they had all been somewhat affected by the altitude and their exertions of the previous day, and only one would accompany me. Though the reward of our efforts had seemed so close at hand, even within our grasp, I now began to realise that I could not go on and leave the coolies where they were, for they would surely have died. With the obstinacy of despair, I went on for about two hours, to a height of, I suppose, some 22,000 ft., and then returned to camp. The snow was very soft, and this served to confirm my misgivings of the previous evening and the effect it would have had on our further progress."

Retreat was imperative, and Slingsby returned to Ghastoli. Thus ended a gallant attempt to climb Kamet. If Slingsby had had expert Darjeeling porters with him, he would in all probability have reached the summit of the Eastern Ibi Gamin. He seemed to realise that this peak was a separate entity and that it would have been necessary to have descended many hundreds of feet before the ascent could have been resumed. Actually, a descent of over 700 ft. from the summit of the Eastern Ibi Gamin to the col between it and Kamet would have been necessary.

It is even doubtful whether the summit above him was the summit of the Eastern Ibi Gamin. His proposal to go to the east and avoid the Eastern Ibi Gamin shows that he was misled by the nature of the ground. Such a traverse would have been quite impracticable, whilst a traverse across the western face would have been equally impracticable.

Any party approaching Kamet from Slingsby's Col would be bound to traverse the summit of Eastern Ibi Gamin. Such a traverse would be a very long one, and would involve at least another two camps above Slingsby's highest camp, whilst the position of a party exhausted on the final slopes of Kamet, or caught there, or on the col between Kamet and the Eastern Ibi Gamin, by bad weather, and faced with a re-ascent over the latter mountain, would be precarious in the extreme.

Undeterred by his reverse, this determined mountaineer returned to the attack during May and early June 1913. The same route was adhered to, but he was again dogged by bad luck. As before, he had difficulty in persuading the local coolies to accompany him at high altitudes; the weather was bad, and finally, a severe snowstorm put an end to his climb at a height of over 23,000 ft.

The credit for the eventual conquest of Kamet belongs to Mr. C. F. Meade, for he solved the perplexing problem as to the right route, and would undoubtedly have reached the summit had not luck been against him.

In 1910, Meade, with the Italian guide Alexis Brocherel and the French guide Pierre Blanc, prospected the western side of Kamet. They experienced very bad weather, and accomplished but little with the exception of an ascent of the Khaiam Glacier to the Khaiam Pass, 19,300 ft.

In 1912, Meade returned to the attack, this time with four Alpine guides, Pierre Blanc, Franz Lochmatter, Justin Blanc and Jean Perrin.

The party left Mana on May 26, and two days later

CAMP FIRE

established their base camp on the Ghastoli Glacier. On May 31 they advanced a camp to 18,000 ft. near the foot of the slopes leading to Slingsby's Col. Bad weather intervened, however, and enforced retreat to the base camp. The weather mending, they returned to their 18,000 ft. camp, and on June 5 ascended to Slingsby's Col in three and a half hours. Like Slingsby, they found the slopes of snow above the col in very bad condition, and were not able to push their camp to a greater height than 21,000 ft. Next day, June 6, they continued to advance, finding the going very exhausting in the soft snow, but they struggled on to a height of over 23,000 ft. Deteriorating weather and mountain sickness again rendered retreat imperative. Fifty-two degrees of frost were registered that night.

They returned to Mana, but on June 19 again set out for Kamet, this time without Franz Lochmatter and Jean Perrin, who had to return to Europe to fulfil engagements. On June 20 they reached Slingsby's Col. Snow again fell, rendering the slopes exceedingly dangerous. Retreat down the steep face below Slingsby's Col under such conditions was no easy matter, but the descent was skilfully accomplished without accident.

Although he ascended but little higher than Slingsby, Meade was convinced by what he saw that the Eastern Ibi Gamin was not a mere spur or point on a ridge leading to Kamet, but a separate and formidable peak. The view he obtained of the Raikana Glacier system also convinced him that, if there was a practicable route at all up Kamet, it must be sought for on the eastern and not the western side of the mountain.

Before crossing to the eastern side of the mountain, he

carried out an interesting exploration up the Satopanth and Bhagat Kharak glaciers, from the combined snouts of which issues the sacred Alaknanda River, the source of the Ganges. In both cases he discovered passes from the heads of these glaciers, a pass across the range from the head of the Satopanth Glacier leading to the Kedarnath Valley system, and a pass from near the head of the Bhagat Kharak Glacier, which appeared to lead into the head of the great Gangotri Glacier, which is about twenty miles long. He then explored a pass from the ice-filled valley above Mana from which flows the Kulhia Ganga. This pass he crossed without difficulty, and descended into the Bhyundar Valley, and, ascending to the Bhyundar Kanta Pass, 16,700 ft., descended to the Dhaoli Valley and Niti.

During July, he thoroughly explored the Raikana Glacier system to the east of Kamet, becoming convinced from what he saw that the only solution of the problem of ascending Kamet was to traverse the East Kamet Glacier, the route which Doctor Longstaff had so uncompromisingly condemned on account of the danger from ice avalanches.

In 1913, Meade proceeded with Pierre Blanc to test his theory. By this time, thanks to their tactful handling by former expeditions, experienced and willing porters, who had lost much of their fear of the heights, were available from Bhotia villages such as Niti and Mana. Meade established his base camp on the Raikana Glacier and Camp One in the same position where Dr. Longstaff pitched his camp. From Camp One he proceeded up the narrow trench-like East Kamet Glacier. Though very forbidding in appearance, this glacier did not prove so dangerous as it looked, and no ice avalanches menaced the party. Camp Two was pitched in a safe place at 18,500 ft., and Camp Three at about 20,600 ft. Above Camp Three the party's difficulties began. It was only after some difficult rock-climbing and heavy step-cutting in steep ice that they were able to gain easier slopes and pitch their fourth camp at about 22,000 ft. This was their highest camp. They had hoped to establish another camp on the broad and easy col, 23,500 ft., now known as Meade's Col, between Kamet and the Eastern Ibi Gamin, but, although they reached the col, they were unable to pitch a camp there, and were beaten by the weather and the terrible snow conditions. In addition to these troubles, they were not properly acclimatised to altitude, and suffered also from lassitude induced by the fierce glare of the sun.

Meade had accomplished great work. He had discovered the only practicable route up Kamet. From his highest point he saw that no insuperable obstacle intervened between him and the summit. That success should have eluded him at the last moment was cruel luck. Had he realised the importance of acclimatisation, and had the weather and snow conditions been better, there is no doubt that he would have gained the summit.

Owing to the war, no further attempt was made on Kamet until 1920. In that year Doctor A. M. Kellas, who died the following year while engaged on the first Mount Everest Expedition, and Colonel H. T. Morshead, who was foully murdered in Burma in the summer of 1931, left Niti on August 29 with twenty-one yaks and forty porters. They established their base camp on the Raikana Glacier on August 31.

Owing to lack of acclimatisation and the incidence of malaria, they did not advance up the East Kamet Glacier until September 3. Having established Camp One, they were delayed owing to transport difficulties, and it was not until September 8 that Camp Two was established. Here Kellas's servant was incapacitated through an accidental night out.

Their third camp was established on September 11. There they were delayed for another week by transport difficulties. The weather was fine, but very cold, temperatures below zero being registered. Owing to the effects of altitude and cold, their remaining servants were unable to go higher.

On September 19 they climbed the steep rocks and ice above Camp Three and camped at 22,000 ft. After a rest day for acclimatisation, they ascended to Meade's Col, 23,500 ft., with three Mana porters. They left their camp at 9 a.m., and reached the col at 3 p.m. From the col they pushed on for a short distance up the final slope of Kamet, and at 3.30 p.m. had attained an altitude estimated at 23,600 ft. This was their highest point. They were well acclimatised to altitude, and were fully fit enough to make an attempt on the summit, but their coolies flatly refused to continue on Kamet, or even to attempt the Eastern Ibi Gamin, which seemed feasible. It was essential to establish a camp in the neighbourhood of Meade's Col, but the coolies refused to carry up their tents, equipment, and food from Camp Four.

Several reasons contributed to the coolies' lack of heart. They suffered from headaches, the stuffing was knocked out of them by a cold wind, and they were terrified by the thought that the first winter snowstorms were due. Another reason for the party's defeat—a small reason but a vital one—was the failure of their paraffin cooking stove to vaporise in the thin air of over 20,000 ft. Thus they were unable to cook for themselves or their coolies.

It is interesting to note the time taken by the party to ascend from their base camp to their highest point. No less than eighteen days were occupied in making the ascent. This was largely due to transport difficulties, and it is doubtful whether Doctor Kellas intended to spend so long a time on the mountain before making an attempt on the summit. Yet, I believe that his experiences on the many, other Himalayan peaks that he had previously ascended had taught him the value of slow upward progression at great altitudes. Meade and Slingsby both suffered from the effects of altitude, but Kellas and Morshead were not seriously inconvenienced, and, had it not been for difficulties other than those of the actual mountain and its height, they might have reached the summit.

Doctor Kellas, besides being a great mountaineer, was a clever physicist and had contributed many valuable papers to various learned societies on the problems of acclimatisation. On this occasion he took with him oxygen apparatus in order to carry out various experiments, and it was the non-arrival of this apparatus from England that delayed his attempt on Kamet. I think it may be assumed, therefore, that, unlike other parties that had attempted to climb Kamet, he realised the importance of besieging the mountain and of acclimatising at each camp before pushing on to the next camp.

No further attempt was made to climb Kamet until the present expedition in 1931.

From the foregoing it will be seen that ten expeditions

prior to 1931 prospected routes on the mountain or attempted to climb it. No other great Himalayan peak has received so much attention by mountaineers. For the convenience of the reader, I append the following table setting out these reconnaissances and attempts.

As regards the secondary object of the expedition, explorations in the Badrinath Range to the east of Kamet, which forms the watershed of the Alaknanda and Gangotri Rivers, the two parent tributaries of the Ganges, this possessed both human and topographical interest. What the Jordan was to the Jews, the Ganges is to the Hindus, for it irrigates and fertilises the northern plain of India and brings sustenance to millions of Indians. Because of this it is revered by all Hindus. As it flows past the sacred city of Benares it receives the living and the dead—the living, who enter it to be cleansed of their sins, and the dead, whose ashes are taken from the burning ghats and cast upon its waters. Yet, the devout Hindu does not consider himself to have completed his religious devotions by a visit to Benares ; he must make a pilgrimage to Kedarnath and Badrinath and pay his respects to the holy and eternal snows whence the Ganges flows from the feet of the gods. Fifty thousand pilgrims toil annually to these places, of which Badrinath is the holier place and the seat of the Rawal, the high-priest and the keeper of the temple.

Benares can be reached by train, but not so Kedarnath and Badrinath ; the pilgrim must brave the heat and disease of the lower Himalayan valleys, and finally the freezing airs from the snows, before he can accomplish his pilgrimage. Some fall by the wayside, and many more perish of cholera, dysentery, typhoid, malaria and other

Expedition	*Year*	*Route*	*Highest Point*
A. and R. Schlagintweit	1855	Tibetan side up Ibi Gamin Glacier and East Ibi Gamin.	22,239 ft.
Dr. T. G. Longstaff and Brig.-General C. G. Bruce and A. L. Mumm with Alpine guides Alexis and Henri Brocherel	1907	Preliminary reconnaissance eastern and western sides. Highest point reached was above East Kamet Glacier.	20,180 ft.
C. F. Meade with Alpine guides Alexis Brocherel and Pierre Blanc	1910	Preliminary reconnaissance western side: Khaiam Glacier and Khaiam Pass.	19,300 ft.
Dr. A. M. Kellas	1911	Preliminary reconnaissance western side: Khaiam Glacier, Khaiam Pass, and peak north of Khaiam.	20,200 ft.
Capt. A. M. Slingsby	1911	Attempted Kamet on western side from Ghastoli Glacier via col between East and West Ibi Gamin.	22,000 ft.
C. F. Meade with Alpine guides Pierre Blanc, Franz Lochmatter, Justin Blanc and Jean Perrin	1912	Attempted Kamet by same route as Slingsby.	23,000 ft.
Capt. A. M. Slingsby	1913	Attempted Kamet by same route as before.	23,000 ft.
C. F. Meade with Alpine guide Pierre Blanc	1913	Attempted Kamet from eastern side via East Kamet Glacier and reached col between Kamet and East Ibi Gamin.	23,500 ft.
Dr. A. M. Kellas	1914	Another reconnaissance of which no record was published.	—
Dr. A. M. Kellas and Colonel H. T. Morshead	1920	Same route as Meade's 1913 route.	23,600 ft.

NOTE.—The above list does not include the early reconnaissances of Strachey and the Survey of India.

tropical diseases. Yet, the greater the tribulation and the immolation the greater the virtue and the forgiveness. To gaze at the sacred image in the temple at Badrinath and purify the body by dipping it into the icy glacier waters of the Alaknanda River is worthy of much toil and suffering.

Unimaginative is he who can gaze upon the Himalaya from the lower foothills or the plains, and not sympathise with the simple, child-like adoration of the Hindus for the eternal reservoirs of snow, the gods of which despatch Mother Ganges to minister to their needs. Dull indeed is he who can gaze unmoved upon the snows—when the maiden of dawn fires them, and the great peaks glow above the slumbering plains.

The explorer and mountaineer who visits northern Garhwal will find much to interest him in the religious mysticism, mythology and folk-lore associated with these holy snows of Himachal.[1] Parties of explorers and mountaineers have been few and far between in this district, and a wealth of virgin peaks and glaciers remain to be climbed and explored. The upper reaches of the Gangotri Glacier, which is not only the greatest glacier in the district, but one of the greatest glaciers east of the Karakoram Himalaya,[2] are unexplored. The Indian Survey map, painstakingly accurate and uniformly excellent in its delineation of the main valleys and ranges of Garhwal, is vague and sketchy in its delineation of the labyrinth of peaks and glaciers between the Gangotri and Alaknanda Rivers. The most ambitious explorations in this range were

[1] Himalaya.

[2] Possibly the greatest, unless there are glaciers of greater magnitude in Nepal.

HINDU TEMPLE

those undertaken by Mr. C. F. Meade in 1912. Although he only descended a few hundred feet on the western side of the range from his pass at the head of the Satopanth Glacier, he could see that the way was not difficult. The discovery of this pass is of particular interest in view of an existing legend that pilgrims in former times, when visiting Badrinath and Kedarnath, used to take a short cut across the range instead of making, as they do now, a long roundabout journey via Joshimath and Chamoli. Meade, however, is of the opinion that the pass is not a practicable one for pilgrims, for it is about 20,000 ft. high, and its traverse necessitates mountaineering knowledge. Having seen for myself the pitifully underclad, shivering pilgrims who toil up to Badrinath, I am inclined to agree with him. Yet, in India, a land of strange and subtle changes, both progressive and retrogressive, anything is possible, and it is not inconceivable that in bygone years a hardier type of pilgrim existed who thought nothing of crossing 20,000 ft. glacier passes in the execution of his religious vows and devotions.

As regards Meade's exploration of the Bhagat Kharak Glacier, he discovered a pass, not from the extreme head of the glacier, but from the head of a side glacier leading southwards. If the map[1] is to be taken as being approximately accurate in its general indications, this pass was across the range where it runs almost due east and west, and, if the map is to be trusted still further, leads into the head of the Gangotri Glacier, which flows from south-east to north-west, but which in its upper portion bends round

[1] Survey of India Map No. 53 N. Badrinath. Scale, 1in. to four miles, or 1:253,440. The main range is shown bending at right angles from a direction approximately north to south to a direction approximately due west to east.

in an easterly direction. Descent was made a few hundred feet on the far side of the pass, and it is Meade's opinion that had he continued he would have found himself on the head of the Gangotri Glacier. He describes the scenery as being of a most magnificent character, and including many terrific peaks which appear to be hopelessly inaccessible.

One of our objects, therefore, in exploring the Badrinath Range was to traverse it from east to west, and cross the watershed of the Alaknanda and Gangotri Rivers, if possible descending to the Gangotri Glacier and thus making the first complete passage of the range.

CHAPTER III

THE CONDITIONS OF SUCCESS

THE SUCCESSFUL carrying-out of an expedition to the summit of a great Himalayan peak depends upon so many factors that it is difficult to enumerate them in order, yet, however well planned an expedition may be, and however well the plans are executed, there is always one link of strength unknown in the chain of circumstances, and that is—luck. That solitary link may be stretched unreasonably and not break ; it may be strong and unyielding or pitifully weak ; when apparently strong, it may develop an unexpected flaw, when apparently weak, it may continue to hold. Luck is blessed and cursed, but without it mountaineering would be a dull, mechanical pastime. Luck depends largely on the weather, and what the weather has done, or may do, to the mountain. Bow therefore to luck, accept it and forget it, making sure at the same time that all other links in the chain are as strong as human ingenuity and forethought can devise.

Himalayan mountaineering depends upon unselfish team-work, and unselfish team-work depends upon having a team of men who are temperamentally in phase. Your friend in civilisation may become your enemy on a mountain ; his very snore assumes a new and repellent note ; his tricks at the mess table, the sound of his mastication, the scarcely concealed triumph with which he appropriates the choicest tit-bits, the absurd manner in which he walks, even the cut of his clothes and the colour of the patch on the seat of his trousers, may induce an irritation and loathing almost beyond endurance. None of these things may matter at sea-level, and why they should matter on a mountain is a problem more within the scope of physiologists and psychologists than the writer of this volume. But the whole success of an expedition depends upon them *not* mattering.

The ideal team is one that includes different interests, paradoxical though this may sound. It is a profound truth that men sharing identical interests seldom get on well together in the wilds. If they do, it is as much of a miracle as a happy marriage. Wide divergencies of opinion seldom matter. It is the small divergencies of opinions that count for so much. I cannot conceive a team of mountaineers composed exclusively of doctors, barristers or politicians.

In the present instance, I was extremely fortunate in securing as my companions men of widely diverse interests in life. I make no apology for putting on record the following scrap of conversation overheard at the end of the expedition. It emanated from Captain Birnie. He said, "When I started on this show I expected that I should hate you all before the end of it, but, strangely enough, I can still tolerate you."

The size of a Himalayan expedition depends largely upon the magnitude of the task to be attempted. For a peak such as Everest, where long and difficult communications must be maintained, where ill-health and high altitude deterioration are certain to reduce the party, and where it may be necessary to make two or three attempts on the summit and each one by a fresh party, a minimum of eight to ten climbers is essential. For a party who aim at summits no higher than 23,000 ft., four climbers, who can be split up into two parties of two, is ample. The next best number above four is six, which can be split up into three parties of two or two parties of three.

What is the best age for high altitude mountaineering? I believe it to be on the average between twenty-four and thirty-five years of age. Opinions differ as to whether men younger than twenty-four should expose themselves to the physical strain of high-altitude climbing. I am convinced they should not. Possibly, I am unduly prejudiced, for I know that at thirty-one I cannot go so fast as I did at twenty-one, but I can go farther and withstand cold and hardship better. There is another and subtler argument against *extreme* youth on Himalayan expeditions. The effort that must be put forth to climb the highest peaks in the world is a mental as well as a physical effort. It is something greater and finer than athleticism. The men who will one day reach the summit of Everest will be men capable of disciplining their minds as well as their bodies. Experience and skill, coupled to the right mental attitude towards a great task, are required of the men who would attempt the highest summits in the world and this is only gained by experience. Athleticism by itself is of no more use to the mountaineer than size and weight by themselves to a boxer. If I have stressed this point, it is because of a suggestion put to me by a well-known traveller and sportsman who ought to have known better. His suggestion was that an ideal Everest party should consist exclusively of the pick of University athletes!

The present party consisted of Wing Commander E. B. Beauman, of the Royal Air Force; Captain E. St. J. Birnie, of Sam Browne's Cavalry, and Adjutant to His Excellency the Governor of Bengal's Bodyguard; Doctor C. R. Greene; Mr. R. L. Holdsworth; Mr. E. E. Shipton and myself. We were fortunate in possessing both a doctor and transport officer who were also mountaineers.

Wing Commander Beauman of the Royal Air Force is a mountaineer of many years' standing. He has a large number of first-class Alpine climbs and ski expeditions to his credit. He served throughout the war, and holds an early flying certificate.

Captain Birnie, our transport officer, had not had a great deal of Alpine experience, although he had some excellent climbs, to his credit, but he was experienced in Himalayan travelling both in Sikkim and the north-west frontier provinces. He speaks fluent Hindustani, and thoroughly understands the simple, childlike psychology of the primitive hill people whence we had to draw our porters. He is one of the best polo and squash racket players in the Indian Army, and an expert big-game shot. His services were invaluable to the expedition.

Doctor Greene practises in Oxford. He is a former President of the Oxford University Mountaineering Club, and was editor of its *Journal* and the *Climbers' Club Journal*. He is a mountaineer possessing both Alpine and British rock-climbing experience. He stands six feet four, and required a specially extended sleeping-bag. He joined the expedition in the triple capacity of doctor, physiologist, and mountaineer. In the second subject he is particularly interested, and has contributed a number of papers to

THE EXPEDITION AT RANIKHET

SHIPTON, BIRNIE, SMYTHE, GREENE, HOLDSWORTH, BEAUMAN. Sitting—DORJE, ACHUNG, ANG NERBU, NERBU, ONDI, NIMA, NIMA TENDRUP, PASSANG, NIMA DORJE

scientific journals on the question of acclimatisation to high altitudes.

Holdsworth is a classical master at Harrow School, and gained a double blue at Oxford for soccer and cricket. He is a fine ski-runner, and is the founder of a flourishing little mountaineering and ski-mountaineering club at Harrow known as the "Harrow Marmots." He was also the expedition's botanist.

Shipton, although the youngest member of the party, is a mountaineer of skill and experience. He plants coffee in Kenya Colony, and made, with Mr. P. Wynn Harris, the second ascent of Mount Kenya which had been attempted many times since the first ascent by Sir Halford Mackinder and two Alpine guides. He has also made first ascents of a number of subsidiary summits in the Kenya massif, and ascended Kilimanjaro, the highest mountain in Africa.

The next consideration after the formation of a team was the best time of the year during which to attempt the ascent of Kamet. Owing to the monsoon precipitating much of its moisture on the foothills and main range of the Himalaya, Kamet is subjected only to its strongest outbursts, and climbing in northern Garhwal is possible from May to the end of September and, under exceptional conditions, into October. During the monsoon season, which may last during the whole of July and August, bad weather lasting for a week or ten days at a stretch must be expected and provided for. It was decided, therefore, to attack Kamet before the monsoon in June. If the ascent was not completed before the onset of the monsoon, we hoped to be established at a considerable height, with plenty of stores and equipment, ready to seize upon any favourable weather that might occur during the monsoon season. It was, however, inadvisable to go too early, for, as Doctor Longstaff warned us, the Dhaoli Valley and its villages, which are deserted during the snowy winter months, are only repopulated by the nomadic Bhotias and their flocks of sheep, yaks and goats towards the end of May or the beginning of June. If we went too early we might find it impossible to obtain food for our coolies, whilst the bridges spanning the Dhaoli River, which are often swept away or damaged during the melting of the snows, might not be replaced or repaired. Reliable information is often hard to come by, and the expedition owes a debt of gratitude to Mr. Hugh Ruttledge for much invaluable advice on local conditions and travel. Mr. Ruttledge also sent a covering letter to Mr. N. C. Stiffe, the Commissioner of Kumaun. Mr. Stiffe replied in the friendliest terms, and generously offered to help the expedition to the best of his power. It may be perhaps as well to mention here that expeditions into the Himalaya are usually a source of trouble and anxiety to the officials administering the territory they are operating in. It behoves an expedition, therefore, to cause the minimum of worry and trouble to those in authority, for an unfavourable impression left in the minds of officials and inhabitants may vastly increase the difficulties of future expeditions in the same district.

The most vital condition of success in Himalayan exploration or mountaineering is successful porterage. Travelling to the foot of a great peak, and establishing a base camp, is only less difficult than the task of climbing the peak. Successful porterage depends on employing a body of loyal and willing men, of interesting them in the objects of the expedition, of treating them fairly, and feeding them well. No amount of bullying or slave-driving will make for successful porterage, and the smooth running of an expedition depends enormously upon the work of the transport officer. Thanks to expeditions to Everest, Kangchenjunga and the Sikkim Himalaya, there exists now at Darjeeling a body of men trained in the peculiar problems, hardships and difficulties of high altitude mountaineering. These men are Sherpas and Bhotias, and they come from the valleys of northern Nepal along the frontier of Tibet. They are half-Tibetans, half-Nepalese, and are the hardest, toughest natural mountaineers in the world. They are born adventurers at heart, and, whatever the hardships, difficulties or dangers, invariably come up smiling. To know them is to love them, and no expedition which intends serious mountaineering on the great peaks of the Himalaya should go without some of them as a backbone to its porterage.

Successful porterage also depends upon mobility, and mobility depends upon cutting down the size of an expedition to the absolute minimum. An expedition small enough to be able to feed its porters from the country is in a happy position, for it must be remembered that where an expedition is so large that this is impossible men must be engaged to carry food for their fellows, and those men who are carrying food must themselves be fed—a vicious circle. Whether local food is obtainable or not depends upon the country and its population. Fortunately, in the Kamet district food is available locally, but how much food depends upon previous harvests and stores of grain. It is essential to make careful enquiries beforehand before assuming that food will be available, even from villages where it is usually obtainable. The amount of food available is limited at the best of times in the upper valleys of the Himalaya, and the advantage of a small party over a large one is obvious. The 1930 Kangchenjunga expedition employed over four hundred porters to carry the expedition's goods to the base camp at the foot of Kangchenjunga. The difficulties of feeding these men were immense, and the consequent anxieties detracted considerably from the pleasure of the expedition for all members concerned, especially the transport officer. I had no intention of risking the same difficulties again, and went into the question of porterage very carefully. By rigorously excluding the unessential from the essential, it was found possible for six Europeans to manage with only seventy porters, and these included ten men carrying cinematographic and photographic apparatus. Thanks to previous arrangements, and the kind help of various officials, I made certain in advance that our men would be fed properly.

While on the question of food, the importance of adequate feeding on the right lines can hardly be overestimated.

As with polar expeditions, the essential vitamins must be carefully considered. I believe that the bodily deterioration supposed to be inseparable from high altitudes is accelerated by lack of vitamin C, the anti-scorbutic vitamin. Fresh fruit should be taken by expeditions, and, failing this, pure lime juice. Fresh meat and vegetables should be eaten whenever possible, and tinned food only reverted to when necessary.

As regards the harmonious working of an expedition, much rests on food. The fads and fancies of each member must be considered, especially above the base camp. Like and dislike are sure guides to good or evil. Palates must be tickled with dainties. The higher the climber goes, the more he realises that his body is nothing more or less than an engine crying out for heat and yet more heat—and heat is sugar. Estimate for as much sugar as you think you will need, then double that estimate, and you may with luck have enough. It is safer to treble the original estimate.

It is not proposed to deal here with questions of health, which in itself is a vital condition of success. It is dealt with by Doctor Greene at the end of this book. Suffice to say that scrupulous attention to detail, both on the part of the medical officer of an expedition and of each individual member, is necessary, if fever is to be avoided in the tropical valleys of the Himalaya, and also those minor stomach disorders which are the bane of Himalayan travelling, and which lower the physical and mental stamina.

Assimilation of the experiences and lessons of previous expeditions is the first duty of an organiser of a Himalayan expedition. To make the same mistakes as one's predecessors is inexcusable. The lessons taught by previous expeditions including three Everest and two Kangchenjunga expeditions were invaluable to us. We knew that it is possible for man's body to acclimatise itself to heights greater than Kamet, and the moral value of that knowledge was inestimable. Among the general public some misapprehension still exists as to the use of oxygen at great altitudes. There are even some people misguided enough to question the fairness of employing such an adventitious aid as oxygen on a mountain. I do not think, however, that those who have climbed in the Himalaya will have any doubts on this question. The odds are so much against the mountaineer that he is fully justified in exercising his mechanical ingenuity. It may be sacrilege to drive a piton[1] into the rocks of Scawfell, but it is common sense to drive it into a Himalayan peak if safety is increased thereby. "Safety first" may be a loathsome slogan, but it is worth remembering in the Himalaya. Were it possible to devise an oxygen apparatus weighing only a few pounds, and giving off gas for some days, no one but a fanatic would deprecate its use. Unfortunately, however, the weight of the apparatus, and consequent labour of porterage, counterbalances any benefit that may be derived from its use. Possibly, for the next assault on Everest, a compromise will be arrived at, and oxygen employed for the last 1,000 feet or so when the climber is too exhausted to continue without it. Yet, I believe that the summit of Everest can and will be reached without oxygen apparatus. Himalayan mountaineers of to-day are labouring under the same moral disadvantages as those who essayed the ascent of Mont Blanc over a hundred years ago. The bogey of altitude is always lurking at the back of their minds. It is safe to predict that in another hundred years, or even less, Himalayan mountaineers will regard with amazement the gasping struggles of their predecessors. They will be acclimatised to altitude physically and mentally, and by then physiologists should have discovered some artificial means of adapting the

[1] Iron spike with a ring on the end.

body to the lack of oxygen at great altitudes. When that time comes, the bogey of altitude will be finally laid, and the greatest and grandest mountain range in the world will be fully opened up to the mountaineer.

Such are the principal conditions of success on a Himalayan peak, and it is to be hoped that from this fragmentary account the reader will be able to gain some idea of the preparations and forethought involved in planning a Himalayan expedition. Such planning is only less interesting than the expedition itself. We left England knowing that we had concentrated our whole attention on the problem before us. We knew that we had one link of unknown strength, luck, in our chain of reasoning, but should that snap we would have done our best.

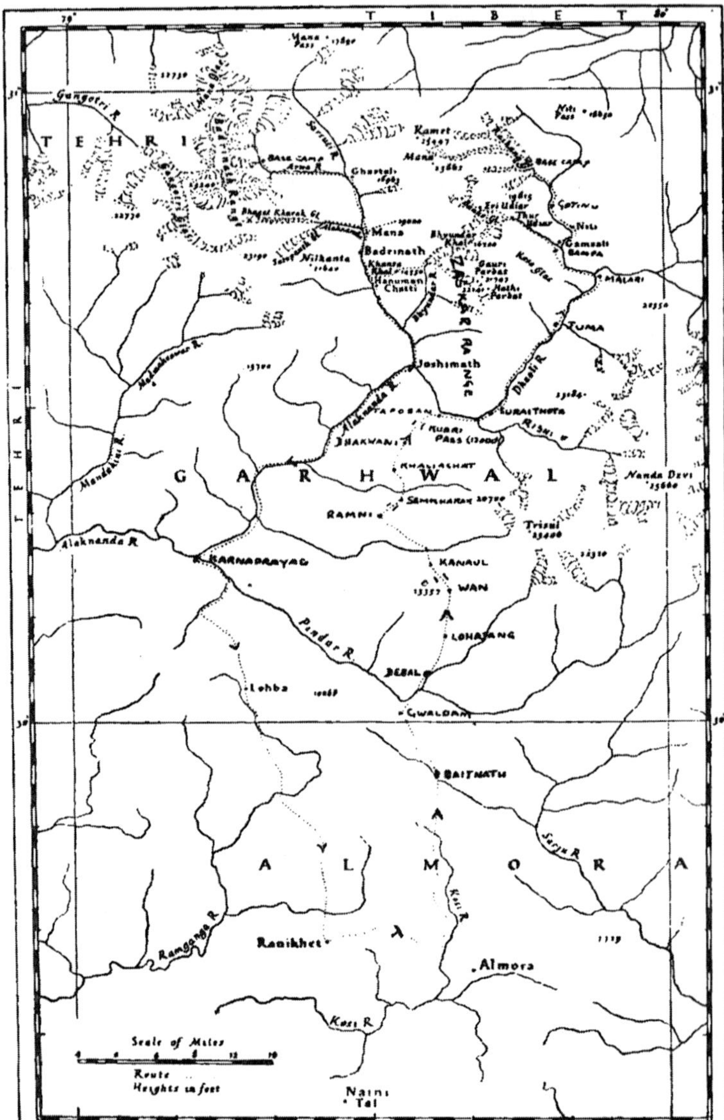

THE APPROACHES TO KAMET

Reproduced by courtesy of the Royal Geographical Society, with minor additions by the Author

CHAPTER IV

TO RANIKHET

THE SMELL of the East came in at the window. Above the rattle of the train hummed and whirred a myriad insects. Dawn came up over the great northern plain of India ; the sun swung over the level horizon like a huge blood orange, then, topping the low hazes, burst into white, eye-searing flame. Somewhere beyond that level horizon were the Himalaya.

Jungle, mile after mile of it, dank, steamy, malarious, and then—a darkening of the heat haze—dim shapes—the foothills of the Himalaya.

Languid after two days of travelling in appalling heat Shipton and I stepped from the train at Kathgodam. We loaded our goods and ourselves into a lorry and set off on the last stage of our journey to Ranikhet, the hill station 6,000 ft. up on a ridge of the Kumaun foothills which was to be the starting-point of the expedition. Forest fires were raging on the foothills, and the atmosphere was blue with smoke. Up and up climbed the lorry. The air was cooler now ; we no longer just lived ; we enjoyed living.

Through a complicated maze of hills wound the road, now up over a ridge, now down into a valley where the heat clutched at us again, lifting itself from the dusty road in suffocating waves.

Along the side of vast-bosomed hills terraced with rice we climbed—an ugly country, with not even the saving grace of the desolate. If this was Ranikhet—— ! We turned a corner of the dusty hillside, and miraculously found ourselves in a cool forest of deodars and chestnuts. Above the noise of our vehicle came the bell-like call of a cuckoo.

At Ranikhet we were met by Captain J. Clarke. He had kindly arranged for us to live at the forest bungalow while we made arrangements for the expedition.

Waiting for us were three of our Darjeeling men who had been sent by Colonel H. W. Tobin. Lewa was to be our sirdar. Nima Tendrup, the Old Soldier, had been my servant on Kangchenjunga in 1930. It was good to see again their merry eyes and broad grins. These Darjeeling men are Sherpas and Bhotias. They come from the valleys of northern Nepal, along the frontier of Tibet, and are Mongolian in type. They are natural mountaineers, and carried loads to over 26,000 ft. on Everest. The third of the trio was Achung, our cook, a quaint, nervous little Lepcha from Sikkim. Lewa and the Old Soldier did not disguise their pleasure at seeing me again. We had had some great times together on Kangchenjunga and the Jonsong Peak in 1930. Mountains can overcome barriers of race and language. Beneath the ragged and odorous exteriors of the Darjeeling Sherpas and Bhotias are hearts of gold. They are adventurers.

The bungalows of Ranikhet are scattered along the crests of wooded ridges. No other nation has such a genius as we for carrying its life and customs to the fringe of its empire. In Ranikhet there are motor roads, and a club, an inevitable adjunct of British life, from the veranda of which the eye can turn from the tennis-courts to the distant Himalaya.

LEWA

NIMA TENDRUP, THE "OLD SOLDIER"

ACHUNG, THE COOK

NIMA DORJE

Shipton and I had three weeks in which to make the final preparations—the hospitality we received while doing so will always remain a pleasant memory. We visited Naini Tal, where we were received by His Excellency Sir Malcolm Hailey, Governor of the United Provinces and President of the Himalayan Club, and Lady Hailey. Mr. N. C. Stiffe, the Commissioner for the Kumaun, loaned us fifty-five of his own Dotial porters to carry our goods to Niti, the last village on the route. Captain Bradford, the Commandant of the 3rd Gurkha Regiment, to whom General Sir William Beynon had written a letter of introduction, loaned us two Gurkha N.C.O.s who were to prove invaluable to the expedition. Meanwhile Birnie worked hard in the stifling heat of Calcutta, ordering and packing our stores, in which work he was greatly assisted by Mr. G. B. Gourlay, who had been invited to join the expedition but had unfortunately been unable to do so, and Mrs. Brown of Ranikhet arranged with the Rawal, the High Priest of Badrinath, to have porters' food ready for us. In England we had heard many pessimistic accounts as to the difficulty of obtaining porters. These difficulties may have existed before the war, but they no longer exist. The real difficulty is, and always will be, the feeding of porters, and for this reason we made careful enquiries as to the stores of grain available along the line of march.

The climate of Ranikhet in spring and early summer is delightful. Seldom does the shade temperature during the day exceed 85° Fahrenheit, and at night it sinks to 65°. The only disadvantage is the dust, which, before the monsoon, rises in clouds when the wind blows. This dust is largely composed of small particles of mica, which find their way into the water and food. The result is an unpleasant stomach disorder, a mild but weakening form of dysentery.

Shipton and I slept on the veranda of the forest bungalow undisturbed save for an occasional leopard and the monkeys which used to prowl around the compound at night. I shall not easily forget how, on waking in the morning, we opened our eyes to the Himalaya. The view extended from the peaks of Nepal and the snowy cone of Nanda Kot to the snows of Badrinath, and the wonderful spire of Nilkanta. But the central glories in the wall were Trisul, 23,406 ft., and Nanda Devi, 25,660 ft., for these were only fifty or sixty miles distant.

Three weeks before I had opened my eyes every morning in a London flat. From my window I had gazed over a few square yards of smoke-grimed garden to a row of houses, a bilious yellow in colour, covered in that horrible stucco which defaces residential London. The roar of London's traffic, the rattle of the milkman's cans and the yowling of cats had been in my ears.

At Ranikhet I awoke to hear the call of a cuckoo vying with the flute of some far-off shepherd, and the tops of the deodars awaking with gentle sighs in the dawn breeze.

Below the veranda on which we slept the forest fell away, a dark green sheet, into the blue trough of a valley, rose again half a score of miles away, and so continued ridge on ridge, like awe-compelling deep-sea rollers, breaking at last in foamy snow on the eternal peaks of the Himalaya.

Sometimes I would awake early and watch dawn's

alchemist transmute the leaden snows to pearl and gold. In that magical hour of dawn, all that I knew of mountains was forgotten, and I saw them again as I had seen them when I was a boy. Once, while the dawn was coming thus gloriously to the world, I noticed my servant, the Old Soldier, standing in the compound gazing towards the snows. Like ourselves, the men from Darjeeling see more in a mountain than inanimate ice, snow and rock. Love and veneration for Nature is part of their Buddhist religion. That religion may be burdened with superstition, but it has one great doctrine; it teaches that God made all life, therefore life is a precious thing. We Christians pride ourselves on our societies for the prevention of cruelty to animals and children, but in Tibet there is no necessity for such societies. Small wonder that the Buddhist looks askance upon a religion that tolerates the disembowelling of horses by pain-maddened bulls and delights in the tearing to pieces of a fear-crazed stag by a pack of dogs.

The fine weather broke; vast clouds massed in the valleys. Thunder spoke from the Himalaya. Grey veils of rain were slashed by blue swords of lightning. Every afternoon storms stalked raging across the foothills. At night this cloudy combat over the Himalaya was weirdly magnificent. There is something intimidating and almost terrifying in such a vast horizon as that on which we gazed from Ranikhet. As I watched the daily miracles of dawn and sunset along the snows, I could feel that strange exaltation and mystification that comes to some in the presence of great mountains. I knew, as the Indians know when they turn their eyes towards the snows, that the mysteries of life and of death must be sought for there.

On May 10 Birnie arrived, looking remarkably fit considering that he had been living in the heat of Calcutta. He brought with him our stores and a gramophone and records. Next day we packed hard. The Dotial porters arrived under the charge of their "mates." We were immediately impressed by them—they were a cheery crowd. They come from southern Nepal, but, unlike the Gurkhas, have more Indian than Mongolian blood in them. On May 13 they left under the command of Lewa. The day after their departure, Beauman, Greene and Holdsworth arrived from England. The following three days were spent making our final preparations. We were to cover the first fifty miles in a motor-lorry which would take us to Baijnath, the terminus of the road. There we would overtake the Dotial porters and thenceforward proceed on foot as one party.

The night prior to our departure I felt that same queer thrill the adventurers of old must have felt when they slipped their cables to venture into the unknown. The plans, theories and preparations of months were to be put into practice. How futile and foolish they seemed that night. The world stretched limitless into the darkness. All along the Himalaya the lightning flamed wrathfully and the still air quivered to the vibration of thunder. I could feel then that "the mystery and thrill of travel is always upon one in the Himalaya, but the mystery is awful and the thrill is sometimes a shudder."

CHAPTER V

THE FOOTHILLS

MAY 18 dawned brilliantly. The recent thunderstorms had scoured the atmosphere of the dust blown up from the plains, and the great Himalayan wall stood out sharp and clear beyond the orderly ranges of foothills. I looked at it with a new feeling ; for nearly a month Shipton and I had been unable to respond to its insistent call, and now, at last, the expedition was ready to start.

On those remote and shining peaks we were about to adventure. The plans, the theories of months, were to be tested.

I stood in the compound of our bungalow and gazed for a few moments between the deodars at Kamet. It was one hundred miles distant, yet every detail was distinct. Through glasses I could discern the sweep of its red granite precipices seamed by avalanche-swept gullies ; the cold gleam of its icy ridges. A small scarf of snow trailed from its square-topped crest. A hurricane was raging, but where I stood only the gentlest of dawn breaths stirred the forest.

Would Kamet be kind to us ? It was just such a morning that we had left Darjeeling last year to attempt Kangchenjunga. High hope had been ours, but we had returned defeated, and we had left one of our number buried in the snow beneath that terrible mountain.[1]

[1]Chettan, a Sherpa porter.

We had ordered the lorry that was to convey ourselves and our luggage to Baijnath, sixty miles distant, for 5 a.m., but it was not until 9 a.m. that we were ready to start.

We experienced a qualm of apprehension when confronted by our vehicle. It was very old and decrepit. Its body, which was absurdly large for its chassis, was constructed of three-ply wood, warped and cracked by tropical suns. But it was the tyres that caused us most anxiety. Of tread there was but little left and here and there the covers had worn through, exposing the inner tubes, which bulged out like sausages. In the worst places gaiters had been affixed, but in other places there was no such protection. The driver was a dark taciturn Moslem. He looked a soured and disappointed man.

Somehow, six Europeans, eight Darjeeling porters, Achung the cook, with his paraphernalia of clattering pots and pans, and 2,000 lbs. of luggage were stowed away into the vehicle.

Before leaving Ranikhet, it was necessary to obtain a pass from the police. Apparently, our load was about three times the maximum allowed legally, but the police were solicitous neither for our safety nor for regulations. After all, if we did go down the *khud*,[1] why worry? It would be the will of God.

This difficulty removed, the clutch was engaged with a fearsome wrench, the gears jerked home with nerve-shattering crashes, and we went rattling, bumping and banging through the bazaar, the cynosure of all eyes. The first stage of our journey had commenced. We could only hope that it would not also prove the last.

[1] Hillside.

We passed the Ranikhet golf-links. These links are both sporting and expensive. Sporting, because it is often necessary to drive off from the summit of one hill to a green on the summit of another, and expensive because a slice or pull may dispatch a ball into dense jungle or down a steep hillside. The links are superbly situated, and between rounds the golfer may find consolation for his misfortunes in the view, which embraces a considerable portion of the Garhwal Himalaya.

The road narrowed ; its hairpin bends were sometimes so acute as to render reversing necessary. Where it traversed open hillsides, there were places where drops of over a thousand feet awaited an error on the part of the driver or the bursting of a tyre.

We smiled at each other—at times a trifle wanly—and strove to make light and airy conversation. Our porters, however, had no qualms, and chattered away merrily in the back of the lorry. Packed tightly as we were, we had perforce to stop at intervals and alight to stretch our cramped limbs.

Down hillsides terraced with rice and dotted with the primitive bamboo thatched huts of the peasants into the steamy heat of malarious valleys rattled our aged vehicle, to wind tortuously up once more to the cooler uplands.

Now and again we caught glimpses of distant peaks, but, though we were approaching them, the vast scale on which even the foothills of the Himalaya are constructed made them seem, if anything, farther away.

Once we were stopped by a native, and a colloquy ensued between him and our driver. The gist of it was that the former wanted a letter delivered, but this commission our driver resolutely refused to undertake until he had satisfied himself beyond all reasonable doubt that the deliverer was, like himself, a Moslem by faith.

It was a striking instance of the antagonism prevailing in India between Hindus and Moslems, for, had the deliverer of the letter been a Hindu, our driver would not have acceded to his request.

At the junction of our road with the Almora road, we found awaiting us the two Gurkha Lance-Naiks[1] who had been detailed off for service with the expedition by Captain Bradford, Commandant of the 3rd Gurkha Regiment at Almora. Their soldierly smartness and alertness was in itself a tribute to British army training. Their names were Budhibal Gurung and Randhoj Kan. Budhibal Gurung was a serious young man, which is unusual among Gurkhas. He seldom spoke unless addressed, but his speckless, tropical uniform, his wide-brimmed, rakish hat, and his quiet air of efficiency betokened a good soldier, and one who would serve us well. Randhoj Kan was of a very different type. Here was the typical Gurkha : broad-faced, thick-lipped, with a wide humorous mouth ready to expand at any moment into a smile and with merry twinkling eyes, he appeared to find life one perpetual joke, and to extract huge amusement from everything he saw or did.

During the halt to collect our Gurkhas, one of the tyres elected to go flat. The driver, with characteristic Oriental laziness, decided to try to pump it up rather than change the wheel for the spare, but happily, as we expected, he had to admit himself defeated and put on the spare wheel.

[1] Lance-Corporals.

DOTIAL PORTERS AND ONE OF OUR GURKHA SOLDIERS

It was fortunate that the next puncture occurred, not on a sharp corner or above a precipitous hillside, but on a safe and level stretch of road. This time, there being no spare wheel, the puncture had to be repaired, and we took the opportunity to lunch in the shade of a wood beside a small stream in which we could see mahseer[1] swimming.

It was with profound sighs of relief that we stepped at last from our chariot at Baijnath.

Lewa was awaiting us, radiating his usual vim and energy. From him we learned the good news that the fifty-five Dotial porters in advance were marching well. Owing to some extra loads that we had brought with us, it was necessary to recruit five Garhwali porters. These men were not to be compared with our Sherpa or Dotial porters, either in physique or morale. They were weak, cringing creatures, and it was obvious that our Darjeeling men regarded them with contempt.

Baijnath is situated in a wide open valley running south-east and north-west, enclosed by low forest-clad hills and grassy alps rising to gentle undulating skylines. The valley was brown and parched with drought, but here and there the bright green fronds of banana trees afforded a pleasing contrast to the prevailing aridness.

The village consisted of the usual collection of thatched and filthy hovels. The ground around these hovels was strewn with rotting garbage black with flies, ready to rise in clouds at any moment and transfer their filth and disease to a newcomer. Mangy dogs prowled about the huts, and languid, dejected-looking cattle, which appeared to have given up all idea of obtaining nutriment, stood

[1] Hill Salmon.

or lay on the withered, sun-scorched fields without the village.

It was late in the afternoon, and as soon as the Garhwali porters had been recruited we set out on the ten-mile walk to Gwaldam.

A well-constructed path passed over or between little tree-clad knolls. In the more open valleys between the low hills banana groves flourished, and their fruit, which could be purchased at the rate of a dozen for one anna, was a welcome lubricant to mouths parched by the heat.

Here and there small brooks chattered over the stones, but we dared not drink from them for fear of cholera, typhoid or dysentery.

As we progressed, the country became more and more like an English park-land. The hillsides were covered in well-spaced deodars, the resinous fragrance of which permeated the warm air, whilst their fallen needles softly carpeted the path. Now and again we sat down to rest in their shade. Only the diapason of insect life, so monotonous as to be almost unnoticeable, was there to remind us that we were within tropical latitudes.

Once from the crest of a hill we saw the summit of Trisul, its summit snows, tinged with gold in the declining sun, couched in lurid thunder-clouds.

Gradually the small and indefinite ridges were replaced by bolder forms. Dusk saw us trudging up a steep hillside, sweating profusely and afflicted with thirsts induced by the heat and our lack of training. As I endeavoured to lubricate my parched tongue with saliva, I reflected that, at this very moment, our friends in Ranikhet were reclining luxuriously in arm-chairs at the club, imbibing long iced drinks.

The sun withdrew into the cloudless west ; the tops of the deodars were steeped in its soft glow. The insect chorus died away into the silence of the forest. From the deepening gloom above glanced a remote star.

Night fell swiftly. Darkness revealed a dozen twinkling points of light on a range of hills to the east. They were forest fires over thirty miles away. Fireflies darted about us like minute lamps of palest blue in the hands of restless fairies.

To those unaccustomed to it, a tropical forest is terrible at night. During the daytime little is to be heard, save the whirr and hum of insects, but at night-time, when the insects are hushed, its potentialities for evil become apparent. There are furtive rustlings ; a twig cracks suddenly with a report like a pistol-shot ; perhaps there is some startling crash of undergrowth, followed by an agonised scream—a leopard has secured its prey. But this last is unusual ; for the most part there is little to be heard save the continual furtive rustlings.

To the newcomer a night walk along a path through a jungle is both intriguing and terrifying. No doubt to those well versed in its lore the jungle loses many of its terrors. To the keen ear and trained intelligence of the shikari, its sounds are full not of menace but of interest, yet Birnie's experience with a tiger must have shaken even *his* nerve.

The usual method adopted in tiger-shooting is to tie up a calf or goat a few yards from a tree the fork of which allows of a platform being constructed. Position on this platform may be taken up either before or after the tiger has killed the bait. In the one case, the tiger returns to the kill, and in the other it is a matter of luck as to whether the tiger appears on the night when the sportsman is ready for him. Birnie loves the jungle, and delights to wander alone in it. Perhaps it is for this reason that he disdains the conventional and safer method of shooting from a tree platform, and prefers to shoot his tiger from the ground seated in some concealed spot near the tied-up animal, with an electric torch tied along the barrel of his rifle. On one occasion, however, he let fly at his tiger when unable to obtain a perfect view of it. He wounded the tiger but not mortally, and the beast charged. Unluckily the shock of the discharging rifle had broken the bulb of his electric torch, and he was unable to see anything in the darkness. There was no time to run for it, and he sat there waiting to give the tiger his second barrel. It is not easy to picture such a situation, or to imagine the feelings of a man alone in the darkness of a tropical jungle at night charged by an infuriated tiger. Birnie says that the whole thing happened so quickly that he had no time to experience any other emotion than an intense excitement. He waited until he thought the tiger was a yard or two away, and then fired his second barrel. He missed completely. The next moment the tiger seized him.

He says his predominant thought at the moment was that it was a very poor way of being "outed," but, with instinctive self-preservation, he beat at the tiger with the stock of his rifle. This saved his life. It diverted the tiger's attention from him to the rifle and it snatched the weapon in its jaws and made off with it.

The next few minutes were mentally the worst for Birnie. He was badly mauled, for the tiger's teeth had met in his shoulder, and he expected the beast to come back and finish him. In the darkness it was not easy to find a tree which he could scale, but at length he discovered one, and, climbing it, passed the remainder of the night in a fork. His wound bled profusely and he was unable to bandage it, but so venomous were the tiger's jaws that within two hours suppuration set in and the bleeding stopped.

Next morning he was joined by his native shikari. Most men after such an experience would have returned there and then to civilisation, and Birnie, in addition, was badly mauled and weak from loss of blood. He decided, however, that the wounded tiger must be tracked down, so, accompanied by his shikari, he followed it for five miles and finally shot it. This delay in receiving medical attention nearly cost him his arm, for blood-poisoning set in, and when at last he reached hospital, it was touch and go whether it was amputated or not.

From ahead came a shout, and presently we were joined by Tikia, the mate of our Dotial porters. All the men and all the loads had arrived at Gwaldam. This was good news, as we had experienced a doubt when sending off the advance-party of Dotial porters from Ranikhet with no European in charge of them.

The path climbed steadily through the forest. At length a cool breath of wind denoted the crest of the ridge 6,000 ft. high on which stands the dak bungalow of Gwaldam, and a minute or two later, the squat, dark mass of the bungalow loomed out of the darkness.

We groped our way round the unlit veranda in search of Achung. Tired, hungry men are liable to become both angry and impatient. Why was there no tea waiting for the sahibs? What was the good of having a cook if he didn't go on ahead and prepare a meal for his employers? Achung spread out his hands with a weak, hopeless gesture. "No tea, no milk, no here," he mumbled. The bungalow was not even unlocked. We roared for the chowkidar.[1] A miserable, ragged man materialised from the darkness; he was the chowkidar, but he had lost the key of the bungalow he was supposed to look after.

With the arrival of Birnie matters assumed a different complexion. Milk was forthcoming, tea, and later food. Naturally, things were in a muddle, and in the darkness it was not easy sorting out from the rest of the baggage the load containing the required food. A kind friend in the person of Lieutenant Carr, who had camped in the compound of the bungalow, came to our rescue, and lent us necessaries, so that soon we were seated in the little dining-room eating ravenously.

The Gwaldam dak bungalow is unprepossessing both within and without. On the spot where it stands there had once stood a large bungalow occupied by some tea planters. They had experimented with tea-growing in the locality, but their experiments had not proved commercially successful, and in the end they had been forced to sell their bungalow to the Public Works Department who required a dak bungalow at Gwaldam. They received a good price for it, but as luck would have it, on the very day that the bungalow was paid for by the Public Works Department it was burnt to the ground. The Public Works Department, undismayed and with commendable economy, collected

[1] Caretaker.

the remnants of their purchase, and constructed the present dak bungalow from the scraps thus obtained. Whitehall should be able to point the moral.

The one bedroom of the bungalow was small and dirty, so we pitched our tents in the compound. It was good to be in a tent once more ; to sniff the faint odour of clean new canvas and the sweet scent of dewy grass ; to peer through the doorway into the kindly night.

Long after I had blown my candle out, I lay in my sleeping-bag, my brain busy with thoughts of the past and the future. The past was already remote. I could review its events almost with the detachment of a god. The remembrances of civilisation passed before me, a procession of phantasms. Of the future I could but speculate in vain. And, so at last, the peace of the hills laid gentle hands upon me and I fell into the deep, dreamless slumber that is the daily reward of those who live and travel in the open.

I awoke next morning to see the broad face of old Nima Tendrup, with its habitual worried expression, peering in at me from the door of the tent. I crawled outside. It was a glorious morning ; water jewels gleamed on the grass ; from the woodlands came the call of a cuckoo and the bell-like notes of the coppersmith bird. From the terrace on which our tents were pitched the forest-clad hills stretched northwards, ridge on ridge, lapping at last in dim blue waves against the ridges of Trisul from the snowy crest of which streamed a small tendril of wind-blown snow. In the limpid atmosphere of early morning, as yet unpolluted by the heat-hazes from the valleys, details were faultlessly distinct, and every dell in the silvery snowfields was revealed by the slanting rays of the sun.

At breakfast, flies introduced themselves to us. We had been warned about these flies, but both in numbers and perseverance they exceeded our most pessimistic expectations. The food was black with them, the air droned with them; they swam in the milk and dragged their foul bodies over the butter; they struggled to extricate themselves from the jam. And there were other flies that bit, and bit viciously. These last were small and black, scarcely larger than sand-flies, and they drove their probosces into our arms and legs and, having sucked our blood, injected their poison, leaving us with itching sores. We could well understand the regret expressed by General Bruce when he travelled in Garhwal that, owing to a defect in the anatomy of these flies, he was unable to make them scream.

After breakfast Birnie re-allotted the loads. The porters were full of good cheer, and they strode off down the hill chattering gaily.

From Gwaldam we had to descend into the steamy valley of the Pindar River. Had it not been so hot we might have appreciated the beauties of the path, which passed through forests of firs and sub-tropical jungle. The Gwaldam dak bungalow is the last dak bungalow on this route, and at the village of Debal we pitched camp. Our tents stood on a grassy shelf above the Pindar River. Behind the camp were the filthy hovels of the village of Debal. Owing to the foul and unsanitary conditions, plus the presence of innumerable flies, disease is rife at Debal, and Greene had his hands full. Apart from venereal disease in its worst and most varied forms, he was asked to treat cases of cancer of the stomach, malaria, and intestinal ulcers. One poor little girl, about six years old, brought to him by her father, had

TRISUL FROM GWALDAM

a terribly septic leg, the oozing sores of which were battened on by swarms of vile flies. There was little he could do save advise the sufferers to go to the nearest hospital, a journey which they seemed loth to undertake. He might have administered morphia in some painful cases, but, as he said, it would not have been fair to let his patients realise that there was a means of affording them temporary relief from their pain which was not available to them. It seemed strange and dreadful finding such misery so near the purity of the snows.

That evening we fished for mahseer in the Pindar River below the camp. Mahseer attain to the dimensions of salmon, and are quite good eating, although decidedly bony. We fished both with small and large spoons, and with fly, but, although we saw many rising fish, we were unlucky. The ragged villagers clustered around, grinning broadly at our unsuccess. Obviously, they considered fishing with rod and line a futile and foolish method, and one of them proceeded to demonstrate his skill with a net below the pool in which we were fishing. We did not see him catch anything, but later a fish weighing several pounds was brought to our camp.

Before turning in that evening we treated ourselves to a gramophone concert. Night brought in its train a delicious coolness, and relieved us of the horde of flies. We sat at peace outside our tents, with only the faintest of breezes rustling the fir tops above us. At such times it is always the old songs that are appreciated most, possibly because one does not wish to be reminded of the busy, teeming life of plain and city beyond the ranges. But some of these old favourites we were, alas, to hear for the first and last time during the expedition, for in the middle of our concert there was an exclamation, a crack, and a crunch. Beauman had sat on the records !

Before leaving Debal, we were shown the village war memorial. On a simple stone slab let into the side of a rickety hut is an inscription which reads : " From this village twenty-two men went to the Great War, 1914-1919. Of these, two gave up their lives." Somehow that primitive little record in this remote corner of the Empire impressed me to a greater extent than have many elaborate memorials to the fallen that I have seen amid civilised surroundings.

The march from Debal to Lohajang is a long one. Officially, it is ten miles. Actually, it is much farther, in effort at least, for the path ascends more than 4,000 ft., and the tropical sun was on our backs. It was grillingly hot. Our lack of training was again manifest. How the porters, carrying 80 lbs. each, did it I do not know, but they marched so well that many of them were waiting for us when we arrived at Lohajang.

Of our two Gurkhas, one, Budhibal Gurung, was in charge of the treasure chest, and it was amusing to see him striding along, immaculately clad, behind the sweating native who laboured under a box of rupees weighing 75 lbs. The other Gurkha, Randhoj Kan, was appointed a general whipper-in of straggling porters. Undoubtedly, the smartness and discipline exhibited by these men was a valuable example to our porters. For this reason we made no attempt to restrain their salutes or the clicking together of their heels whenever a sahib appeared.

Camp was pitched on a grassy ridge fanned by a cool and refreshing breeze. As we wanted to conserve our tinned meat as far as possible, Lewa was sent to buy a sheep. He returned later leading one on a halter, and explained that as he had been unable to find the owner he had appropriated the sheep from the pasture on which it was grazing !

The sheep was slaughtered in a masterly fashion by Budhibal Gurung. We had often heard of what a kukri is capable. It is said that this heavy sickle-shaped knife can, in the hands of a skilful Gurkha, sever a bullock's head from its body at one stroke. I can well believe this. In the present instance a rope was tied to the sheep's horns, and, with one man holding it and another man the sheep's hind legs, the animal was held in position without movement.

The sun was setting over the hills, and in its dying gleams Budhibal Gurung, with his uplifted right arm grasping the kukri, looked like some Druidical figure about to perform a sacrifice. The next moment, in a curve of crimson light, the knife descended. There was a dull crunch, and the sheep's head rolled on the ground.

This had scarcely been done when we observed a gesticulating and agitated figure, its rags flying in the breeze, running along the ridge towards the camp. It was the shepherd of the flock ! As soon as he reached us the floodgates of his eloquence were unloosed. What was he to do ? The sahibs had taken his sheep. What would his master say ? He had betrayed his trust. He was a ruined man.

Laughingly, Birnie took hold of his shoulders and forced him into a kneeling position.

" Now," he said, " be quiet or we will cut off your head too." But this little pleasantry was lost on the shepherd ;

he still chattered volubly. " All right, then. Cut off his head," Birnie ordered Budhibal Gurung. I looked at Budhibal Gurung. There was no trace of a smile in his eyes. " Cut off his head," reiterated Birnie. Budhibal Gurung's hand seemed to tighten on the hilt of his reeking kukri ; there was a curious look in his eyes ; these men are used to obeying orders. I don't think we realised at the time how near that order came to being carried out.

The shepherd's wrath waned ; suddenly his weather-beaten face cracked into a broad smile.

Yes, he would take money for the sheep. Seven rupees was the usual price, but we gave him eight annas extra for the insult. He was vastly pleased. After all, he could always tell his master that the sheep had died or had fallen down a precipice—and he was seven rupees eight annas to the good. " If the sahibs would like another sheep . . . ? "

We dined well off the sheep's liver and kidneys, while our men gorged themselves on a fearsome concoction the principal ingredients in which were the sheep's entrails.

The next morning, before leaving camp, Greene was called upon to do some more work. One of his patients was a small boy, who complained, apparently, among other things, of a sore throat. Greene examined him, but could find nothing in particular wrong. He decided, however, that, as the boy's tonsils were none too healthy, it would be a good thing if they were to come out on the spot. He was preparing to perform this operation when the terrified boy explained that it was not he who was ill, but his father in the village below, and that he had come on his behalf, and had merely tried to enact his ailments.

The march to Wan was a charming one. The scorched

ridges across which we had passed for the first three marches were behind, and we found ourselves on more fertile hillsides. The Himalayan oak predominated: its stocky, weather-beaten trunk and gnarled branches make it a fitting comrade to the great peaks beneath which it grows.

Shoots of bracken which were growing in the forest near the path were collected eagerly by our porters, for they are prized hereabouts as an excellent vegetable.

The valley bent north-westwards, disclosing bolder ridges, no longer dominated by forests but bare and craggy with streaks of winter snow lingering in their gullies.

The sun beat relentlessly down upon us, but the breeze was sweet and clean, and brought with it a fragrance of woodlands and wild thyme. The stream below us was no longer the sullen thing we had fished in at Debal, but rushed joyously along its rocky bed, halting here and there to dream in quiet pools among the grey boulders.

In a glade beneath a hoary old oak, a shepherd-boy was sitting minding his flocks. Clad in ragged sackcloth, he made a picturesque figure, and I stopped to photograph him. He glanced at me shyly out of his dark, sloe-like eyes, and would have fled had it not been for a grin on the part of Nima Dorje and a voluble explanation as to the harmless nature of the proceedings.

Passing through fields of ripening maize, the path turned and zigzagged up the north-eastern side of the valley. Standing at a corner of the path were three villagers busily twirling their shuttles of wool, and regarding us curiously the while. We seldom saw a native in Garhwal without his shuttle of wool. In one hand he carries a mass of wool;

from this he draws out a thread, which is wound on to a shuttle suspended by the thread itself and twirled so that the wool is both attenuated and woven into a compact strand before being wound on to the shuttle. Such of this wool as is not required for their own hand-looms they sell to the agents of the Cawnpore woollen mills, or trade it for salt and borax. They were a cheery and smiling trio, and were vastly intrigued with my cinema camera.

The majority of Garhwali men possess an abundant crop of hair. This they bob in feminine fashion until two knots of it project from under their tight-fitting little caps on either side of their heads. Although, as a rule, clad in clothes of the most ragged and disreputable description, they are fond of ornamenting themselves, their wives and children, and it is a common sight to see a woman clad entirely in rags hung around with a costly array of jewellery.

The path entered a grove of magnificent pines. They were the largest conifers that I have ever seen. Some of them must have been 150 ft. in height, and their timber would be most valuable were it possible to export it. As we passed through their dim-lit aisles, thunder boomed threateningly, and large drops of rain began to fall.

We had barely pitched camp on a grassy terrace beyond the pines when the storm burst. It was the first time our tents had been exposed to rain, and we were gratified to find that not a drop from the heavy deluge that accompanied the storm penetrated their fabric.

So delightful a spot is the camping-ground at Wan that Carr, who had accompanied us from Gwaldam, decided to stop there and make it his centre for some days ; but,

BETWEEN WAN AND KANAUL

before we parted from him, he very kindly insisted on presenting us with some excellent large-scale maps of the Badrinath and Kamet districts.

We awoke to a morning of delightful freshness. The sun shone brilliantly. Overnight there had been a hint of frost and the air was sweet with the fragrance of resin and wild roses. Just such a morning may be experienced in the Lake District or the Scottish Highlands after rain.

In the valley beneath the camp, the blue smoke from the brown huts of Wan rose lazily above a patchwork of yellowing barley-fields. From the valley, noble forests swept upwards in a deep blue-green sheet, to straggle out at last in vain attempt to win the crests of the snow-friezed ridges.

From the camping-place a stony path passed between banks ablaze with creamy wild roses, and then mounted towards the ridge we must cross to reach Kanaul. Ram Singh, an Indian Assistant Commissioner, who had accompanied us as far as Wan, now parted from us. He had taken a lively interest in the expedition, and had helped us by arranging food for our coolies. His work was taken over by Hukam Singh. Both of these men were the finest types of Indian Assistant District Commissioner. Hukam Singh possessed that introspective, far-away look in the eyes peculiar to those who dwell among the hills, whilst his thin, almost ascetic countenance, seamed with innumerable wrinkles, was of that weather-beaten, leathery quality found only among those who expose themselves to hot suns and cold winds.

Shipton had left at dawn to ascend a peak of 13,357 ft. to the south-west of the pass between Wan and Kanaul. We envied him his view from the summit, but our envy was forgotten as we mounted the last slope, covered in oaks and rhododendrons, to the crest of the ridge we must cross.

A cold wind met us, rustling the gnarled and stunted oaks and rubbing their twisted branches like the bones of a skeleton hung from a gibbet on a windy heath. Before us were the snows of the Badrinath peaks, a confused jumble of mountains. Before them stood their queen, Nilkanta. It is one of the loveliest mountains in the world : above the broad buttresses from which it springs its graceful lines lead the eye upwards to a perfectly proportioned summit, a sheer spire of gleaming snow and ice. Nilkanta stands watch and ward over the snows of Himachal. It is from its flanks that the sacred Alaknanda River falls " like the slender thread of a lotus flower."

We descended through woodlands and glades gay with dwarf gentians to the pastures of Kanaul, where we camped beside some shepherds and their flocks. Greene busied himself the same afternoon with blood-pressure tests, while some of us amused ourselves playing deck-tennis, using a fir-cone in lieu of a quoit. As I reclined on the close-cropped turf, I could not help comparing my companions to the immaculate young men they had once been. The ladies who had given us dances at Ranikhet would have looked askance could they have seen us now with our sun-tanned faces and rapidly growing beards.

It must not be thought that we grew beards out of sheer laziness. We did so because they afford protection from the ravages of the sun at high altitudes. But at this early stage in their development they presented an unpleasant spectacle. Greene, Shipton, and myself had so far developed

SUNSET FROM KANAUL

little more than straggly fluff. Birnie's fiery red growth was, however, beginning to inspire respect, whilst the appearance of Beauman and Holdsworth, both of whom are dark-haired, can only be described as blackguardly.

That evening, Greene and I strolled up a small hill covered in barley-fields to watch the sunset. The tall cumulus clouds that had been built up fold on fold, layer on layer, and turret on turret by the moist warm valley airs during the afternoon were being dissipated, and their apparently solid bastions were melting into the evening sky. The summit of a peak stood forth. A cloud still hung to one of its supporting ridges, concealing it. The effect produced was that of a peak of height and breadth but of negligible thickness, something cut out from cardboard, or a photograph. A solitary pine-tree was pencilled darkly against a sky of vivid green. Long, zeppelin-shaped clouds flared and sank into the abysses of night.

As we turned downhill towards camp, there came to our nostrils the scent of burning pine and juniper, and to our ears the care-free laughs of our porters.

CHAPTER VI

THE KUARI PASS

THE PATH beyond Kanaul descended into the Nandakna Valley. Banks of honeysuckle and wild roses lined the way. Flocks of horned and shaggy sheep were streaming up the path, many of them carrying little bags of grain, slung on either side of their backs for the nutriment of their shepherds and for trading purposes.

On entering the gorge down which rushes the torrent bearing the snow-waters from the western glaciers of Trisul to the Alaknanda River at Nandaprayag, we were made to realise for the first time that we were in the immediate presence of the High Himalaya, for, looking up between the precipitous walls of the gorge, we could see the ice-crowned buttresses of Trisul, vignetted by the silvery mists of morning.

Crossing the torrent by a log bridge, we toiled up a steep hot path and then traversed horizontally along the northern slopes of the Nandakna Valley. The sun burned down with a piercing heat that presaged a storm. I developed a thirst of which a fireman might have been proud. This thirst was not relieved by Greene, who, looking at me sadly, murmured something about long iced lagers at Ranikhet.

We lunched by a stream in company with a large lizard, which took a great interest in us. Beyond our lunching-place, the path passed across one of the steepest grass-clad hillsides that I have seen. The steepness of the valley sides is a feature of the higher Himalayan foothills. Formidable landslips occur frequently, whilst stone and mud avalanches render dangerous many of the paths between villages during the melting of the snows or the monsoon rains.

The camping-place at Ramni was shadeless, and had been befouled by sheep and oxen. Shipton was taken ill, and, as there was a possibility that he was beginning an attack of dysentery, Greene injected a special anti-dysenteric serum he had procured from the military hospital at Ranikhet. Probably, he was only suffering from an acute form of the stomach disorder that so often afflicts travellers in the more unhealthy valleys of the Himalaya, for in three days he had completely recovered.

The heat was relieved that evening by a sharp thunderstorm. From the west a smooth, dun-bellied pall of nimbus slid up over the hills. Battalion after battalion of giant cumuli followed. The hushed landscape seemed to quiver to the hollow bellow of thunder. Crooked blue swords of lightning drove at the crests of the wooded ridges. The thunder's clamorous roll was resolved into an angrier crackle. A giant rent strips of calico from mountain-top to mountain-top. Rain rushed down upon the camp with a roar.

The lightning was exceedingly vivid. One stream of mauve flame, that connected with a hilltop across the valley, seemed to last for at least one second : possibly the cloud from which it emanated discharged the whole of its energy in a single violent " flash-over."

The grey skirts of rain, lashed by furious lightning, swept up the valley towards Trisul. The storm was superseded by a calm sunset of vivid opalescent green, into which the foothills carved purple wedges. The crests of the retreating thunder-clouds were steeped in the glare of the setting sun ; their bases, merged in the darkness of the storm, flamed wrathfully with lightning. Night fell ; a delicious coolness and fragrance of moist turf ushered in her stars.

Ramni had been selected previously as a halting-place for our porters. The marches on this route are not long ones, but they involve tedious ascents. Load yourself with 80 lbs. and walk ten to fifteen miles in a day, included in which is an ascent of 3,000 ft. in a shade temperature between 80° and 90° Fahrenheit, and you will be glad that you were not born a Dotial porter. And, if you believe in reincarnation, you will pray fervently that you are not born a Dotial porter in the next life. Load-carrying over long distances is of course a matter of knack and experience, but this cannot alter the fact that it requires so many foot-pounds of energy to carry 80 lbs. a distance of fifteen miles and lift it through a height of 3,000 ft. There is probably no better load-carrier than the Himalayan Dotial porter, and even Lewa, ever jealous of the reputation for load-carrying of his Darjeeling men, told us that he had never seen a finer body of porters than our Dotials.

They had worked so well that on the following morning we gave them each eight annas *baksheesh*, and they departed happily in search of such pleasures as the ramshackle village below the camp might afford.

Greene, Holdsworth and I, unwilling to spend a day in the shadeless camp, with its filth and its swarms of pestering flies, climbed up to the ridge immediately to the north of Ramni, which separates the Nandakna and Gohna Valleys.

As we topped the ridge we hailed with enthusiasm—Kamet. It was the first time we had seen it since leaving Ranikhet. It was no longer an insignificant point, but a great peak dominating the ranges of northern Garhwal.

To the west, Nilkanta stood out magnificently, whilst immediately to the east rose Kamet's sister mountain, the Mana Peak. The massively proportioned peak of Dunagiri was visible in the extreme east, but minor peaks were hidden by the nearer range of Pilkhunta, over which we had to cross by the Kuari Pass, 12,000 ft. Almost immediately opposite, on the northern side of the Gohna Valley, was the great scar in the side of the Maithana Mountain caused by the landslip of 1893. As this landslip was the greatest that has occurred within living memory, a few details may be of interest.[1]

The portion of the Maithana Hill which fell was a spur of 11,109 ft. The fall was due to several causes. The dip of the dolomite rock of which the Maithana Hill is composed was the primary cause. The beds of rock are inclined at an angle of about 45° to 50°. As the dip of the rock on the northern side of the Gohna Valley is greater than the angle of repose of dolomite, sliding tends to take place when the necessary facilities are presented. As long as the slope of the surface of a mountain does not exceed in average angle the dip of its strata, there is no danger of a slip. In the present instance, however, the foot of the slope was undermined by the action of a river and of springs. Thus, the average angle of the slope was increased, and an enormous fall resulted. It is perhaps as well to mention that if

[1] I am indebted to His Excellency Sir Malcolm Hailey, Governor of the United Provinces, for the following details, which are embodied in a Governmental report entitled *Report on the Gohna Lake*.

rock beds are well cemented, and subject only to the influence of their own weight, the surface slope may greatly exceed the dip before sliding commences. In the landslip at Gohna, however, not only was the support removed by undermining at the foot of the slope and loosening of the beds, but the beds were impelled outwards by a series of changes following as a natural consequence of the processes which destroyed the originally compact nature of the strata. These causes combined to precipitate a mass of material, which dammed the Birahi Ganga and formed the Gohna Lake.

The causes producing a loosening of the strata were rainfall and melting snow, which resulted in a reduction of the coefficient of friction.

The southern side of the Maithana Hill became thoroughly unsafe, and in September 1893 occurred the huge landslip that now blocks the Gohna Valley. Two falls took place. It is difficult even to imagine a fall estimated to contain 12,500,000 cubic feet of rock. The fall was catastrophic in its magnitude, and continued for three days with deafening noise and clouds of dust which darkened the neighbourhood and fell for miles around, whitening the ground and tree-branches like snow. Great lumps of rock weighing tons were precipitated through the air like cannon-shots, striking far up on the slopes of the opposite side of the valley.

Providentially, the actual fall was unaccompanied by loss of life, only a few uninhabited fields being overwhelmed. Small wonder if the villagers thought that the end of the world had come. The Birahi Ganga was dammed by the huge mass of débris. The dam was nearly 1,000 ft.

PATH NEAR RAMNI

high, and formed an impenetrable barrier to the stream. Steadily the water collected behind the dam, forming a lake which attained to a maximum length of about three miles. The rise of this lake against the dam was watched anxiously. There was little likelihood of the dam collapsing owing to its thickness, but a very real danger was to be apprehended when the lake finally overflowed it, as the rush of water in the loose débris of the dam would soon form a deep channel through which the lake would quickly empty itself, with disastrous consequences to life and property in the Alaknanda Valley. Every precaution was taken by the authorities to prevent loss of life, so that when, at 11.30 p.m., on August 25, 1894, the waters of the lake overflowed the dam and started to carve a channel through it, every place along the path of the flood-waters had been evacuated and towns as far distant as Hardwar, 140 miles from the dam, were warned to expect a heavy flood. Thanks to this prompt action of the authorities, the loss of life was limited to a man, his wife and three children, who were killed by a slip of débris from the dam some time before the water flowed over. The man was known as the Gohna Fakir, and he persisted in remaining in a very dangerous position below the dam, although he had been ordered to leave it. Twice he and his family had been forcibly removed to a safe place, but had returned each time.

The flood must have been a terrifying affair. The enormous mass of water released from the lake roared down the valley at a speed between twenty and thirty miles an hour to Chamoli, which stands at the junction of the Alaknanda and Birahi Rivers. The flood was estimated to be 280 ft.

deep at the point where it left the lake. At Chamoli it was 160 ft. deep. The river-bed was raised 50 ft. by the mass of boulders borne down by the torrent. The bridge, abutments, temple, bazaar, and dispensary were washed away. All down the main Alaknanda Valley enormous [damage was done. The entire city of Srinagar, including the rajah's palace, dispensary, police station and dak bungalow, was destroyed.

Some idea of the volume of water released from the lake, and the rapid erosion of the dam, may be gauged from the fact that during the nights of August 25 and 26, the level of the lake fell 390 ft. The lake now left is 3,900 yards long and 400 yards broad. The depth averages about 300 ft. Recently, it has been experimentally stocked with trout, so that now it is possible to fish from waters covering what was once a dry valley floor.

While Greene and Holdsworth slept I wandered into the forest. These primeval forests that stretch along the feet of the Himalaya are grand, savage and untamed. Their great trees lift themselves proudly from a tangle of impenetrable undergrowth, draped with tendinous creepers, and their dim aisles are pregnant with mystery, I sat down in the shade. The afternoon was warm and slumbrous. Even the brain-fever birds had ceased to call. It was a relief to hear the buzz of a fatherly old bumble-bee and to watch him fly with noisy importance through the undergrowth.

Next day we continued our march. It was a brilliant morning charged with freshness. As we walked uphill through groves of oaks we could almost fancy ourselves on a Sussex hillside. Shipton, who was still a little weak from his bout of stomach trouble rode a pony, but he soon found walking preferable to the uncomfortable and primitive saddle.

Kamet welcomed us once more as we stepped on to the ridge above Ramni. It was the first time our porters had seen it since leaving Ranikhet, and, as each Darjeeling man breasted the ridge, he halted, doffed his hat, and muttered a few prayers. Even Nima Dorje's face assumed an unwonted solemnity. Of what were they thinking ? Doubtless of the gods whom they believe dwell on the heights, and in particular of the god whose throne is the solitary pyramid of Kamet. Other gods had not been kind. Chomolungma,[1] Goddess Mother of the World, had swept six of them to destruction ; Kang-mi, the vengeful snow god of Kangchenjunga, had claimed the life of " Satan " Chettan, bravest and best of Himalayan porters.[2] Prayers to these deities had been of small avail, but perhaps the god of Kamet might prove kinder ; and so, facing the great mountain, they prayed.

On a pasture just below the ridge on which we were standing, a ragged shepherd was sitting minding his flock. Like many another shepherd of these hills, he was whiling away time on a flute. The air he played was the essence of the hills translated into sound. Like most Eastern music, it was rhythmical rather than tuneful. As in Tibetan music, there was a *motif* of mystery and sadness and acceptance of life, but, now and again, a cheerful upward trill seemed to denote courage and hope. Play the same music on the plains or in the city and it would sound but mean, but played on the slopes of the Himalaya,

[1] Everest.

[2] Passang, a porter with the Bavarian 1931 expedition, has since perished on Kangchenjunga.

it spoke of the slow night wind, the torrent, and the little brook hastening between the ranks of golden kingcups. Two annas will purchase a shepherd's bamboo flute, but a king's ransom will not purchase its music.

Descending the northern side of the ridge, we entered a forest of oaks, pines and rhododendrons. Here and there were little glades blue with dwarf gentians. Holdsworth discovered a rare primula, and just before our camping-place at Semkharak we passed a dell of creamy peonies.

Our tents were pitched on a grassy ridge fringed with pines. Between the pines we could see the graceful peak of Nanda Ghunti. The sky was no longer hazed by the dust from the plains, or by steamy vapours rising from low tropical valleys, but was a deep rich blue sprinkled with lazy galleons of cumulus cloud.

Near our camp was a shepherd's bivouac, from the filth of which the usual swarm of flies arose to pester us.

That evening we ate our supper seated by a fire built around a tree-stump. After supper we opened one of our precious bottles of whisky, lit our pipes, and yarned. What happy evenings those were on the march ! Even now it needs but a whiff of smoke from burning pine or juniper to take me back in spirit to the Himalaya.

Next morning I was awakened as usual by Greene's stentorian bellow of " Passang ! Passang ! Garram pani ! " The volume of his voice is commensurate with the inches of his frame. Beauman said that he had been awakened in the night by some animal sniffing at his tent. He thought it was a leopard, but it was more likely an inquisitive sheep-dog, or possibly imagination stimulated by some horrific ghost-stories narrated by Greene the previous evening.

We were now approaching the Kuari Pass. From Semkharak we descended to the Birahi Ganga which drains the western snows of Nanda Ghunti. The valley-sides hereabouts are so steep that they have in places slipped away, exposing long slopes of loose rocks and rubble. During the rainy season or the melting of the snows, landslides occur frequently, and travellers and villagers traversing this route must be prepared to run the gauntlet of these as well as falling boulders and mud avalanches.

During the march Beauman attempted to photograph a small shepherdess, but narrowly escaped being stoned for his pains. Possibly, she mistook his camera lens for the evil eye.

It was a long, hot climb up the northern side of the valley. As we ascended, we saw large numbers of the little black beetles which infest the paths in this district. They are almost always to be found firmly fastened to the round dropping of a sheep at least twice as big as they are. This they roll down the path, clinging to it resolutely the while. The dung, doubtless forms their meal, though why they roll it about in this fashion must remain a mystery. Perhaps they do it to work up a satisfactory appetite.

The camping-ground at Khaliaghat had been so befouled by the villagers that Hukam Singh, gave orders for us to camp on one of the villagers' rice-fields. " It is the villagers' duty," he said, " to preserve a clean camping-site for such sahibs as may pass."

The local shikari came from the village to greet us. He was a typical hillman, lean and stringy of figure, with deep, far-seeing eyes set in a lined, cadaverous face. As he carried good *chits* from former travellers, it was arranged that Birnie and Holdsworth should start at dawn next morning and try their luck with the local bear, thar (wild goats) and bharhal (wild sheep).

That evening there was another heavy thunderstorm. Approaching from the south, it burst furiously upon a range of rock-peaks above the camp. It was a scene of wild magnificence. We stood outside our tents watching the blue rapiers of lightning lunging at the crest of the rocky pinnacles. Now and again, the overcharged clouds seemed to deliver themselves of their electrical burden all along the crest of the ridge, and a curtain of flame would fall, followed by a tearing crash of thunder, that boomed and reverberated from peak to peak.

We left early next morning for the camping-ground known as Dakwani, on the southern slope of the Kuari Pass.

Above Khaliaghat, the path meanders along the hillside and then zigzags upwards to the crest of a wooded ridge. It was again a glorious morning, with the faintest suggestion of frost in the air. We could see plainly the huge scar left by the Gohna landslip on the face of the Maithana Mountain, whilst reposing in the valley at our feet was the turquoise Gohna Lake.

We passed over the breast of an alp bright with buttercups, and descended through woods to a waterfall that leapt from the jaws of a rocky cleft. Birnie and Holdsworth joined us here. The shikari had shown them some thar, but they had not been able to get near enough for a good shot.

The hillside above the waterfall was clothed in rhododendrons, which early in the season must afford a gorgeous spectacle. Even now many were still flowering.

Budhibal Gurung approached with a baby musk deer he had found by the side of the path, a mile or two back. It was a pretty little beast, with a coat of iron grey and light brown. It had long ears, laid back like a rabbit's ears, and brown eyes barely opened, which stared pathetically upon the world. Its legs, which were long and gawky, could scarcely support it. I was annoyed with the Gurkha for stealing it from its mother, and would have returned it had it been possible, but to have done so now would have meant certain death for it. So we adopted the poor little beast as the expedition's mascot, naming it Rupert. It was doubtful whether Rupert had been weaned, and Greene's medical skill was called upon to combat the problem of feeding him. By means of a mugful of milk, a syringe and a rubber tube, he tried to inject nutriment down Rupert's unwilling throat, but Rupert objected strongly to this procedure, and his pitiful bleat showed that he considered a syringe a poor substitute for his mother.

Camp was pitched on a grassy terrace, mauve with dwarf irises, about 1,500 ft. below the Kuari Pass. Behind us, a broad gully, set at a steep angle and half-choked with beds of slowly melting snow, led up to the parabolic notch of the pass.

Southwards, the foothills stretched wave upon wave towards the violet hazes of the distant plains. We were on the threshold of the High Himalaya.

There was the usual evening thunderstorm, but it did not approach near to us, and vented its wrath upon the foothills. Later, however, there was a sharp little hail-storm and a cold wind, which made us glad to employ for the first time both layers of our eiderdown sleeping-bags.

As we wanted to view the magnificent panorama for which the Kuari Pass is famed before it was obscured by clouds, we arose early. It was a cold morning, and the grass was rime encrusted. For the first time since leaving Ranikhet, we were able to appreciate to the full the value of a plateful of hot porridge. Achung had a peculiar culinary knack of rendering the most palatable food tough and leathery. The liver that morning was no exception. Fortunately, however, the worst he could do to the porridge was to render it lumpy, or reduce it to an attenuated broth, and so we came to regard it as our stand-by on the march.

It was a goodly sight to see the long train of porters zigzagging up the last slope to the Kuari Pass. I must confess that of late I had experienced some misgivings as to our porterage—misgivings founded entirely on the experiences of Kangchenjunga in 1930, when difficulty succeeded difficulty. I had no fear that our Darjeeling men would let us down—they were picked men, as keen as we were for the success of the expedition. But our Dotial men were an unknown quantity : had they chosen to " play up " or desert us, our position would have been an awkward one, for porters would have been difficult to replace from the scanty population of the district through which we had passed. But the Dotials had marched, and were marching, magnificently, and everything had gone without a hitch, thanks to Birnie's tactful handling of them.

We tramped upwards towards the pass in the frosty calm of a cloudless morning. We expected to be rewarded with a beautiful view, but what we did see exceeded our greatest expectations.

THE KUARI PASS

As we emerged from the head of the gully on the last grassy slope leading to the pass the sun crept up over a neighbouring spur. For a few moments the rime glittered like fairy spear-points on the grass, then was resolved into shining drops of water.

We breasted the slope and halted, silent, on the pass. No words could express our delight. The Himalaya were arrayed before us in a stupendous arc. Our vision swept from the gorges of Trisul to the peaks of Kedarnath. Was it from the Kuari that the Hindu sage of old gazed upon the Himalaya and penned those inspired lines :

" He who thinks of Himachal [the Himalayan snows], though he should not behold him, is greater than he who performs all worship in Kashi [Benares]. And he who thinks on Himachal shall have pardon for all sins, and all things that die on Himachal, and all things that in dying think of his snows, are freed from sin. In a thousand ages of the Gods I could not tell thee of the glories of Himachal where Siva lived, and where the Ganges falls from the foot of Vishnu like the slender thread of a lotus flower."

The snows before us were the snows of Himachal. A curving belt of purple haze marked the course of the Alaknanda River, sacred to every Hindu as the principal tributary of the Ganges. We saw Kamet as we had not seen it before—a queen among mountains. Nilkanta was draped in clouds, but to the west the square-topped summits of Gauri Parbat and Hathi Parbat rose like fabulous monsters from a sea of lesser ridges. Remote in the east, the icy crest of Dunagiri gleamed in the sun.

Clouds were forming, and one slid jealously athwart Kamet's pyramid of granite, concealing it from our gaze.

The path traversed for a while almost horizontally across beds of snow along the northern side of the Pilkhunta ridge. At one point a subsidiary spur jutted outwards, forming an ideal belvedere. On it we sat for a long time, all save Holdsworth, who was anxious to descend as soon as possible and look for flowers. It was the only occasion during the expedition that I was glad not to be a botanist.

So we lingered awhile on a couch of fragrant turf. Clouds were born in the valleys and floated slowly upwards, caressing the hillsides. I wish we could have camped there for a night, and watched the passage of eve and dawn along the ranges. Aurora must sometimes stand on the Kuari Pass to witness her handiwork.

We descended from the pass towards the Dhaoli Valley, passing flocks of sheep with their shepherds, toiling up to the pass. Soon the last snowdrift was behind, and we halted to lunch on an alp gay with flowers, the music from a dozen little brooks in our ears. Below us was the verge of the pine forest, with one sentinel weather-beaten tree standing out before the others. Above the forest were the peaks, smoky blue and mysterious in the mid-day haze.

As we descended into the heat we felt again the runnels of sweat coursing down our bodies. Pines gave way to peaches, plums, almonds and cherries, but, none were ripe. The porters, who had arrived long before us, had pitched camp on the usual camping-ground near the village of Tapoban. It was a foul spot, strewn with filth, swarming with flies and crawling with vermin, so our tents were removed half a mile up the valley and pitched on the grassy talus of a former landslip.

Birnie and Budhibal Gurung had parted from us below

the Kuari Pass in order to go to Joshimath to fetch our mail, which had been sent there. They arrived late that evening bringing letters from home, and newspapers. As regards the world's news, I must confess that the first thing I turned to was the cricket reports. How Kent was faring in the county championship seemed of greater importance than the latest political crisis, divorce scandal or arsenical poisoning. As a nation we are often accused of lacking a sense of proportion in regard to our love of the open air and of sport. In other words, the foreigner means that we enjoy fresh air and hard exercise more than we ought to. Obviously I must have been suffering from an excess of both, and as a result the things that ought to have mattered had ceased to matter. The things that mattered to us were the machinations of Achung, the length of a day's march, and our internal economy. The mountaineer, if not a throw-back to the ape, is certainly a throw-back to some sort of primitivism.

CHAPTER VII

TO NITI

We rested our porters for a day at Tapoban, and on May 30, set off on the last stage of our journey to Niti, which was now only four marches distant. The march over the foothills had been, save for flies and heat, a most enjoyable experience, but memories of the march up the beautiful Dhaoli Valley will remain bright when much else has passed into oblivion. We are likely also to remember a particularly bad smell which was encountered two or three miles from Tapoban. Our gaze was directed to the spot whence it emanated by the drone of a million flies. It was a dead bullock—a very dead bullock—that had died by the side of the path. Another smell of approximately the same wavelength was met with a mile farther on. Again it was a bullock, but in this case the animal had apparently been killed by falling from the path down the precipitous hillside.

But it is not of these unpleasant things that I would write, but of other scents and scenes : the scent of pines and dewy turf in a hot sun ; little alps set in a chaos of giant crags ; splendid precipices veiled in gauzy waterfalls or steaming with tumultuous torrents ; and deep gorges where the overhanging crags flung back the voice of the torrent, so that we could imagine ourselves walking in some whispering-gallery of the gods.

We camped that evening on the grassy plain of Surai

Thota, and were lulled into dreamland by the dull roar of Kamet's snow-waters hastening to join the Alaknanda at Joshimath.

Before leaving Surai Thota we were told of a belief which we were to hear repeatedly in the Kamet and Badrinath districts. When Doctor Longstaff climbed Trisul in 1907, one of his Gurkhas, Karbir by name, who accompanied him to the summit, was questioned by the villagers on his return as to the view he had seen from the top. Being of a somewhat inventive and mischievous turn of mind, Karbir replied with a grave face that they had seen far over the foothills to the great plain where they could see the cities of Delhi and Bareilly. And then, of course, it was easily possible to see Bombay, and beyond Bombay was the Black Ocean, and beyond that England, and he knew it was England because he'd been there ! Thus does folk-lore originate, and we were questioned more than once as to whether we were climbing Kamet in order to see England from the summit.

Another belief existing in this district is that on the summit of Kamet there is a palace of pure gold tenanted by a powerful god. It seems a pity that Mr. Snowden was not informed of this national asset before he decided to abandon the gold standard.

During the night there was a storm that dusted the peaks with snow, but the morning dawned gloriously fine, and we walked along the path breathing keen, invigorating airs, so different now from the steamy, languorous vapours of the lower valleys. Only Rupert was unhappy, and he, obviously unwell, was bleating hoarsely and pitifully. During the marches he had been carefully carried in a small string bag similar to those borne by the sheep, slung to the belt of one of our porters. Now, his head drooped weakly from the mouth of the bag and his eyes were dull and glazed. I wish we had known what to do with the poor little beast, but there was little hope of its living separated from its mother. We were not surprised to learn, after an hour's march, that Rupert had died.

We buried our short-lived mascot by the side of a torrent beneath a sheer precipice of red granite that swept regally into the deep blue sky.

A short distance from Rupert's last resting-place, Greene and Shipton narrowly escaped being hit by falling rocks. At the spot where this occurred, the path traversed beneath vertical or overhanging cliffs, and the rocks fell free through the air with tremendous velocity, giving no warning of their approach save for sudden screams like shells. Greene was almost struck by a block as big as a man's head, that crashed to the ground beside him so viciously that his boots were covered with its dust and splinters.

Every half-mile or so we overtook families of Bhotias who were coming up the Dhaoli Valley to re-populate its villages, which are deserted during the winter months. They were driving before them herds of sheep and goats, carrying panniers laden with grain, home-spun cloth and other goods which they were taking over the Niti Pass into Tibet to trade for salt, borax and gold ornaments. These Bhotias have both Mongolian and Hindu blood in them. In appearance and temperament, however, they are more Mongolian than Hindu. They are friendly, happy-go-lucky people, with the same broad grin and merry, twinkling, almond-shaped eyes as our Darjeeling porters. Like

DHAOLI VALLEY

most nomadic people, they are fond of brightly coloured clothes and gay ornaments, and it was a pleasure to meet them after the sullen-faced natives of the lower hills and the plains.

Geologically, there is much of interest in the Dhaoli Valley. In its lower portion, for some ten miles above Joshimath, it passes between mountains, the strata of which has a dip of about 30° from south to north. This results in abrupt cut-offs on the southern sides of the peaks and inclined slopes on the northern sides, which in the case of the lower peaks are thickly wooded. There are abundant traces also of previous glaciation. Moraines issue from the mouths of side valleys, and in places line the main valley consisting usually of hardened mud in which are imbedded stones of all sizes, varying from a pebble to boulders weighing tons. Where the path passes beneath them, they form a danger to travellers, for boulders constantly fall from them, particularly during rain, when the cementing mud becomes softened. What might easily have been a fatal accident occurred but a few yards from our camping-place at Juma, when one of our Dotial coolies was struck on the head by a falling stone. Fortunately, he only received a scalp wound, which was sewn up by Greene, an operation which vastly amused his comrades.

The fine weather we had so far enjoyed was steadily deteriorating. Heavy rainstorms were developing earlier every day and lasting well into the night; the peaks were becoming plastered with snow. We went to sleep at Juma with the patter of rain in our ears, and awoke next morning, June 1, to find the pines a thousand feet above the camp white with freshly fallen snow.

At Juma, we were joined by Alam Singh, who had been sent from Mana by the Rawal of Badrinath to help organise our local transport and secure for us coolie food. He had been Meade's servant during his expeditions to Kamet, and we expected to find him a great help to us in many ways. He was a man of medium height, spare and slightly stooping in figure ; his hair was greying, and his face, which was long and sheep-like, was ornamented by a straggling, uneven and ill-nourished moustache. His most pronounced physical characteristic was what novelists describe as a " flashing smile." His greatest use to us lay in the fact that he had been appointed by the Rawal to look after our interests, for the Rawal, although not possessed of executive power, is the spiritual ruler of Garhwal and the high-priest of the Badrinath district. We therefore appointed him sirdar over our local men at a salary of sixty rupees a month.

Alam Singh is a Hindu, and Lewa a Sherpa Bhuddist, and it was interesting to compare the two men. Lewa, the hard-visaged fighting man, abrupt, brutal in his diction, never giving an order which he was not prepared himself to carry out, a man of magnificent physique, tough, alert, wiry, loyal to the core, sparing neither himself nor his comrades in the service of his Sahibs. Alam Singh, willing yet weak, intelligent yet lacking initiative, shelving responsibility whenever possible, expecting the expedition machine to run of its own accord, helpless in the face of a small difficulty or danger, frightened of offending either his superiors or his inferiors, a passenger not a captain on stormy waters, leaving most things to chance and God, yet, withal, a likeable man, who faithfully did his best to help us, and one whose cheery smile will ever remain a pleasant memory.

In places the path disappeared beneath smashed and uprooted pines—brought down by spring avalanches. Small wonder that the Dhaoli Valley is uninhabited during the winter months, for, apart from the depth of snow, the paths between villages are swept by many avalanches.

It was an interesting walk to Malari. Every turn in the path revealed new beauties and grandeurs. The peak of Dunagiri was visible from our lunching-place. Its delicate snow summit is formed by the intersection of ice ridges, ribbed in their turn with gleaming flutings of ice. Two of these ridges were visible—the north ridge and the west ridge. Neither appear practicable save to an expedition prepared to spend weeks of arduous work hacking a way up their thin, razor-like crests, and over their rickety pinnacles of ice. The west ridge looks practicable in its upper portion, but is protected from assault in its lower portion by a cut-off. Probably the eastern side of the mountain is accessible from the Bagini Pass, traversed by Doctor Longstaff's party in 1907.

Our eyes, wearied of dazzling snows, sought relief in the green depths of the Dhaoli Valley, where a pleasing contrast was afforded by a number of rocky pinnacles crowned with sentinel fir-trees.

Nima Dorje was unusually talkative as we tramped along the path after lunch. His knowledge of English was greater than I had imagined, and he chattered gaily about Everest and Kangchenjunga. Like Lewa, he was profoundly optimistic as to the eventual conquest of Everest. It was obvious that three Everest expeditions had done something more than inculcate a spirit of loyalty into the Darjeeling porters ; they had stimulated in them an enthusiasm for mountaineering. Future expeditions should continue to foster this spirit. By doing so, they may eradicate some of the fears and superstitions these men have for the high snows.

Two miles below Malari, hundreds of cedars grow from the hillside. Possibly, they are the survivors of a forest felled before the advent of British Rule and the forest conservation laws. Among them are many lordly trees, hundreds and possibly thousands of years old. What inscrutable process of nature decreed their growth in this particular spot, far from their fellows of the lower valleys ?

The sky darkened and the usual afternoon rain began to fall. Seen under a lowering mist, the slopes in the neighbourhood of Malari assumed a melancholy appearance suggestive of a Derbyshire moorland.

Malari is a quaint little village, the grey houses of which, clustered together as though for mutual protection, melt peaceably into a stony landscape.

Camp was pitched in pouring rain half a mile beyond the village. Shipton greeted us gloomily. Being in charge of our commissariat, he was always anxious to procure for us as much fresh food as possible. His most roseate dream was of the eggs and chickens awaiting us at the next village, dozens and dozens of chickens and hundred and hundreds of eggs. He would talk to us of chickens, roasted and succulent, and of eggs—boiled eggs, poached eggs, curried eggs, scrambled eggs, fried eggs, and huge omelettes, steaming and savoury. Alas ! these dreams had not materialised (see p. 304). Yet, despite disappointment after disappointment, Shipton remained undaunted. He had started out from Juma that morning with the stern light of a fixed resolve in his eyes. Malari was, he told us, the largest village in the Dhaoli Valley. There *must* be chickens and eggs. Now he was seated on a biscuit-box. The light of stern resolve had died from his eyes and had been replaced by a look of settled gloom. There were no eggs and no chickens in Malari. But near the camp someone had caught and killed an unfortunate bird that was fluttering about with a broken wing. The remains were handed solemnly round, and, after a prolonged examination, declared by a majority to be those of a cuckoo. And so, as the corpse was much too small to divide among six, our dinner that evening started with cuckoo soup.

When making up our list of stores we had, as previously stated, made an allowance for food obtained locally. Our provisions of late had been disappearing at an alarming rate. Jam in particular was being consumed at the rate of a pot a meal. We deemed it advisable, therefore, to augment our larder by as much local food as possible. In lieu of porridge we had already sampled a kind of meal composed almost exclusively of husks. This had not proved a success. Hardened campaigners, such as General Bruce, who have travelled in Garhwal, are reputed to have lived almost exclusively on chupattees. Without desiring to cast any aspersion on the gastronomical integrity of these pioneers, I must confess that I find this as difficult to believe as I find chupattees are to digest.

It was for reasons of economy that dinner began with cuckoo soup and ended with a native meal called sattu. Both dishes were accompanied by chupattees, into which

Achung had managed to impart a consistency and texture resembling well-seasoned boot-leather. Holdsworth, who, up to date, had been the foremost to insist that living on the country was essential, was enthusiastic as to the excellence of sattu. This enthusiasm was maintained, verbally, up to the last spoonful. It is remarkable, therefore, that on no future occasion was he observed to eat this excellent and nutritive food, nor did that pearl of Himalayan philosophy, " living on the country," again fall from his lips.

In appearance and taste, sattu resembles powdered cement. This comparison is not based on imagination.

A friend and I were ski-ing in the Austrian Alps. The weather was perfect, and we enjoyed excellent sport. Unfortunately, however, our provisions ran out, and it seemed necessary to return to civilisation from the remote hut which we had made our headquarters. To avoid doing this, we ransacked the hut for food. My friend was outside the hut attending to his ski when, in a corner of the kitchen, I discovered a sack, and, plunging my hand into it, encountered a soft powder which I took to be flour. Our problem was solved, we could subsist for another day or two. I took a large pinch of the flour to taste. It was certainly a harsh and gritty flour, and in flavour decidedly peculiar. Saying nothing to my friend, I proceeded to mix a quantity of it with water and knead the resulting pasty mixture into a number of little cakes, which I placed on the stove to cook. Then I went outside to declaim the joyful news to my friend. He came in, eyed the results of my labours hungrily for a moment, picked up one of the cakes, and took a hearty bite. But, alas ! the paste had changed miraculously to stone. The bagful of " flour " I had discovered was a bagful of cement !

That evening it rained heavily. For some reason—probably because they were dirty—our tents leaked a little, and once or twice I was awakened by drops of water impinging on to my face with maddening accuracy. It was, however, the sole occasion during the expedition that the " Willesden " canvas displayed the least inclination to leak.

Next morning was again brilliantly fine. Snow lay low on the grass slopes above Malari, and the peaks gleamed virginal white in a sky of deepest blue. The hills north-east of Malari with their blue, brown and purple slopes merging into snow-crested ridges reminded me of the Scottish Highlands.

Presently, the path, after plunging through a pine forest, ran out on to fertile meadows hemmed in by savage rock peaks. General Bruce once told me that the Gastern Thal, near Kandersteg, in the Bernese Oberland, is Himalayan in the character of its scenery. I can bear him witness, for the Dhaoli Valley above Malari bears a striking resemblance to the Gastern Thal, only the Dhaoli Valley is on a more lavish and magnificent scale. The splintered rock peaks of reddish granite, of Alpine size in themselves, are mere outposts of greater peaks behind.

Near the junction of the Dhaoli and Banke Valleys are the two little villages of Bampa and Gamsali. The former village actually boasts a post-office. It is the last post-office in the Dhaoli Valley and must be one of the highest post-offices in India, standing, as it does, at an altitude of nearly 10,000 ft. above sea level. That postal communication should extend so far up these remote valleys speaks well for the initiative of the authorities concerned.

At Bampa several of our Darjeeling porters prevailed upon the local natives to relieve them of their loads and to carry them, for a consideration, to Niti. I think, however, that they were not actuated solely by laziness, but because, in their own estimation, they were great men specially picked to climb Kamet, and also selected by the Sahibs as their personal servants. Strolling along like Sahibs, able to pay for substitutes to carry their loads, their prestige in the valley would be enormously enhanced; not only would the villagers offer them liquid refreshment, but they would find favour in the eyes of the village belles. I noticed that, among our Darjeeling men, Ondi, who was the first to find a substitute, invariably appeared to find favour with the feminine element of the villages through which we passed, although when we looked at him we used to wonder why, for he is by no means prepossessing in appearance.

We were no longer within range of Gandhi's activities, and, after the insolent stares of the "Congress Wallahs" of the lower hills and plains, it was pleasant to be greeted with a respectful and friendly "Salaam, Sahib" or "Salaam, Huzoor" from the villagers we met on the path.

A dozen or so ponies, driven by Tibetans, passed us, laden with merchandise. They were probably the first traders to cross the Niti Pass that year.

Half a mile above Gamsali, the Dhaoli Valley narrows to one of the grandest defiles in the Garhwal Himalaya. From either bank of the Dhaoli River the precipices rise smooth and sheer, as though sliced by a titan's knife. Here and there time and weathering have rifted the rocks

NITI GORGE

into chimneys and clefts, which spring upwards as straight as spears for 1,000 ft. or more. But, for the most part, the precipices are unbroken, and rise in a series of smooth "boiler-plate" slabs of terrific aspect.

Through this awesome rift the Dhaoli River rages in unbridled savagery, and its cold spray blasts upwards like smoke from a cannon. The path is in places a mere platform of wooden boards laid on iron stanchions driven into the side of the cliff, and a sheer drop of 300 ft. into the boiling torrent awaits an unwary step.

We crossed a vibrating and swaying log bridge, turned a rocky corner, and emerged on to the stony fields of Niti. We had passed, as it were, through the gorge of the Styx to the pastures of Avalon.

Arriving at our camping-site, which was at a height of nearly 11,000 ft., about one mile below the village of Niti, we were surprised to find another camp pitched not far away and be greeted by an English lady, Miss Gertrude Benham. She told us that she had already been several times round the world, and had chosen this quiet retreat in order to be alone and undisturbed while making some sketches of the country and the people; she hoped later to obtain permission to cross the Niti Pass into Tibet and visit the sacred peak of Kailas.

On the hillside immediately above our camp several bharhal could be seen moving about among the patches of scrub on the long scree slopes. Bharhal are wild sheep, and some of them are larger than ordinary sheep. They have curved horns, and are almost as active as chamois. Owing to the fact that they are seldom stalked in the remoter parts of Garhwal, it is sometimes possible to approach within a hundred yards of them. Birnie and Holdsworth, who were first in camp, watched one of the Niti villagers stalking one along the mountain-side above the camp. Finally he shot it, and it was rolled down the scree slope to the camp. The old axiom that " the mountain sheep are sweeter, but the valley sheep are fatter," does not apply to bharhal, for their flesh is tougher than that of ordinary sheep. The mincing machine was our gastronomical stand-by, and often there would go up a pean of praise and thanksgiving to General Bruce. His last words whispered into my ear before I left England had been, " Don't forget the mincing machine." Was it chance or providence that, soon after Shipton and I had arrived at Ranikhet, we received a note from a lady : " I understand that you require a mincing machine. I have for sale a second-hand one in excellent condition." We bought it. Its operation, however, entailed a certain amount of work, and, because of this, Achung conceived a hatred for it. One day we were given chops for dinner instead of the usual minced meat. A Gurkha could have stropped his kukri on those chops. We summoned Achung and questioned him. Achung spread his hands helplessly ; there was an unholy gleam in his eyes. " Mincing machine no good. No go," he replied. He had " lost " a vital screw, and, as he said, the mincing machine would " no go." All the mechanical ingenuity of the expedition was called in to solve the urgent problem of making the mincing machine work again. It was finally solved by Shipton, who substituted an artfully carved plug of wood for the lost screw, and the digestion of the expedition saved. After that we would see Achung seated on the ground, turning the handle of the mincing machine round and round and round with the dull, hopeless look of a beaten man. He was a slave to the mincing machine.

It was a cheery party that congregated round a table built of packing-cases in the mess tent for dinner that evening. Everything had gone well so far. Porterage had worked without a hitch and we had not lost a load; we had been blessed with glorious weather, and had enjoyed every mile of a march which, as Greene said, was worth an expedition in itself. We were lean, tanned and fit.

CHAPTER VIII

A STALK AFTER BHARHAL

I ROSE at dawn the next morning and set off with Budhibal Gurung for a day's stalk after bharhal. It was a frosty and cloudless morning. My legs levered me uphill with that effortless gait that is the product of physical well-being; my lungs drew deep breaths of pure air. We mounted rapidly up the stone-strewn hillside, not halting until we were a good 2,000 ft. above the sleeping camp.

The black carbons of night glowed redly in the current of dawn, then brightened to radiant white; blue shadows stole down brown hillsides. A small bird burst into twittering song. Only the valley slept beneath a tenuous shawl of chill, white mist.

No bharhal were to be seen, but Budhibal Gurung who was well versed in their habits, said that we must traverse the hillside in a northerly direction.

Traversing was not easy, for the mountain-side was seamed with steep gullies, the earthen beds of which were hard frozen. Care was needed in crossing these gullies, for they were studded with sharp stones ready to rip the flesh to ribbons in the event of a slide.

A crag projecting from the mountain-side was an obvious coign of vantage, and we made for it. As we clambered on to it, there was a sudden and startling rush, and a large eagle flew up from the rocks and circled round, obviously annoyed at our intrusion. We kept a wary eye on it for a minute or two, but it did not attack us, and presently made off. Had its nest been on the crag, we should have been in for a warm time of it, even though we had a rifle with which to defend ourselves.

Long we lay on the crag, scanning the rough hillside before us. No bharhal were visible, but presently I saw something moving across a patch of open ground half a mile away. It looked like a small brown bear, but, before I could get my monocular trained on to it, it disappeared into some bushes. We approached the spot carefully, but, finding nothing, continued traversing the hillside. As we did so the sun swung up over the range we were on and glared down upon us with ever-increasing intensity.

The hillside bent round a corner. Budhibal Gurung was ahead. As he gained the corner, he sank down with a sharp warning hiss. I crawled up to him. " Bharhal, Sahib ! " he said. I gazed in the direction in which he was pointing, but could see nothing. Before us the ground sank into a deep hollow, the far slope of which rose some 2,000 ft. to a gentle sky-line. It was on this opposite slope, at least a mile away, that the bharhal were grazing. I strained my eyes, but still could not see them. It was not until Budhibal Gurung had sighted the rifle on the spot that I could make them out. Even then it required a long look through the monocular to convince me that what I at first took to be seven small white stones on the slope, amid many other similar stones, were indeed bharhal. Budhibal Gurung has eyes like a hawk.

To gain the far side of the hollow we had to cross the head of the widest and steepest gully we had so far encountered. We would have given much for ice-axes. But we got across at last by clinging to tiny pebbles projecting from the frozen earth.

Taking advantage of the scanty cover afforded by scattered bushes two or three feet high, we toiled up the hillside.

Luck was against us. The morning air, which until that moment had been perfectly calm, began to stir. Light puffs came up out of the valley beneath us, wafting our scent straight to the noses of the bharhal. We were not surprised, when they retreated beyond the ridge, bounding the hollow far up the main mountain-side above.

We were dripping with sweat, but we decided to follow them. The bharhal were clearly visible some 1,500 ft. above us, congregated on a broad grass ledge, running across a minor buttress of the hillside. Their leader, a magnificent ram, was standing apart from the rest of the herd, doubtless on the *qui vive*, and was silhouetted sharply against the blue sky.

Direct approach was hopeless, both on account of the breeze and lack of cover. The best we could do was to make a wide circling movement to the right, and approach diagonally up the hillside. Had we the time and the energy, we might have made an even wider circling movement, climbed the steep hillside half a mile to the right of them, traversed it, and descended on to them. But we were climbing at 15,000 ft., and we should have been far too slow.

Utilising the scanty cover as well as we could we toiled on. Half an hour passed and the bharhal remained stationary. Four hundred yards, three hundred, two hundred and fifty. Suddenly, the big leader, who had been looking down into the valley, turned and gazed straight at

YAKS ON MARCH

us. The remainder of the herd did likewise. We " froze " immobile in our tracks. " Shoot, Sahib ! " whispered Budhibal Gurung. But to shoot was hopeless at such a range. I was panting and trembling from my exertions and for such a long shot steadiness was essential. I did not want to wound the quarry, for I was not prepared to follow up ; I was tired ; we had climbed over 4,000 ft.—sun and altitude had done the rest. So I lay watching whilst heart and lungs gradually reassumed a quieter rhythm, hoping meanwhile that the suspicions of the bharhal might be allayed. But it was not to be. At first they were merely curious, but in a few moments fear supervened. The big ram turned suddenly and darted off, disappearing down the far side of the buttress. The remainder of the herd immediately followed his example.

As it was possible that their fear might be forgotten and they might stop when out of sight of us, we ascended another 500 ft. of steep grass and broken rock on the opposite side of the buttress to which the bharhal had descended. Cautiously we poked our heads over the crest of the buttress. No living thing was to be seen on the expanse of mountain-side before us. To make sure that they were not concealed in " dead ground," Budhibal Gurung climbed several hundred feet farther up the buttress, while I made myself comfortable in a convenient turfy hollow. Presently he returned without having seen any sign of them.

I had one regret. For me it is a greater pleasure to photograph wild animals than to shoot them. Had I taken a camera with me, equipped with telephoto lens, I might have obtained some interesting photographs.

Holdsworth had started soon after us to ascend on ski a peak of some 15,000 ft. to the south of the camp. We could now see him descending, a tiny black speck, tracing out a wavering line on the northern snow slopes of the mountain. From where we sat, the summit of Dunagiri was visible. That this mountain, although placed well to the north of Trisul and Nanda Devi, receives a greater precipitation of snow than the Niti district is evidenced by a lower snow-line and the absence of rock. Dunagiri, like Kangchenjunga, is a beautiful mountain to look at, but, from the northern side at least, a dangerous one to climb, for its accumulated snows bulge out over its precipices in hanging glaciers, ready at any moment to sweep the glaciers beneath in huge avalanches.

It was now about mid-day, and towering thunder-clouds were creeping up from the foothill valleys. Ere night-fall they would expend their energy on the main range. They were not likely to reach Niti, and, even should they do so, they would receive short shrift from the dry Tibetan wind.

For a long time we lay on our couch of turf while the hours sped and the shadows swung round to the east. I wondered of what Budhibal Gurung was thinking. Was his enjoyment of such a day merely an adventurous enjoyment? Was it only the excitement of the hunt that appealed to him, or could he see farther than the brown rocks and the blue sky?

We heaved and stretched ourselves to our feet, and raced each other down the long slopes of grass and scree. Late afternoon saw us back in camp.

CHAPTER IX

THE BASE CAMP

AT NITI, Birnie paid off the Dotial coolies, and they departed happily on their long trek to their homes in the foothills.

Hukam Singh also left us at Niti. He had helped us considerably, particularly in regard to the feeding of our coolies along the line of march, and we parted from him with many expressions of goodwill.

Alam Singh, meanwhile, was busily recruiting Bhotias from Niti, Gamsali, Bampa and Malari. In addition to the men he collected, others had come from villages as far away as Mana, Alam Singh's own village, to offer their services to the expedition. At first appearance they seemed a wild, almost ruffianly-looking crowd. Their faces had never seen, or their bodies experienced, soap and water. They exuded strong odours of yaks and other things. Their tattered garments consisted for the most part of coarse sackcloth. They walked either barefoot or with their feet encased in clumsy cloth Tibetan boots or layers of sackcloth. But their gait was the gait of the hillman—slouching and slow on the level, rhythmical and deceptively fast uphill.

At first we were puzzled by their sullen and suspicious demeanour. Later, we discovered the reason for this. It was Lewa. Not only was he anxious to demonstrate his own personal superiority, but he regarded the Garhwal Bhotias as being racially inferior to the Darjeeling Sherpas and

Bhotias. Therefore, he adopted a bullying, truculent, parade-ground attitude, which he had been wont to use when dealing with the Dotials. But the Bhotias of northern Garhwal are a very different type of men to the submissive and easily cowed Dotials : not unnaturally they resented Lewa's attitude and their resentment caused them to shun their work. In the beginning Lewa would exclaim passionately, " These men are no good ! " and almost we believed him, for their morale did indeed seem poor. It was not until we had discovered their unspoken grievance, and warned Lewa to exercise more tact, that we won their confidence, and then we discovered that beneath their unsavoury exteriors beat hearts every whit as courageous and loyal as those of our own Darjeeling men.

So far, with the exception of Shipton's illness at Ramni and minor stomach disorders, we had all been very fit. At Niti, however, Greene went down with a sharp attack of fever, accompanied by a splitting headache, aching limbs and general lassitude. The attack passed away within thirty-six hours ; it was probably a touch of the sun. In the coolness of the upper Himalayan valleys the traveller is liable to become careless of the sun, but its rays are, if anything, more penetrating than at lower elevations, and it is not safe even to sit in the shade of a tree without protecting the head. A great deal of nonsense is talked about sunstroke by those who have never experienced a tropical sun, or by those whose skulls are so thick that they can do without a solar topee and assume that others can do likewise. The ideal sun-hat for Himalayan mountaineering is the planter's terai, which consists of two wideawake hats, one within the other ; to ensure complete protection, a piece of red cotton may be inserted between the two hats.

Birnie was not fit either. Possibly "living on the country" had something to do with it. At all events, we agreed that local food had better be left severely alone until we had finished with Kamet.

By June 4, thirty local coolies and thirty yaks and jhobus (half-bred yaks obtained by crossing yaks with oxen) were in readiness to start.

On the morning of June 5 we set out on the last stage of our march to the site of our base camp. The recent unsettled weather had mended, and the winter snows, although lying exceptionally low for this time of the year, were melting fast beneath a brilliant sun.

In some ways June 5 was the most anxious day of the whole expedition. Now that our willing and faithful Dotial porters had been dismissed, we relied upon the local men, the yaks and jhobus. Many of the former had been rendered sullen and resentful, thanks to Lewa's tactlessness. As to the latter . . .

At first sight, there is nothing more inoffensive in appearance than a yak. Its large brown eyes survey the world with the placidity of a White Knight. Its clumsy, lumbering body covered in long hair, which droops down concealing all but the lower portion of its legs, resembles a walking doormat, or one of those little yapping flat-nosed dogs, adored by some ladies. Never are appearances more deceptive. A yak will stand calmly contemplating the infinite while a heavy load is being laboriously strapped on to its back. Suddenly, however, it awakes from its day-dreams, and, finding to its surprise that there is something on top of it that it does not at all like the feel of, it proceeds to get rid of the encumbrance as quickly as possible. It tears itself free from those who are holding it and dashes away, bucking and jumping, until the ropes tying the boxes to its back are wrenched loose and the boxes distributed violently over the surrounding landscape. Directly the yak has freed itself from its load, the devil departs from it and it stands quite still, surveying the ruin it has wrought with a puzzled expression in its brown eyes, as though wondering how the boxes came to be lying on the ground.

The boxes, having been collected, and any that have had their sides stoved in or their lids wrenched off repaired, are re-loaded, to an accompaniment of many curses, by the yak drivers. But this time the yak displays not the slightest interest in the proceedings. Having registered its official protest and disapproval, it bows to the inevitable and moves peaceably off, maintaining an " all out " speed of one and a half miles per hour for the rest of the day.

Unfortunately, the yaks employed by us had done little or no load-carrying for a long time, and continued to register protests throughout the day. The more fragile of our belongings seemed to have been placed on the backs of the most obstreperous yaks. Starting late from the camp, I was just in time to see a box containing my photographic plates and spare cinema camera crash to the ground, and all but roll down the steep hillside to total destruction.

The yak drivers were largely to blame for the frequent stampedes, for they did not seem to know how to tie on the loads securely, and the yaks were irritated into stampeding.

From Niti a stony track zigzagged upwards for about 1,500 ft. and then traversed more or less horizontally across

NITI

Photograph, E. St. J. Bernie

YAK

broken hillsides. The path was in places a mere goat-track, and had not yet been built up after the ravages wrought by avalanches and streams due to the melting of the winter snows. It was interesting to observe that all the devil departed from the yaks when the ground became difficult, and they walked across the dangerous bits with sober circumspection. There was one steep rocky gully where the path petered out altogether. Seated on the far side of the gully, I waited for the yaks. With their heavy loads, it seemed scarcely possible that they could safely negotiate such a place. The first of them appeared, a lumbering, ungainly beast like a walking tank. It halted a moment, eyed the path critically, and proceeded to cross with stately *sang-froid*. Considering that its projecting load forced it to walk on the very edge of the rocky ledges, it was a remarkable piece of work. The remaining yaks and jhobus followed their leader, one by one, unaccompanied by their drivers, who evidently considered it the wisest policy to let their charges work out their own salvation. A slip would have resulted in a fall of a thousand feet or more, but not a yak faltered. It was not until they approached close to me that they showed any signs of perturbation. A European, particularly one with a reddish beard, appeared to unnerve them.

It was probably my appearance that caused a stampede. This occurred on a steep slope of loose stones. One yak bolted. Two or three others immediately followed its example. Beauman and I had to leap aside for our lives. In the general *mêlée*, several boxes fell to the ground, and one of them rolled down the hillside. Lewa leapt after it in hot pursuit. The lid of the box was torn from its hinges and

Shipton's pyjamas emerged; they were caught by a bush, and remained bravely fluttering in the breeze. The gramophone shot out and bounded valley-wards, but, before it had gone far, Lewa pounced upon it. We thought it must be irreparably damaged, but from another unbroken box we unpacked a record and placed it in the machine, scarcely expecting anything to happen. It was with profound thankfulness that we heard Caruso's passionate "O sole Mio." Whether this had a steadying influence on the yaks I do not know, but thenceforward they proceeded soberly.

We turned a corner and gazed into the gently inclined valley up which stretched the pastures of Goting. It was a desolate valley, and save for a solitary clump of scraggy, weather-beaten trees in its lower portion contained nothing but grass and stones. Above the Dhaoli River long slopes of reddish-brown screes swept upwards to cliffs of decaying rock and a frieze of shattered pinnacles that leant wearily against the sky. These valleys on the edge of Tibet suggest a slow, never-ending symphony of solitude and sadness. As the snows deepen and melt on their hillsides, so do nations and men wax and wane on the far-off plains, but on the borders of Tibet only the voice of the torrent, the occasional rattle of a falling stone, and the growl of avalanches breaks a silence that is akin to the silence of death.

Sharp and hard on the still air came the report of a rifle. Before its echoes had ceased clamouring there came another and another—nine in all. Budhibal Gurung, who had gone on ahead to look for bharhal, was having a merry time.

Camp was pitched on a stony pasture by the Dhaoli

River. There, Budhibal Gurung turned up with the good news that he had shot two bharhal. We were particularly glad to hear this, because the Niti villagers had demanded ten rupees for a sheep—an exorbitant sum. We had refused to purchase one, and now the gods had provided us with two large bharhal, an object-lesson to the villagers, illustrating not only the sagacity of the Sahibs, but the impartiality of the gods.

Budhibal Gurung said that he had sighted a herd of about a dozen bharhal, and had blazed away at a range of over two hundred yards, killing two of them. Both he and Randhoj Kan are in the army " marksman " class. One of the bharhal was deftly skinned by our Darjeeling men, and we supped off its liver and kidneys.

We were already beginning to learn something of our new porters. Living as they do on the Indian side of the Himalaya, the Garhwal Bhotias are, theoretically, Hindu by religion. But in practice, their creed is as accommodating as that of the Vicar of Bray, and it is probable that when in Tibet they revert for the time being to Buddhism. Alam Singh was the only one among them who showed signs of being a devout Hindu, and this was doubtless because he had been the servant of the Rawal of Badrinath.

Because of their religious unorthodoxy, the Garhwal Bhotias are less prone to superstitious terrors than are the Darjeeling Bhotias and Sherpas, whose orthodox Tibetan Buddhism is impregnated with Lamastic superstition. Yet, although the two had many traits in common, they would seldom mingle during the day or share a fire at night. The most intelligent among these local men was Natar Singh, who was capable of keeping written accounts and of exercising authority in some small degree over his undisciplined companions. One man, whom I remember vividly, was a crotchety old fellow, with weak watery eyes and a querulous mouth. He was seldom without some new grumble or complaint. His name was Pomo.

Garhwal Bhotias are simple and childlike in disposition. Most simple and childlike of all appeared Kesar Singh. We had yet to learn that behind his disingenuous and self-deprecating smirk lurked the brain of a schemer and a scrounger. Of all the local men, he is the one I remember best, not so much for his outstanding work on Kamet, but because of the disarming grin of conscious guilt with which he invariably met well-merited rebukes from Birnie.

We rose early next morning, for the march to the base camp site promised to be a long one. Old Pomo grumbled that it was two marches from Goting to the Raikana Glacier, but, as other parties had done it in one march, we saw no reason why we should not do likewise.

A hard day's marching had evacuated the devil from the yaks, and no one seeing them now as they lumped peaceably along would have attributed to them anything but the most harmless of dispositions. The Darjeeling men had purchased local cloth at Niti, and the Old Soldier had blossomed forth into a pair of remarkable breeches, made from a white cottonish material, the bagginess of which suggested a Zouave or an American baseball player. Some of the local men had affected broad-peaked caps, which lent to them a sportive and rakish appearance, whilst one, who had wrapped a dark blue scarf round his neck, might easily have been taken for an oarsman in an Oxford crew.

For two miles we followed the main Dhaoli Valley,

which is almost flat above Goting. It was a brilliantly clear, frosty morning, and as the sun lit the pinnacled ridges and slowly stole down the long slopes of reddish rock and screes, I was forcibly reminded of Mr. T. Howard Somervell's paintings of the valleys in the neighbourhood of Everest. There were the same crude, almost bizarre colourings, in which reds and yellows predominated. The shadows were hard-edged, like shadows thrown by an electric arc lamp. Such a scene would induce despair in a conventionally-minded artist. To those accustomed to the diffused lighting and soft atmospheric effects of Europe, Somervell's paintings appear harsh and brutal in their lighting and colouring. Yet, were they to see the country for themselves, they would realise that only by brutal daubing can the spirit of these strange valleys on the edge of Tibet be transferred to canvas.

Above the junction of the Dhaoli River and the torrent from the Raikana Glacier we had to cross the former stream. Other parties had experienced difficulty here and had been forced to build bridges, but, luckily for us, the Dhaoli River was spanned by a great drift of avalanche snow.

At the lower end of the Raikana Valley is a stretch of level, grassy ground where spring onions flourished. We breasted a rise, and gazed for the first time at the Raikana Glacier and our base camp site. It was not an inspiring view. All the great peaks were hidden. The terminal moraine of the Raikana Glacier blocked the valley like a vast slag-heap from some demon mine.

According to their map, Kellas and Morshead followed the western bank of the Dhaoli River above Niti. Early in the season, however, the route is very dangerous, and we saw boulder after boulder leap down the hillside and dash into the river beneath.

Winter snow lay down to 12,000 ft., and soon we were trudging across wide drifts of it. Below the terminal moraine of the Raikana Glacier is a level alp on which the Niti shepherds graze their flocks. It was now mostly snow-covered, but the warm sun was already arousing many little flowers from the scanty patches of sodden turf.

We crossed a stream and trudged up the terminal moraine, noting with satisfaction that abundant fuel in the form of dwarf juniper bushes was present. The higher we went, the larger became the snow patches, until we were trudging through almost unbroken snow of the usual abominable type met with during a hot afternoon in the Himalaya. It was seldom of the same consistency for more than a few yards, and we sank sometimes boot-deep and sometimes knee-deep into it.

Nothing is more tedious to walk over than a Himalayan terminal moraine, and we toiled to the crest of ridges a hundred feet high only to find that we had to lose the height so laboriously gained by descending an equal distance into hollows on their far sides. Providence must provide Himalayan terminal moraines for the express purpose of humbling presumptuous mountaineers.

At the foot of the moraine we said arrogantly, "We will be pitching the Base Camp within an hour." But it was three hours before we swung our rucksacks from our backs on a boulder-strewn ridge projecting from the snow which we decided was the least uncomfortable of all the boulder-strewn ridges in the vicinity.

BASE CAMP, 15,500 FT., ON RAIKANA GLACIER

LOCAL HIGH CAMP PORTERS. KESAR SINGH STANDING ON RIGHT

The Darjeeling porters set to work with such right good will that in less than an hour level platforms had been constructed for the tents, and walls built to protect them from the wind. It is surprising how the roughest and most desolate mountain-side can be rendered habitable. The height was 15,500 ft., almost equal to the summit of Mont Blanc.

The local men and yaks arrived in fine fettle, despite a long day's marching, and the former, after a short rest, went back down the moraine to collect juniper wood.

Towards evening, the clouds hanging about the peaks dispersed. Kamet appeared : only the summit was visible over an intervening ridge, and we were unable properly to appreciate its grandeur or to grasp its scale. Both the southern and northern faces were visible in profile. It was the northern face we must ascend from Meade's Col. The angle was steep—steeper than we had anticipated—and we realised immediately that it was going to be something more than a walk to the summit. Great bulges of ice on the upper slopes could be seen through glasses. They appeared to present ugly obstacles. It would, however, be rash to jump to any premature conclusions as to technical difficulties, for we could only see the slope in profile, and there was no telling how broad it was and how many opportunities it might present for out-flanking obstacles.

From the Base Camp we could gaze up the Raikana Glacier. For perhaps three miles the moraine débris stretched, a silent witness of the forces that disintegrate the great peaks, but beyond, the glacier stretched smooth and unbroken towards a wall of snowy peaks, which forms a natural frontier between Garhwal and Tibet. Many of these peaks invite the mountaineer to test his strength and skill. One of the most striking was a cone-like snow peak so simply constructed that it might have been drawn by a child.

The northward view was a fascinating one, but it was to the south that we turned at sunset, to watch the twisted masses of ashen thunder-clouds passing like tall ghosts into the night, and the summit of Nanda Devi glowing for a few minutes like a red-hot casting from a Titan's forge before being quenched in a cold bath of stars.

It was strangely silent ; the avalanches were hushed ; not a pebble fell. Night distributed her stars. And what stars ! Stars that flashed and glittered a bright electric blue, stars that pulsated eagerly and fiercely. And across the stars stretched the Milky Way, a tenuous banner spanning the breadth of heaven.

The frost was a sharp one, and we were glad to don warm clothing. As we sat in the mess tent facing candles that no longer leaned wearily from the heat, it was strange to think that a few days previously we had laboured in tropical heat and that the sweat had rolled from our foreheads.

After dinner we celebrated the completion of one stage in our journey with a ration of rum apiece. Everything had gone well ; porterage had worked without a hitch ; despite the obstreperousness of the yaks, we had not lost a single load. Shipton manipulated the gramophone, and the well-remembered favourites floated out into the still night, whilst we sat around on packing-cases puffing at our pipes, at peace with the world.

As I turned into my tent, I could see the fires of our porters about the camp. Soundless lightning was flickering in the south as I slipped into my sleeping-bag.

Frost jewels were sparkling on the roof of my tent when I awoke next morning. The bass roll of a distant avalanche heralded the rising of the sun. It was a busy day. Time was vital now ; in another month the monsoon would be upon us ; we must take full advantage of the present fine weather. On the morrow we must establish Camp One.

The local men were paraded before Birnie, and volunteers were called for to work between the Base Camp and Camps One and Two. Thus far they could go without any special equipment save snow-glasses, for Camp One was to be pitched at a height of only 16,500 ft., and Camp Two at 18,500 ft. For the work of helping our Darjeeling men to establish the higher camps, six additional men were selected. These were doled out with the same warm clothing as supplied to the Darjeeling men.

The local men were now more cheery and confident than they had been at the outset. Even old Pomo ventured a smile—after he had been warned that any more grousings would ensure his instant dismissal. We could not afford to include an agitator in our little army.

The plan of attack was as follows. Our first object was to establish an Advanced Base Camp. At what height this would be depended on the condition of the mountain and the weather. We hoped, however, that it would be at a height of over 20,000 ft., and if conditions permitted, on Meade's Col, 23,500 ft. Relays of unequipped men were to work between the Base Camp and Camp Two, bringing up food and fuel, and relays of equipped men between

Camp Two and the Advanced Base, until the latter had been fuelled and provisioned for at least a month. During the period while this was being done, the climbers would be acclimatising steadily to altitude. When this Advanced Base Camp was established we should be in a strong enough besieging position and capable of lasting out long periods of bad weather without having to retreat far down the mountain at the expense of valuable time and acclimatisation. Indeed, it would not be of vital consequence if, owing to bad weather, communications between the Base Camp and Advanced Base Camp broke down completely once the latter had been well stocked with provisions and fuel. We were even prepared to dig ourselves ice caves similar to those made and utilised so successfully by the Bavarians on Kangchenjunga.

As a halt at Camp One for acclimatisation was unnecessary we were to push on after one night there and establish Camp Two. At Camp Two, we were to remain some days to acclimatise before pushing on to Camp Three. At Camp Three there would be another halt for acclimatisation before pushing on to Camp Four, and the same would apply to Camps Four and Five. We must not rush Kamet. Success depended on acclimatisation to altitude. Even the temptation of pushing on owing to good weather must be resisted until we were acclimatised.

It was arranged that, on June 8, Greene, Holdsworth, Shipton and myself, with 36 men, including Lewa, Budhibal Gurung, and 12 high-camp men, were to establish Camp One. Directly this was done, 25 local men were to return to the Base Camp, leaving the remaining 11 men to continue with us to Camp Two. Birnie and Beauman were to remain at the Base Camp, and, on the same day that the advance party established Camp Two, ascend to Camp One with the 25 local men, carrying more loads. Twenty yaks and jhobus were to be retained by the expedition and kept on the nearest pastures, to graze until they were wanted again.

Both our Gurkhas were keen to go high. We told them that, if they did, they would have to carry loads, as we could not afford any passengers. To this they agreed with enthusiasm, and spent the remainder of the afternoon practising the use of rope and ice-axe on the snow slopes around the camp. Meanwhile, Holdsworth and Shipton ascended a small eminence of 17,230 ft. which stands near the junction of the East Kamet and Raikana Glaciers, from which they obtained a view of the East Kamet Glacier, up which we had to go to reach the foot of Kamet.

Our plan was simple, but, like all Himalayan plans, depended for its success on the weather. We watched the sky anxiously that evening, but the sun dipped into a cloudless west, flooding peak and snowfield with a peaceful rose. Even Greene's presumptuous announcement that any party he accompanied was always favoured with fine weather failed to arouse the wrath of the gods, and we turned in with high hopes of the morrow.

CHAPTER X

CAMPS ONE AND TWO

JUNE 8 dawned brilliantly. The first task was the correct allotment of loads. Among our local men were some whose ambition was to carry a lighter load than their fellows. If they could escape observation with an empty box instead of a full one, they would do so without any qualms of conscience, believing, like children, that work existed only to be evaded. If they were not detected, well and good, the sahibs were to blame, but if they *were* detected they shrugged their shoulders philosophically, grinned broadly, and accepted without question a heavy load. We had already caught out one young man, who had been apparently bowed down beneath a load of empty petrol-tins and food-boxes. But now we were wary, and Birnie lined the men up and inspected every load.

Thanks to the muddling of Alam Singh, who had not understood properly which loads were to be taken and which left at the Base Camp, it was not until the sun was high in the sky that we bade farewell to Birnie and Beauman and set out for Camp One.

The snow was soft, and Holdsworth demonstrated the utility of ski on the Raikana Glacier ; where Greene, Shipton and I sank in above the tops of our boots, he was able to slide along the surface.

From the Base Camp we slanted diagonally across the glacier, until we found ourselves beneath the cliffs of the little peak climbed the previous day by Shipton and Holdsworth.

It was grillingly hot, and a fierce sun beat down upon us with a glare that absorbed our energy like blotting-paper. But if the snow was soft, it was at least consistent, and we advanced steadily.

Below its junction with the East Kamet Glacier the Raikana Glacier is concealed beneath a wilderness of moraine mounds, but these were now, for the most part, snow-covered. We had not expected to find so much snow, and we hoped that the tardy spring presaged a summer of exceptional fineness. Himalayan snow melts and evaporates at an astonishing rate, and the sun was now hard at work. Boulders the size of cottages were beginning to appear from beneath their winter covering ; ice and snow were being stripped from the cliffs, and tumbling to the glacier in miniature avalanches, the ice with a silvery tinkle and the snow with a heavier thud.

We pressed on eagerly, anxious to obtain a view of the East Kamet Glacier. We turned a corner of the 17,230 ft. peak and saw the glacier spread out before us. At first sight it was not possible to appreciate Doctor Longstaff's reluctance to traverse it. Where we stood the glacier was at least a mile broad, and only minor rock or snow avalanches could fall from the peaks on either side of it. Indeed, the mountains bounding the glacier to the north had long, unimpressive rubble-covered slopes which could easily be walked up. But some five miles higher the glacier narrowed to a gorge, less than half a mile wide. Here again the peaks bounding its northern side were gently inclined, but those bounding its southern side were of a very different nature. Here was a mountain wall typical of the Himalaya. Six thousand feet above the glacier rises the range culminating in the Mana Peak, 23,862 ft. It is a range that bears a slight resemblance in outline to the range bounding the south-eastern side of the Lauterbrunnen Valley, in the Bernese Oberland, the northern side of which forms one of the greatest mountain walls in the Alps. But there the resemblance ends. The angle of the Mana Wall is not Swiss, but Himalayan. Owing to plasticity induced by temperature range, Himalayan ice can cling to rocks set at a terrifically steep angle. Had this wall been in the Alps, where, owing to a lesser temperature range, ice is of a more brittle nature, there would have been few, if any, hanging glaciers adhering to the rocks. As it was, the precipices were crowned with walls of ice hundreds of feet thick, some as clean cut as though chiselled by an expert mason, others broken and tottering, with fantastic towers and pinnacles leaning precariously over the cliffs. It was a place that reminded me vividly of the Nepal side of Kangchenjunga, for here were the same forces held in leash ready at any moment to sweep the precipices in avalanches of ice-blocks weighing tens of thousands of tons, the momentum of which is sufficient to carry them far across the level glacier beneath. Even as we gazed, there came a deep growl that swelled to a thunderous roll.

Yet, the danger was not so great as I had expected to find. Ice avalanches and large ones must be expected to fall into the East Kamet Glacier, but it takes an avalanche of Kangchenjunga calibre to sweep a glacier over half a mile wide, and although there were hanging glaciers fully capable of discharging avalanches sufficiently large to do this, there were no ice-walls so huge as those that defend Kangchenjunga, and avalanches that traverse the breadth of the East Kamet Glacier can seldom fall. He who ascends the East Kamet Glacier must take a chance, but it is a fair and not an unjustifiable chance.

From the junction of the East Kamet and Raikana Glaciers we passed across to the northern side of the former glacier. It was irritating travelling. We were either climbing up the side of a moraine mound, or descending into the hollow between two of them. It must have taken us well over an hour to march a mile.

Along the northern side of the glacier stretched a convenient side moraine on the crest of which we were able to walk with comparative ease. Side moraines are a boon to the Himalayan mountaineer, as they enable him to avoid wearisome détours and ascents. Another useful line of least resistance is a trough between the glacier and the mountain-side formed by the sun's heat and radiation from the rocks.

Here and there, the way along the sharp crest of the moraine was barred by great boulders many of which were so ill balanced and unstable that circumspection was needed when traversing beneath them.

We lunched on some slabs of Kamet's red granite. How many decades had passed since these rocks formed a part of the great mountain we were assailing? Time and weather are pulling the noblest mountains to destruction, but this destruction is so gradual that centuries hence, when civilisation as we know it now has crumbled to dust, the great peaks of the Himalaya will challenge the hardihood of man.

After lunch we basked in the sun, watching lazily between half-closed eyelids the play of light and shadow on the peaks.

Continuing on our way, we tramped along the broken crest of the moraine until we came to a hollow in the mountain-side just above the glacier which the local men affirmed was the camping-site of " Kellas Sahib." Now it was half filled with snow, and we pitched our tents on a rock-strewn slope above it.

The local men were in fine fettle, and, putting down their loads, grinned farewell and started off for the Base Camp, chattering gaily among themselves. It seemed scarcely possible that they were the sullen, dispirited creatures we had engaged at Niti. They strode along the crest of the moraine as though they were at the beginning and not at the end of a day's work. We had won their confidence.

Platforms were constructed for the tents, but, before the tents had been pitched, slate-coloured clouds poured down the glacier, bringing a biting wind and a drift of snowflakes. The snowstorm was a mild, desultory affair, and at sunset the clouds rolled back, disclosing peaks wedging a cold sky of greenish purple. A solitary avalanche roared like a questing lion ; the stars blazed forth ; frost gripped the snowfields ; the last zephyr of wind died away—and the world knew silence.

We supped luxuriously in our sleeping-bags. Fortunately, Achung had been relegated to the Base Camp. We had parted from him without regret. His cooking of late had reached the ultimate zero of inefficiency, and no makeshift cooking on the mountain could be worse than his. As luck would have it, both Nima Dorje and Ondi displayed an unexpected talent for cooking, and the former at least should go far in that abused but profitable calling. Their inventiveness that evening was not taxed, for we supped off pemmican soup, tinned fish, fruit and biscuits. At periodical intervals, the broad countenance of the Old Soldier inserted itself between the flaps of my tent and his horny hand passed in some fresh delicacy. When the idea happened to occur to him, he would pull an *exceptionally* greasy rag from his pocket and solemnly wipe my knife and fork upon it.

Supper was followed by a steaming cup of "Ovaltine," and the last thing I remember was a bottle which inserted itself at regular intervals into my tent. I believe its career ended in Greene's tent, where its remaining contents were taken care of until the following morning. As an example of the implicit confidence reposed by the layman in the medical profession, this deserves to be recorded.

A miniature snowstorm falling on to my face rudely awakened me next morning. The sun had risen, and its warm rays, striking the tent, were detaching the ice-flakes adhering to the inside of it, formed by the condensation and freezing of my breath.

We had decided the previous evening that an early start was undesirable. This decision was dictated by the possible danger of avalanches falling into the trench-like East Kamet Glacier. In my own experience, I have often noted that the greatest ice avalanches fall during the early hours of the day, and some of these *within a few minutes of the sun first touching the peaks*. The explanation for this possibly lies in the fact that, though the downward movement of the hanging glacier due to gravity is constant, the internal tension of the ice is affected considerably by temperature change. Thus, a hanging glacier will continue to move down over the edge of a precipice during the night, but, though a large mass of it may be in unstable equilibrium, it will remain bound to the stable ice by frost. It often happens, however, that the first touch of the sun is sufficient to shatter the frost shackles and detach the unstable mass of ice. Frost is also responsible for detaching ice avalanches in the evening. In this case, the freezing and consequent expansion of any water in cracks may just give the necessary outward impetus to a mass of ice already on the point of reaching unstable equilibrium. If the mountaineer is forced to expose himself to the risk of ice avalanches, by traversing beneath hanging glaciers, he can minimise that risk considerably by avoiding the hours of dawn and sunset. Ice avalanches may occur at any hour of the day or night, but they are more likely to occur during these two periods. Two Himalayan expeditions have, however, gone some way towards teaching me that it is seldom wise to compare Alpine conditions with Himalayan conditions. In the Alps, the number of avalanches falling at dawn and sunset is markedly greater than at any other period of the day, but on Himalayan peaks, where hanging glaciers are twice as thick as Alpine hanging glaciers, this is not so evident, as the ice is not so affected by temperature change. During the monsoon season, however, when the air temperature is appreciably higher than it is during the spring and autumn, avalanches are constantly occurring at all hours of the day and night, and I am convinced that during that period of the year the traverse of the East Kamet Glacier would be very dangerous. Had we followed

ABOVE CAMP ONE

out the plan that was at one time mooted of attempting Kamet during August, it is more than likely that we should have run a grave risk. As things turned out, however, the danger during June was negligible, and, as was subsequently proved, our porters were able to proceed safely between Camps One and Two during all hours of the day. By starting early, when the snow was hard frozen they were able to traverse the East Kamet Glacier with the minimum of effort, and so quickly that any slight additional risk they may have incurred by ascending it during the dawn hour was more than compensated for by the speed with which they traversed the dangerous area.

We left Camp One at 8.30 a.m. Descending slopes of loose rubble and frozen earth, we reached the East Kamet Glacier. Walking was considerably easier than on the previous day. Instead of being forced to toil up and down in a wilderness of moraine mounds, we progressed easily over the gentle undulating surface of the glacier, having to make only an occasional détour to avoid a crevasse or heap of boulders.

It was a lovely morning, and so long as we went reasonably slowly we could appreciate it to the full. But presently, when the snow, at first frozen hard, became softened by the sun, we sank in several inches at every step and pleasure degenerated into toil. Holdsworth, however, slid easily along upon his ski. Why were the whole party not equipped with this labour-saving device? The answer is that someone must make a track for the heavily laden porters. "But," argue my ski-ing friends, "if ski conserve the energy, they should be taken by the Europeans, who will require all that energy at some later period." One way out of this impasse is unladen porters who make the track for their fellows. The obvious disadvantage of this is that there are extra mouths to feed. Holdsworth considers that these men's loads might be distributed among the Europeans, but in that case the advantage of ski becomes doubtful. Another suggestion is that every porter should carry a pair of short light ski, but this is open to the disadvantage that all the porters must know how to ski, and they would have to carry their ski up places where ski-ing is impossible in addition to their loads. I doubt also whether a Himalayan porter, who carries his load by a head-band, would find ski practicable. Recently, there has come into prominence a snow-raquette-cum-ski. I hope that some Himalayan expedition will give these a trial, for they appear to be an excellent compromise between ordinary snow-raquettes and ski. Long stretches of suitable ski-ing snow are, however, seldom encountered on the greater Himalayan peaks.

We halted to rest on some boulders. The backward view was an interesting one. We gazed down the East Kamet Glacier to the jumble of moraine mounds at its confluence with the Raikana Glacier. We were now as high as the little peak climbed by Shipton and Holdsworth. Next to it on the range of peaks forming the southerly retaining wall of the East Kamet Glacier was a graceful rock peak over 20,000 ft. high, the dark precipices of which provided a welcome relief to the eye after the monotonous glare of the snow. This glare would, we expected, soon mutilate our countenances, and to counteract its ravages we generously smeared our faces with a special cream the brick-red colour of which is said to eliminate the ultra-violet rays of the sun at high altitudes. So efficacious was this preparation that we experienced none of the facial misery usually inseparable from high-altitude mountaineering.

Above our resting-place the East Kamet Glacier narrowed abruptly into a huge gorge. Although we were nearly half a mile from this gorge, the great peaks rising 6,000 ft. above it seemed almost to lean over us, and their precipices of reddish granite crowned with gleaming masses of ice threatened us with destruction. Suddenly, there came a thunderous roar, a small puff of snow-dust hung suspended for a few moments from the crest of a precipice and gradually melted away. The echoes reverberated sullenly from side to side of the glacier gorge, dying away at last in the distant recesses of Kamet. Only a small avalanche, a few hundred tons of ice-blocks, ground into powder before reaching the glacier, but it set my nerves quivering, for fresh in my memory was that terrible avalanche that killed poor Chettan on Kangchenjunga.[1] Was it a warning shot, fired across our bows, or was it the scornful laugh of the mountain gods at sight of this pitiful little cavalcade of men about to dare their stronghold?

We trudged onwards. It was heavy going. In that glacial trench the sun's heat, reflected upon us from either side by snow-clad peaks, was almost suffocating. Our bodies and minds became the unwilling slaves to that insidious drug, glacier lassitude. But glacier lassitude, if it saps the energy from the limbs and renders each forward step a

[1] *The Kangchenjunga Adventure*, pp. 250–7.

mental as well as a physical effort, has at least one good thing to be said for it—it dulls appreciation for danger. We looked at the wall above us and its suspended bastions of gleaming ice with indifference. The beauties and grandeurs of the immense defile through which we were passing appealed not one whit. Our eyes lifted not heavenwards, but sought the featureless snow before us. Our thoughts were concentrated, not on completing the day's work, but on the next halting-place where we might rest our leaden limbs. We longed for shade, but a sun almost vertically overhead scorched us relentlessly.

The distance to be covered was no more than five miles, but it seemed interminable. At last we reached the point where the glacier bends north-westwards. As we turned the corner, Kamet appeared. Lassitude was momentarily forgotten as we gazed upon it. From the Base Camp we had seen only the summit peeping over the nearer ridges, but now the mountain appeared in all its grandeur. The eastern precipice, nearly 7,000 ft. in height, which falls in one sweep from the summit to the East Kamet Glacier, confronted us. Our gaze passed up and over escarpments of rock towards the level plateau of Meade's Col, and then continued to mount slopes of snow and ice to the summit. How remote was that final point ! A small, gossamer-like cloud formed suddenly, rested there for a few instants, and was absorbed again into the deep blue sky.

Beyond the bend the glacier rises steeply. At the foot of the slope is a level plain. This was littered with ice-blocks. Many of them, weighing tons, had been cast right across the glacier, and it needed but an upward glance at the tottering walls of ice, thousands of feet higher, to assure us that others might be expected to fall at any instant. We did not linger, but toiled on. If this plain formed a bowling-ground for the gods, we could only hope that they would not make us their jacks.

We crossed the danger-zone and commenced to ascend the slope above. This was the most trying part of the day. In spite of the steps that we stamped out in the sodden snow, the porters were making very heavy weather of it and were halting every two or three hundred yards to rest. One man was so affected by glacier lassitude that he was unable to carry his load. Lewa refused to abandon it, and with indomitable energy insisted on shouldering it *in addition to his own.* He was already carrying about 50 lbs., though, being sirdar, he was not expected to carry anything. Thus, he bore on his back a total load in the neighbourhood of 100 lbs.

I went on ahead to look for a camping-site. A block of rock the size of a cottage formed an excellent shelter for a kitchen. Water was obtainable from a hollow close by. This was important, as we must conserve our fuel, for the amount of heat required to melt snow is almost as much as the amount of heat required to raise water from freezing-point to boiling-point.

I expected to find that the porters after their heavy day were too tired to return to Camp One as arranged, but after a drink of tea they quickly recovered their vitality, and at about 4 p.m. Lewa, Budhibal Gurung and ten porters set off back to Camp One.

We hoped that the Base Camp party, consisting of Birnie, Beauman, and 21 porters carrying rations for two days, had arrived at Camp One the same day. I felt doubtful, however, whether the local men would be able to stand up to the gruelling march from Camp One to Camp Two, a march that had tired our strongest Darjeeling men, so I sent back a note by Lewa advising an early start when the snow of the glacier was hard and frozen, for the danger of ice avalanches had proved far less than anticipated. I also suggested that if, on the morrow, it was found impossible to get all the loads to Camp Two in one day, the men who were too tired to carry them the whole distance should dump them as far up the East Kamet Glacier as possible. Actually, this proved unnecessary. We had yet to learn that beneath the unprepossessing and unwashed exteriors of our local men beat valiant and strong hearts.

After Lewa, the best load-carrier among our Darjeeling porters was Passang, Greene's servant, who lumbered along with an ungainly gait. No one would credit him with intelligence or initiative, but, as Greene said, "What he lacked in grey matter was more than compensated for by his prodigious strength." On this occasion he arrived at the camping site no less than fifty minutes before any of the other porters. I fear that Passang's lot was not altogether a happy one. As I have said, he was not conspicuous for his intelligence, and for this reason his leg was pulled unmercifully by his comrades. I shall always remember Passang as the good-natured and willing horse of the expedition—one who never ventured a complaint, and who conscientiously strove to do his best. As Greene's servant he made many mistakes—he was no Jeeves—but he tried so hard that it was impossible to upbraid him for slow-wittedness. He was a pearl of great price.

SUNSET FROM CAMP TWO

Late that afternoon there was a drizzle of snow. Battalions of mist flooding up from the south-west poured over the ridges to the south of Kamet and assembled in the gloomy trench of the East Kamet Glacier. There they remained, a sullen army, undecided as to their next move.

The sun passed behind Kamet ; the mists rising uneasily from the crests of its ridges were illumined until it seemed that we gazed at some astral body fringed by the flames of the sun's corona. The ice walls of the Mana Peak stood out redly like the fortifications of some aerial Verdun steeped in the blood of stricken attackers.

The lights died. The clouds about Kamet shrank grey and wraith-like into the dusk. The ice walls relapsed from red to a cold, malevolent green. The snows about us assumed a deathly pallor. Frost gripped the world. We crawled into our tents and slipped into our sleeping-bags.

Night enwrapped our small camp, her stars glancing down on a scene of stupendous desolation.

CHAPTER XI

CAMP THREE: THE ADVANCED BASE CAMP

I SLEPT badly, troubled by worrying dreams. The incidents I dreamed of were trivial, yet in my dreams they assumed an absurd importance. Strangely enough, these dreams were very similar to those I used to have on Kangchenjunga. For instance, I dreamt of a rucksack buckle that had broken, or some trivial object that I had lost. But the most worrying dream of all, and one that persistently recurred, was of the porters having got into some difficulty. In this dream I invariably had to stand by, powerless to extricate them from their plight. Such dreams are peculiar to high altitudes, yet, in my case, it was only at heights between 18,000 and 20,000 ft. that I was troubled, either on Kangchenjunga or on Kamet. In addition, I never felt well at these moderate altitudes, and apart from dreaming, slept badly. At higher camps I dreamt less, slept better and was undoubtedly fitter. It is interesting to note that two weeks later, when I descended to Camp Two from the higher camps, I dreamt exactly as I had done before. Mine is by no means an unusual case, for many Himalayan mountaineers have felt ill at moderate altitudes and some at heights as low as 15,000 ft. Are such things symptomatic of some physiological change that occurs at a certain altitude? Here is an interesting problem for physiologists, and one which may have an important bearing on acclimatisation.

At Camp Two, also, I was afflicted with jarring headaches for which aspirin proved a certain remedy. These headaches, unlike dreams, did not, however, recur on descending from higher camps to Camp Two; it is probable, therefore, that they were due purely to lack of acclimatisation and not to any physiological change independent of acclimatisation at a certain height.

Next morning we decided to move Camp Two farther up the East Kamet Glacier. This was rendered necessary by the hanging glaciers of the Mana Peak. There were no indications that ice avalanches ever swept the whole width of the glacier at this point, but the Himalaya have a habit of producing the exceptional, and at all events the débris of avalanches soon disappears beneath snowfalls. A quarter of a mile farther up the glacier we should be safe from the largest ice avalanches that might fall from the Mana Peak.

A good camping-site was discovered beneath the rocky slopes of a peak about 21,500 ft. which forms a south-easterly spur of the Eastern Ibi Gamin. Above our camp the East Kamet Glacier broadened into a gently sloping plain that extended to the foot of Kamet's eastern precipice. After this plain, the main ice-stream of the glacier narrows and bends in a west-south-westerly direction, finally widening out again into a series of snowfields, riven by ice-falls, which lead up towards the long western ridge of the Mana Peak. One branch of this great reservoir whence the East Kamet Glacier draws its strength ascends to a well-defined col in the ridge between Kamet and the Mana Peak.

Beauman and Birnie turned up in good time. Their local porters were not nearly so tired as we had expected them to be. They had carried heavy loads, and had well earned the extra eight annas each which had been promised them if they went all the way from Camp One to Camp Two. They had left Camp One at 8 a.m. and arrived at Camp Two at 2 p.m.

All the unequipped local men and nine equipped men returned to Camp One the same day to join Lewa and Budhibal Gurung. Birnie reported that arrangements had been made for the relaying of wood and provisions between the Base Camp and Camps One and Two. Camp One was already well stocked with juniper wood. This was important, as wood was disappearing at an alarming rate. That evening we discovered that its rapid disappearance was due to the fact that the Darjeeling men and local men refused to share a common fire. For economy's sake this difficulty had to be adjusted. One of the local men was interrogated by Birnie.

" Why will you not share a fire with the Darjeeling men ? " he was asked.

" Because we are of a different religion. They are Buddhists and we are Hindus," was the reply.

We knew that this was not strictly true, for the Bhotias of northern Garhwal care little for religious differences. The schism was more likely due to a mutual distrust resulting from Lewa's contemptuous attitude towards the local men at Niti ; the plaint of religious inequality was a mere excuse. Then Birnie asked a cunning question of the local men.

" How do you cook your food ? "

" In cooking-pots," was the reply.

" But you have none."

CAMP TWO AND EAST KAMET GLACIER

"Oh, as to that, we borrow them from the Darjeeling men," was the naïve answer.

"Well," said Birnie, "how can any devout Hindu refuse to share a fire with an unbeliever and at the same time eat from the pot he has defiled?"

There was no answer to this, and thenceforward our Darjeeling men and our local men shared a common fire. Prejudice and mistrust gradually vanished and were replaced by mutual esteem and respect. Mountains have a knack of bringing men together.

June 11 was a rest-day for everyone with the exception of 12 local men, who, as previously arranged, ascended from the Base Camp and stocked Camp One with wood. During the afternoon a postman arrived with our mail. Men had been specially selected as runners between our camps and the post and telegraph office at Joshimath. These men were well paid, and their reliability justified to the full the confidence reposed in them. We were shocked and saddened to read in the newspapers of Lieut.-Colonel H. T. Morshead's tragic death in Burma. The association of mountaineering in the past with mountaineering in the present is a very real one. Those who climb the Matterhorn without remembering the pioneers who toiled and struggled against its at one time impregnable defences, and those who can gaze at Kangchenjunga or Everest without a thought for the hopes and fears and tragedies of the past, are blind to that essence of the mystical and the romantic in which mountaineering has its roots. In the shadow of Kamet, in the silence and the loneliness about us, we felt that the pioneers who had crossed their "last pass" were watching our progress, even perhaps instilling into us their own determination, and passing on to us the bright torch of their pioneering. If success was to be ours, we should be completing work well begun, and in realising our own ambitions realise theirs.

Although it was a rest-day, Holdsworth's enthusiasm for ski-ing took him for an excursion up the glacier. I followed on foot for a short distance. I had just erected my cinema camera to take a film of his descent when there was a sudden roar. A mass of ice on the lower slopes of the Mana Peak had collapsed and fallen from the edge of a hanging glacier. Its fall left unstable a still larger mass, and even as I watched, an enormous square chunk of ice, the size of a cathedral, slowly lent away from its parent glacier. With deliberate yet irresistible force and with the stateliness of a felled factory chimney, it toppled on to the slope below and, rent into a million fragments, thundered down to the East Kamet Glacier, preceded by whirling clouds of wind-driven snow-dust. Luckily, I had time to train my cine-camera on the spot and obtain a "shot" of the avalanche.

Holdsworth enjoyed an amusing little ski-run, but he found the snow heavy and slow. We spent the remainder of the day lounging in the sun. We were already becoming acclimatised, and though I slept no better that night and suffered from occasional headaches during the day, I felt my strength increasing so far as walking uphill was concerned.

The weather was none too promising. Snow-showers were frequent after mid-day, and as the rate at which snow was falling higher up was greater than the rate at which evaporation and melting were taking place, the rocks

THE ROUTE ABOVE CAMP TWO

above 20,000 ft. were becoming plastered. This was, however, of no immediate consequence to us, for we knew that the difficult climbing was to be expected *above* Camp Three, and we anticipated no difficulty in establishing that camp unless exceptionally heavy snowstorms supervened.

Half a mile above Camp Two a wide snow gully was visible, running up between steep and broken rocks. At first sight it appeared an unpromising route to Camp Three, but we knew from Meade's and Morshead's accounts that it formed the only route leading up to the small glacier plateau on which Camp Three had to be pitched. From Camp Two this glacier plateau was invisible, and the precipices into which the gully cut seemed to run up unbroken to a great rock peak forming a buttress of the Eastern Ibi Gamin. Were it not for this gully it would be a long and difficult rock climb to reach the glacier plateau. We could distinguish above the glacier plateau, the upper part of a steep rock and ice precipice crowned by a bulge of ice. On this bulge, at 22,000 ft., must be pitched Camp Four. We knew the 1,000 ft. precipice of rock and ice between Camps Three and Four to be the crux of the climb so far as reaching Meade's Col was concerned.

With the exception of the difficult section between Camps Three and Four, the route to Meade's Col is a remarkable line of least resistance, and the greatest credit is due to Meade for its discovery. It is the one chink in the armour of a giant.

June 12 dawned brilliantly fine, but in my rough diary of the expedition I wrote : " Too cold to start until the sun reached us at 8.30 a.m. How one longed for it. Temperature 10° Fahrenheit in my tent."

The first of these references applied to every camp on the mountain. The temperature might not be very low—to a polar explorer 20° or 30° of frost is negligible—but one effect of altitude is to render sluggish the circulation of the blood, so that it is possible to be frost-bitten in but a few degrees of frost. Another difficulty in high-altitude climbing is to induce porters to start off from camp when they are feeling cold, for, although a Sherpa porter feels the cold less than a European, he has not the strength of will nor the detachment of mind to combat what he does feel of it. He is even less able to withstand wind, and nothing paralyses his faculties or knocks all the stuffing out of him so quickly as the pitiless blasts which sweep the upper regions of the Himalaya. It is scarcely to be wondered at that the Tibetan believes in a cold hell. Whether education will ever overcome these natural and inborn mental disabilities is doubtful. The intelligence of a Sherpa may be quickened, but as long as he glimpses his hell in the cold of the snows, and the wrath of the gods in the storm, he will be fit only to follow, not to lead, on a mountain.

Greene, Holdsworth, Shipton and I were off soon after 9 a.m., leaving Beauman and Birnie to spend a complete rest-day at Camp Two after their strenuous trudge the previous day.

We reached the foot of the gully without difficulty, although the glacier was somewhat rough, and choked crevasses insecurely bridged with snow necessitated small détours. The lower portion of the gully was wide, and filled with snow. The snow was soft, but we mounted with comparative ease. I noted, I must confess with a certain selfish satisfaction, that those on foot were making height more quickly than Holdsworth who was on ski. On the East Kamet Glacier he had had the laugh on us, but slopes of good snow steep enough to necessitate zig-zagging by a ski-runner can be ascended direct by the foot-slogger with less effort and in less time.

The gully led upwards into a rocky hollow. Sheer walls of rock rose to the right and to the left. In front, suspended over a low cliff of smooth " boiler-plate " slabs, was the snout of the little glacier covering the plateau on which was to be pitched Camp Three. Only a small quantity of broken-off ice lay at the foot of the snout, suggesting that the downward progression of this glacier is a slow one. The glacier snout was impervious to direct assault, but between it and the cliff to the east was a steep and narrow snow couloir. This couloir formed an obvious line of least resistance, but after a heavy fall of new snow it becomes a natural chute for any avalanches that may fall from the cliffs above. Even under normal conditions it cannot be described as absolutely safe, and as we sat resting on a rock we heard the vicious ping and whirr of a falling stone.

From our resting-place we gazed downwards and outwards between the walls of the gully across the East Kamet Glacier to the dazzling snowfields and icy steeps of the Mana Peak. From Camp Two we had been unable to appreciate the vast scale of this mountain, and what we had taken for points on its summit ridge were now disclosed as subsidiary buttresses thousands of feet below the summit. Swelling snowfields, shattered ice-falls, tottering séracs, polished ice-slopes, knife-like edges, curling cornices, and granite precipices such is the Mana Peak, one of the noblest and loveliest of mountains.

The snow in the couloir was in good condition, and taking it in turns we advanced, kicking steps. Increasing shortness of breath, necessitating frequent halts, made us realise that we were climbing now at over 20,000 ft. The couloir was deceptively long, but its angle gradually eased off, and Holdsworth, who had been forced to carry his ski over his shoulder, was able to put them on again.

As we mounted we were aware of a low booming, rushing sound in the cliffs above, like distant breakers on a rocky coast. Now, on gaining the gently sloping surface of the glacier plateau, we were met by a spiteful gust of wind that seized the loose snow and flung it stingingly into our faces. In the couloir we had dripped with sweat, but that first gust of wind seemed to go through our ribs and out of our backs like a rapier-thrust, and we hastily donned every stitch of spare clothing, including balaclava helmets.

The Meade and Kellas expeditions had pitched their camps on or near the crest of the ridge which formed the southernmost retaining wall of the glacier plateau and also the crest of the precipices above the East Kamet Glacier.

It was a stern, hard plod up to the ridge, for we were now sinking above the boots at every step into crusted, powdery snow similar to that met with on Alpine peaks in winter. Shipton was going better than anyone, and broke the trail for most of the way.

As we slowly made height the wind assaulted us more vigorously, and we had to bow our heads to its gusts. The sky darkened, and clouds rushing out of the west brought in their van desultory flakes of snow.

We gained the crest of the ridge and gazed for a few

moments at the East Kamet Glacier 1,800 ft. beneath. Then we turned to seek a more sheltered spot for Camp Three. We found it in a snowy valley 200 ft. below the crest of the ridge. Here the wind was unable to harry us, and we sat down and rested for a while.

The ascent of nearly 2,000 ft. from Camp Two had taken us little more than two hours, a speed indicative of an increasing acclimatisation to altitude. There was no reason, therefore, for deferring the establishing of Camp Three. Whether or not it would be made our Advanced Base Camp depended upon the nature of the difficulties that must be overcome on the 1,000 ft. rock and ice face separating the plateau from the top of the ice bulge on which Camp Four had to be pitched. From our resting-place this rock and ice face was in full view. It was heavily plastered with new snow and ice, and its ascent under such conditions was not going to be easy. Even should it prove possible to relay a month's provisions and fuel up to Camp Four the work of doing so would be excessively fatiguing, and might leave our porters incapable of carrying loads to Meade's Col, where we hoped to pitch Camp Five. Also, in the event of a heavy snowstorm, communication with Camp Four might be entirely disrupted for more than a week. But, assuming reasonably fine weather conditions and a practicable route to the summit, the length of time spent above Camp Three depended upon our ability to acclimatise. Supposing all these things proved satisfactory, a day or two at Camps Four and Five should prove long enough for an attempt on the summit. At all events, the first thing to do was to get as much food and fuel as possible to Camp Three.

We returned to Camp Two in a mild snowstorm. I was suffering from a splitting headache, due, I think, more to wind than altitude, but under the influence of ten grains of aspirin it vanished in less than ten minutes.

The following day, June 13, we set out to establish Camp Three. Birnie volunteered to remain behind at Camp Two in order to superintend transport arrangements, as another convoy of provisions and fuel was expected from Camp One. We set off gaily, expecting that an ascent of two hours would bring us to the camp, as it had done on the previous day, but now conditions were different. In my diary I wrote, "Misty snowy day. Very trying. Heavy work for porters. Took hours. Arrived with severe headache. Pitched camp in driving powdery snow." Much lies behind those terse phrases. The previous day we had ascended at an Alpine speed, but now glacier lassitude had us within its toils. Every step was an effort. We had frequently to halt and pant for breath. Only an inch or so of snow had fallen in the night, and, as we had our steps of the previous day to follow, walking should have been easy, especially as we were not tired from our previous exertions. It was simply and solely the climatic conditions. Sluggish shawls of mist draped the peaks. The air was lifeless. The sun shone through the mist with a blinding glare. Sunglare is particularly unpleasant at high altitudes, and no doubt contributes to lassitude, but the primary cause of the peculiar languor which affects both acclimatised and unacclimatised mountaineers is due to humidity, and, were observations to be taken, I believe they would disclose that it is on days and in places of marked humidity that the Himalayan mountaineer feels at his worst. The maximum

CAMP THREE AND KAMET

humidity in the air is found in hollows and on slopes sheltered from the wind. Directly the mountaineer experiences a breeze or escapes on to a crest of a ridge his languor quickly disappears. When ascending for the first time to the site of Camp Three, a constant draught had been blowing up the gully, but now the air was close, breathless and heavy with water vapour.

It was a hard day for the porters. They cannot have taken less than six hours to make the ascent. The mists closed down upon us as we plodded up the last slope to the camp. The scene was inexpressibly dreary. The snows about us were dull, lustreless, shadowless ; dark precipices scowled through rents in the shifting murk ; pale green walls of ice seemed to regard us with feline malevolence. Wind rose, and powdery snow began to fall heavily as we pitched our tents. I sank into my tent too tired, headachy and listless even to help Holdsworth and Shipton fetch some slabs of rock from the ridge above for our kitchen.

Our little tents were pitched in two regular lines, the snow between which was soon trampled down into a miniature high street. It is curious how the most inhospitable waste can be made homely by the addition of a few tents.

The wind rose in fury, and a blizzard whirled past the camp. We snuggled into our sleeping-bags. I started to write a dispatch. But my brain seemed incapable of coherent thought, and preferred to dally lightly with general events rather than concentrate on their detail. So putting down the pencil I lay listening to the hurried tread of the snowflakes on the roof of my tent.

Towards sunset the snowstorm abated and I crawled outside. The scene was wintry in the extreme. Several inches of snow had fallen. The last wisps of grey scud were being absorbed into a cold green sky. In the fading light Kamet's huge precipices were terribly forbidding.

Shipton and I preferred the warmth of the cooking-fire to the coldness of our tents, and sat huddled around it with the porters. At periodical intervals the sinewy arm of Nima Dorje grasping a wooden ladle shot out to serve the " mess of pottage " that constituted our supper. The leaping flames of the juniper fire illuminated the faces of the porters squatting around it. If, in civilisation, I wish to recall the memories of those days in the Himalaya, I have only to sniff the smoke from burning juniper. Still more vivid memories will be recalled by the *taste* of juniper, for most of the things that we cooked over it were impregnated with its acrid smoke. The tea tasted of juniper ; the porridge reeked of it ; however strong the soup, juniper invariably won.

It was bitterly cold, and as I sat by the fire with the front part of me roasting and the back part of me freezing, I was forcibly reminded of winter evenings spent by the draughty firesides of England. A minute or two of that excellent exercise practised by cab and taxi-cab drivers revived sluggish circulation, although at that height it was impossible to persist for long.

The green fields of sunset had been long swamped by the dark floods of night as we crept once more into our tents.

CHAPTER XII

CAMP FOUR

THE PORTERS were in poor shape next morning. Several of them were suffering from the effects of altitude. Among our veterans, the Old Soldier and Ondi were *hors de combat*, whilst Ang Nerbu was groaning from a severe headache. Nima Dorje, Nima and one or two others were their usual cheery selves, but it was obvious that the whole party needed acclimatising before pushing on farther. Personally, I felt reasonably fit, despite a night of broken sleep caused by a rebellious stomach. Beauman, however, was not feeling fit and was not so well acclimatised as were the rest of us.

Unwilling to face the boredom of a day in our tents, Shipton and I started out to prospect the route up the rock and ice precipice leading to the ice bulge on which we porposed to pitch Camp Four. The weather was dull and calm. To reach the foot of the precipice we had to traverse the glacier plateau for perhaps the third of a mile. It was hard work plugging through the soft snow, and we sank in half-way to the knees at every step.

Directly we left camp we began to realise the importance of rhythm in high-altitude mountaineering. Below Camp Three rhythm had mattered little, and we had walked uphill in much the same way as we were accustomed to walk in the Alps, albeit more slowly and with more halts. Apart from the necessity for walking slowly and systematically, it had been unnecessary to keep breathing in time with stepping. But over 20,500 ft. we found that if we were to conserve our strength and proceed with the minimum expenditure of energy, we must consciously adopt a rhythm of breathing to stepping. The beneficial effect of rhythm in walking or climbing at high altitudes may be entirely psychological, for Greene told me that he could see no reason why it should be physiologically beneficial, but the fact remains that the adoption of a rhythmical progression benefits a man bodily as well as mentally. A conscious rhythm, of course, implies measured breathing, and measured breathing implies deep breathing. Possibly, therefore, the greater part of the benefit ascribed to rhythmical progression is due to increased oxygenation of the blood. On the other hand, deep breathing alone will not carry a man along with the minimum of effort. Breathing must be attuned to stepping if rhythmical progression is to be maintained with a minimum expenditure of effort.

One of the peculiarities of the Himalaya is that their mountain-sides invariably prove to be steeper than they look, unless they have been viewed exactly in profile. This optical delusion is fostered by the vast scale on which Himalayan peaks are built, and consequent foreshortening ; it is also due in part to an exceedingly clear atmosphere. From the camp the rock and ice precipice had appeared moderately steep, and its only obvious difficulty was its plaster of freshly fallen snow. Now, as we approached the foot of it, it became more formidable every moment. What had appeared from the camp to be rock slabs set at an easy angle became rock slabs set at a steep angle, whilst steep but apparently climbable rocks were resolved into vertical or overhanging cliffs. The best route seemed at first sight to start from the left and then slant diagonally upwards to the right across the face to a point about half-way up it, then straight up the final slopes of snow or ice to the right of the steepest portion of the ice bulge.

We accordingly started to ascend a preliminary snow-slope. The snow had been disagreeable enough on the glacier plateau, but it was even worse here, for wind had hardened its surface into a breakable crust. Our lack of acclimatisation was made evident by our breathlessness and need of frequent halts. As we slowly gained height, the view ahead of us appeared more and more unpromising. Could we but gain a ledge running across the face to a rocky corner the route we had planned should be possible. But how to gain the ledge? For it was separated from the snow-slopes up which we were climbing by a smooth and repellent rock cliff 100 ft. in height. Even if the ledge were gained, further progress would be by no means easy, for it was laden with snow, piled at an angle of over 50°, whilst the appearance of the granite slabs projecting from the snow showed plainly that an icy glaze must be expected. Doubtless any pessimism we felt was induced by altitude, but we returned to camp as disgruntled as the weather, which ushered us into our tents with a brutal flurry of snow.

During our peregrinations above the camp Birnie had ascended from Camp Two with porters carrying food and fuel, so that if our preliminary reconnaissance of the route to Camp Four had been unsuccessful we could at least console ourselves with the thought that time was not being wasted and that, thanks to Birnie's painstaking work, our position at Camp Three was being steadily consolidated.

June 15 dawned fine. We decided to make a determined attempt to find a route to Camp Four. Between the ice bulge and the red cliffs of the Eastern Ibi Gamin the glacier flowing downwards from Meade's Col ends abruptly in an ice-fall which overhangs the rocks in walls of ice two or three hundred feet high. Occasionally, masses of the glacier are detached, which fall in cataracts of ice-blocks to the glacier plateau beneath. Our camp was well out of range of these avalanches, but it would be extremely perilous to venture upon the precipice beneath this hanging glacier. Between the hanging glacier and the cliffs of the Eastern Ibi Gamin there was a breach formed by a long couloir which connected the glacier plateau to the upper slopes. In its lower portion this couloir was too steep to contain snow, whilst shelving rock slabs sloped awkwardly outwards. It appeared, however, as if this initial pitch could be avoided by an upward traverse from the right into the snow-filled bed of the couloir. From this point the couloir appeared practicable throughout its entire remaining length. Assuming safe snow conditions, the most serious objection to this route was the risk of stones falling from the great cliffs of the Eastern Ibi Gamin into the couloir. From the camp these cliffs appeared to be built of firm material, and their reddish granite showed little signs of disintegration, whilst the glacier plateau at the foot of the couloir was unscored by falling stones. Owing, however, to the recent snowstorms which had probably concealed traces of débris, we could not be certain that this risk did not exist. The chief advantage of this route

THE PRECIPICE BETWEEN CAMPS THREE AND FOUR

over a more direct route up the cliffs to the upper slopes was that it was less steep.

The party that left the camp consisted of Shipton, Holdsworth, Greene, Birnie and myself, with Nima Dorje as our only porter.

Crossing the glacier plateau was scarcely less trying than it had been on the previous day, for its concave formation caused it to radiate sun glare, and we felt like flies in the focus of a burning-glass.

At the foot of the rocks Birnie, who was not feeling too fit and who was still one day behind us in acclimatisation, decided to return to camp. Once more we discovered that we had been deceived as to the apparent angle of our proposed route. The couloir was much steeper than it had appeared from the camp. Its lower pitch of shelving slabs had, from the camp, appeared possible to climb but preferably avoided by an easy sloping terrace to the right. Actually, the lower pitch was completely unassailable, whilst the easy looking terrace to the right resolved itself into a steeply sloping shelf covered with snow banked at a fearsome angle.

We started up the shelf. If the snow had been avalanchy we should have turned back at once, but, despite the recent bad weather, it was reasonably firm. Its surface consisted of the loose powdery snow which had fallen during yesterday's storm, but the snow beneath this had been consolidated by sun and frost and the boot could be plunged into it to make a firm step.

The angle of the banked-up snow was such that when standing upright, the slope could be touched with the outstretched hand. A slip was not to be thought of, and we moved one at a time with extreme caution, plunging our ice-axes in up to their heads and belaying the rope whenever possible.

At the outset we were scarcely gratified to observe a block of rock the size of our portable gramophone fall from the cliffs of the Eastern Ibi Gamin into the couloir, down which it rolled at a terrific rate before plunging into a patch of soft snow. This in itself was a damning indictment of the couloir, but before turning back we decided to satisfy ourselves beyond all reasonable doubt that no safe route could be made up it.

The shelf merged gradually into the bed of the couloir, which above its initial rock pitch was some fifty yards broad. It was no longer possible to drive in the ice-axe to its head—there was ice beneath the snow. Had it not been for the security afforded by rocks around which the rope could be securely hitched, we should have turned back. The sun shone with relentless vigour upon our backs and our pace was funereal.

The angle steepened still more. Bidding Shipton to anchor himself securely, I advanced slowly up the snow, utilising the rocks as hand-holds. Turning a corner, I found that the rocks petered out, and that it was necessary to traverse the mouth of a subsidiary couloir descending from the precipices of the Eastern Ibi Gamin. Wandering down this couloir was a ragged furrow caused by the falling rock we had seen. Here and there this furrow disclosed the gleam of ice. Plunging in my ice-axe before me, I found that about a foot of soft avalanchy snow covered the ice. To have ventured upon such a slope would have been suicidal. If further evidence was needed as to the impracticability of the main couloir as a route we had merely to glance upwards to where in its upper portion it steepened still more. There the soft snow had slipped away altogether, disclosing a sheet of black ice hundreds of feet in length.

I glanced downwards. The couloir allowed little latitude for life but an overwhelming margin in favour of death, and an unchecked slip or an avalanche would bring about certain destruction.

My companions' countenances expressed feelings similar to my own. The sooner we were out of the couloir the better, for the tropical sun was softening the snow every instant. Only Nima Dorje seemed unaware of the general pessimism, and his broad grin came up from the depths like a fine day in an English summer.

It was with considerable relief that two hours' later, after a careful descent, we found ourselves once more in safety on the glacier plateau. Our proposed route up the couloir had proved a fiasco, yet, curiously enough, we marched back to camp feeling by no means dispirited. As Shipton remarked, " We have had a grand day's mountaineering." It was our first piece of serious mountaineering on Kamet, and we felt that we had pulled as a team should pull—together.

The sole alternative left to us now was the direct ascent of the precipice to the ice bulge. We were becoming well acclimatised—our strenuous efforts in the couloir had been an invaluable aid to this end—and it was with a certain feeling of determination that we set out next morning, June 16, to solve the problem of forcing a route to the site of Camp Four.

Opinions as to the most promising line of attack were not unanimous, so we decided to divide into two parties.

Shipton and Holdsworth were to attempt a narrow couloir just to the left of that part of the precipice liable to be raked by falling ice from the hanging glacier above. This route had the initial disadvantage of commencing with a steep pitch formed by several jammed boulders which had wedged themselves into the narrow neck of the couloir. Snow had piled up on this obstruction, and the effects of sun and frost had combined to form a bulge of green ice. From the bulge there projected one large boulder weighing a ton or more, the stability of which appeared doubtful. Higher, however, the route was more promising, and the couloir should take them a long way up the precipice. Leaving Shipton and Holdsworth to find a solution to this problem, Birnie, Greene and I turned our attention to the snow and rocks on the left of the couloir. The snow here was soft, but its consistency was not such as to render it liable to avalanche. Later in the season, when the precipice is free of snow, its broken granite slabs must afford a comparatively easy scramble. Now, every hold was masked treacherously by powdery snow, whilst an icy glaze on the slabs made extreme caution imperative. The work of clearing away snow from the holds with the gloved hand or the ice-axe was slow and tedious. The first fifteen feet must have taken us as many minutes to climb. Even when the holds were discovered and cleared, raising the body by them was no easy matter. As Birnie and Greene followed, they improved the holds by scraping away additional snow or ice with their axes. We were now well acclimatised to altitude, but what would in the Alps have ranked as a simple piece of gymnastics was an effort that taxed the strength of both heart and lungs at 21,000 ft.

Above these preliminary rocks we found ourselves in a steep shallow couloir filled with snow. Climbing here was hard work, but not technically difficult. At the outset we trod the slope with extreme caution, but, although soft, it was not in a dangerous condition, and our feet plunged through a layer of loose incoherent snow into firm consolidated snow beneath. Breaking the trail was an arduous business, and my companions must have chafed inwardly at my slowness, although their patience was commendable.

Toiling upwards, we reached the foot of a rocky wall cutting across the couloir. There was no avoiding this, for an outflanking movement was impossible—it had to be climbed. The wall was not more than 20 ft. high, but it must have taken nearly half an hour to surmount. What rocks showed through the snow consisted entirely of granite slabs. Loose powdery snow had to be shovelled away with hand or axe. I retain vivid memories of the place. There was a splayed-out shallow groove from which the snow had to be cleared. The holds disclosed were barely sufficient. The upward movement was an awkward one, the landing on a sloping glacis of rock, snow and ice still more awkward. Friction was at a discount, and temporary exhaustion due to altitude tended to upset my balance. It was a great feeling to haul myself over the top, and plunge the axe up to the head in the firm snow above.

After my own heavings and strugglings it was somewhat disconcerting to see Greene ascend after a few moments' pause with leisurely elegance. True, the hard work of clearing the holds of snow and rendering the place climbable had been done, but Greene's six and a half feet of height, combined with a proportionately long reach, enables him to grasp holds far beyond the reach of ordinary mortals.

Another stretch of snow followed, studded with small rocks. These rocks were of a friendlier nature than the smooth slabs below, and were broken into great blocks piled one on the other. Snow and ice had been stripped from them by the sun, and it was a joy to grasp their clean-cut edges and feel the nailed boot grind on their honest ledges. The rocks brought us with little difficulty to an easier snow-slope forming the crest of a broad ill-defined ridge. We sank thankfully down into the snow. It was the first place we had come to where a rest was possible on the precipice—and the going had been strenuous.

From our resting-place we gazed down to the glacier plateau across which we had trudged in the morning. The slopes fell away beneath us at a terrific angle. We had climbed them, and could climb them again, but what about the porters? Under such difficult conditions it would be no easy matter for them, even though ropes were fixed on all the difficult sections.

But worries as to the future could not long predominate during that few minutes of delicious repose. I found my gaze wandering dreamily along the irregular track we had scrawled across the glacier plateau to the dark blob of Camp Three, the sole evidence of man in a seemingly unending expanse of ice, snow and rock. My gaze passed over it and beyond, across the unseen trench of the East Kamet Glacier, from which little clouds were nosing upwards to the icy ramparts of the Mana Peak, and still farther over range upon range to the violet hazes of the south where towering thunder-clouds were massing for their daily march along the foothills.

We heaved ourselves to our feet and turned once more to our task. Above the snow-slopes on which we stood the granite precipice rose proudly. There was no climbing it; it was overhanging and impervious to direct assault. Somehow it must be turned; not to the left, where the rocks overhung, but to the right, where a slanting shelf piled steeply with snow led up to a corner. Had the snow not been in safe condition, the traverse of this shelf would have been impossible, but sun and frost had done their work well, and the substratum of snow was firmly consolidated.

We gained the corner and congregated on an almost level slab of rock. The next few feet reminded me vaguely of a section on the well-known North Climb up the Pillar Rock in Cumberland, known as the "stomach traverse." A slab some 12 ft. high, slanting up to the right across the corner, had to be climbed. The slab presented no difficulty once a load of snow masking it had been cleared away, but the awkward angle at which it sloped outwards over the precipice to the right induced me to utilise a crack on the left into which I inserted my left knee and safely wriggled upwards in a painful and serpentine-like fashion. Later, when the snow had all been cleared away and fresh holds disclosed, the ascent of the slab was a surprisingly easy matter.

As we gained the easier rocks above the slab we heard voices, and discerned Shipton and Holdsworth on a snow-slope to the right of us. We also noted with satisfaction that no impassable obstacle intervened between us and the top of the ice bulge on which Camp Four had to be placed.

Broken rock, and a shallow gully filled with snow,

brought us to the foot of the final slopes of snow and ice leading up to the bulge. There was no room to sit until we had scraped the snow away from a rock. This done we were able to investigate the edible contents of our rucksacks. But our lunch was marred by the activity of Shipton and Holdsworth who were now immediately above us. They decided that they had gone far enough and would join us. Descending the snow-slopes they dislodged masses of snow, which bounded down and bombarded us ruthlessly. They brought with them the news that, although the wedged stone in the ice of the gully they had ascended had proved perfectly safe, it was only after some difficult climbing that they had conquered the pitch. Above the pitch they had climbed, for the most part, up very steep snow. They were doubtful as to the feasibility of getting porters up by their route, and, as we felt the same pessimism about ours, we all agreed that it was essential to discover a route which, when roped up, would afford a relatively easy ascent for laden porters.

The slope down which Shipton and Holdsworth had descended consisted of ice overlaid with firm snow well frozen to the ice. But, above their highest point the snow thinned and thinned until it petered out on a forbidding slope of blue-black ice 300 ft. high. To cut a staircase up this ice-slope was going to take time.

The afternoon clouds had blown up and flakes of snow were falling as we commenced to descend. The sole possibility of finding an easier route lay in making a downward traverse along a slanting shelf from the first resting-place on our upward route. This possibility we decided to investigate, although Shipton and I, remembering the view we had previously obtained of the precipice when we first prospected it, did not feel optimistic as to a satisfactory route being worked out.

As we had plenty of rope with us, we decided to leave as much as possible fixed to the precipice. A piton was driven into the rock at the upper resting-place, and a long length of rope let down to the foot of the corner, the sloping slab of which was not easy to a laden man. Another length of rope was placed along the snow-covered shelf below the corner.

From the lower resting-place the route along the shelf did not, at first sight, appear promising. The banked-up snow on the shelf was exceedingly steep, whilst beneath the shelf the rocks fell sheer for 100 ft. to the lower snow-slopes up which Shipton and I had made our reconnaissance. If only this cliff could be climbed, all would be well. But direct descent was hopeless, for the granite slabs were smooth and devoid of holds. Our one chance lay in finding a break in the cliff below the far end of the shelf.

The snow on the shelf was similar to that on the shelf leading up to the corner, and, although very steep, was in excellent condition. Save where it lay thinly over slabs, the ice-axe could be plunged into it up to the head, and the rope firmly belayed.

Soon I had run out the whole length of the 100 ft. rope to which I was attached. Below the point where I stopped only about 30 ft. of slabs separated the shelf from easy slopes of snow leading to the glacier plateau, but they were unclimbable slabs, smooth and repellent. Shipton came along and joined me, and I descended a few feet to investigate whether there was any possibility of climbing them, but, as nothing short of a rope ladder would suffice, I returned. The sole remaining possibility was to traverse the shelf to its extreme end, though from where we stood the rock face appeared higher and, if anything, steeper than that immediately below us.

Leaving Shipton securely anchored, I continued traversing the shelf. The snow held well, and only in one place where some slabs lay a foot or so beneath it was the foot not able to make a secure step. Above me the red precipice rose sheer, and once I heard the whirr of a falling stone. On the shelf, however, there was little danger from stones, for the precipice deflected them outwards.

The shelf ended against a minor buttress of the overhanging precipice. Suddenly, and unexpectedly, I noticed a narrow snow-filled couloir between the rocks of the shelf and the buttress. It was an obvious and easy route between the lower snow-slopes and the shelf. Here was the last link in the route between Camp Three and Camp Four. The problem was solved ! I could not restrain a delighted shout to the others. The reason for our not having previously noticed this couloir was that from the highest point reached on our first reconnaissance the couloir is not to be seen; it is cunningly concealed by the buttress, and the effect when the shelf is seen from below is of a smooth unbroken rock wall running across the whole width of the face beneath it. It was the first time in my experience that anything Himalayan had proved possible when it looked impossible, and I felt it to be a happy omen.

Pitons were driven in at either end of the shelf and a hand-rail of rope, 200 ft. long, stretched between. Now the porters could ascend safely. It only remained to make the staircase in the upper ice-slopes, and the crest of the bulge would be gained and Camp Four established.

One by one the others traversed the shelf, and, led by Birnie, kicked out a secure staircase down the snow of the narrow couloir. Once again the Fates were kind, for, although the couloir was very steep, and by rights should have been a sheet of ice, steps could be kicked throughout its whole length.

At the commencement of the descent the weather had threatened the usual afternoon snowstorm, but this for some reason had not materialised. As Shipton and I drove the lower piton into the rocks above the shelf, the last wisps of cloud were melting into a daffodil sky. It was strangely calm, and the dull thuds of the wooden mallet striking the piton sounded weak and muffled in the thin frosty air of 21,000 ft.

After some difficulty the piton was driven firmly into a crack, and the lower end of the rope securely tied to it. As we turned to go we glanced with satisfaction at the long line of steps and the slender hand-rail of rope suspended above them, mute evidence of work completed and another step forward in our venture.

We descended the couloir cautiously ; the frozen surface of the snow crunched and creaked beneath our feet. Once the slopes below were gained we moved quickly and easily.

Night was draining the red wine of day from the peaks as we trod the glacier plateau ; in the half-light the great wall on which we had laboured all day looked terribly forbidding. Above and behind it rose the huge peak of Kamet, blazoned on a shield of awakening stars.

At Camp Three good news and bad news awaited us. The good news was that Dorje, Birnie's servant, who had been left at the Base Camp with stomach trouble, had arrived, having, according to his own account, ascended from the Base Camp in one day. It was an amazing performance, and showed what can be accomplished by a seasoned veteran of Everest and Kangchenjunga. It showed also his enthusiasm and keenness for the task of climbing Kamet.

The bad news was that several Darjeeling men were complaining of mountain sickness, and the Old Soldier, who had been relegated to Camp Two a day previously, for that complaint, was reported as being unfit to return to Camp Three. Fortunately, all the local men were working splendidly ; already they had carried up enough provisions and fuel to last us a month.

Next morning, June 17, Holdsworth was feeling a little unwell, a sharp attack of earache having kept him awake most of the night. Beauman was still unacclimatised, and Greene felt in need of a rest after the exertions of the previous day. This left only Shipton, Birnie and myself to continue with the work of forcing a route up to the site of Camp Four. It was arranged that Shipton and I accompanied by Lewa, should go on ahead and commence the task of cutting steps up the final ice-slope. Birnie was to follow with four porters carrying provisions, which were to be dumped as far as possible up the precipice.

We left the camp early, while the snow of the glacier plateau was still frozen hard. After the gruelling work of the previous day, it was surprisingly easy to utilise the steps, on the making of which we had expended so much energy, whilst the hand-rail of rope was most comforting.

Climbing rapidly, we soon reached the rocks on which we had halted the previous day for lunch. Here hard work began. The downhill track in the slope above made by Shipton and Holdsworth was of little use to us, as we had to make an uphill track, the steps of which were sufficiently close together for ascending porters to use comfortably. The snow was in excellent order, and, although hard ice lay two feet below its surface, it was unnecessary to cut any steps, as it was safely frozen to the ice.

Above the highest point reached by Shipton and Holdsworth, the snow began to thin ; soon it was barely a foot deep, and it became questionable whether it was safe to proceed without cutting steps. To the left of us were some scattered patches of rock, and, turning aside to them, we sat down for a snack of food. The view ahead was both encouraging and discouraging ; encouraging because it could be climbed, discouraging because of the length of time and the hard work that would be required to climb it. Above the granite slabs on which we were sitting the slope rose, unbroken by any projecting rocks, to the crest of the ice bulge on which must be placed Camp Four. But it was ice—green-black ice—that reflected the sun with a steely glitter. The slope was 300 ft. high, and its steepness precluded anything but buckets of steps being cut for the porters. If, as appeared, cutting was necessary throughout its entire length, at least two days' toil were in prospect, and no light toil at nearly 22,000 ft.

To the right of us snow concealed the ice, but it appeared to lie in too thin a layer over the ice to be utilised successfully. It seemed better to climb the slope where it was pure ice, rather than involve ourselves in the additional labour of having first to clear away snow before a step could be cut.

Leaving Shipton firmly anchored to the topmost rocks, I addressed myself to the task of cutting steps. The first half-dozen blows of the ice-axe convinced me that it was one involving the hardest possible labour. The ice was hard, tough and rubbery, of a consistency similar to that encountered on the ice-wall of Kangchenjunga. The axe-pick sank into it with a dull thud, frequently without releasing a flake or chip of ice, and had to be wriggled about in order to detach it for the next blow. Under such circumstances, rhythm, so important at high altitudes, was impossible, and I had to halt every few strokes and grasp for breath.

A quarter of an hour passed ; I looked down. The steps I had made were adequate, but the height I had gained was pitifully inadequate ; it was not more than a few feet ; Shipton, comfortably ensconced on a granite slab, grinned encouragement. If my progress had been funereal in its slowness, he exhibited no sign of impatience, and only suggested that it was his turn to do some work. To this I assented readily, for the breathlessness of altitude and the sun blazing on my back had rendered me weary. But before I retraced my steps I glanced to the right, where the ice disappeared beneath the snow. Close to us the snow was only an inch or two deep—not deep enough for a step. The odds against it being deep enough and safe enough farther along were a hundred to one, for the slope appeared far too steep for snow to cling to it in any depth. Yet, when I rejoined Shipton, we both agreed that before committing ourselves to the ice, and the immense labour

THE ICE SLOPE BELOW CAMP FOUR
TELEPHOTOGRAPH FROM CAMP THREE

Photograph, E. St. J. Birnie
CLIMBING TO CAMP FOUR

involved by cutting steps up it, we ought to investigate this new possibility. If the slope was dangerous, or threatened to become dangerous, we could but retreat. Apart from the time and labour required for the bare ice, several hundred feet of rope would have to be fixed if porters were to be got up and down in safety, and although we had plenty of spare rope, the accounts of the Meade and Kellas expeditions had not led us to believe that a thousand feet or more of fixed topes would be required between Camps Three and Four, and to sacrifice so much would leave us short of it. It was the bad conditions caused by a lingering winter and recent snowfalls that were responsible for the difficulties, especially those lower down, which obviously do not normally exist.

We traversed downwards and to the right along the topmost slabs of rock to the snow. At first it was a mere skin above the ice, but the farther we progressed to the right the deeper it became. Soon, to our delight, the ice-axe could be driven into it almost up to the head. We kicked at it tentatively ; unless it was firmly consolidated and frozen to the ice, we should have no option but to continue with the work which we had just abandoned. But sun and frost had done their work well. Here was not a loose layer of sloppy snow such as might have been expected after recent snowfalls, but snow firmly crusted two to three feet in depth, adhering tenaciously to the ice. I saw Shipton's eye light up, and next instant he went at the slope with the energy of the boxer who, after months of training, sees his opponent before him. I followed, barely able to keep up with him although I had merely to follow in the steps he kicked.

Progress directly upwards was impossible without step-cutting, as the slope steepened high up, and the snow had slipped away, exposing bare ice. The obvious line of least resistance slanted diagonally upwards to the right. The snow gradually thinned inch by inch. Presently, we could only drive the axe in half-way before encountering ice, but so firm was the snow that it was still possible to climb without cutting steps. It was not until the snow was less than a foot deep that, with a sigh of resignation, we resigned ourselves to the task of cutting steps in the last hundred feet or so of the slope. Quickly now, the snow thinned and we found ourselves once more on bare ice, but it was not the tough, rubbery ice that we had at first encountered, but white, brittle and flaky, ice that had not long since been snow, and which had not yet been converted by pressure, and temperature change into glutinous ice.

With hope animating our hearts and putting new strength into our arms, we went to work with a will. There was no hesitation now. The ice-axe met the slope with a firm, confident thump, the dislodged fragments of ice skipped and hissed continually down the slope ; even our gasps had in them something of exultation. We were tasting the real joys of mountaineering, joys of work doing, of work done and its forthcoming reward.

Above us, the crest of the slope formed a silvery edge against the deep blue of the sky. A small cornice curled over the edge, sun caressed above and blue shadowed below. We avoided it easily on the right. The angle eased off. Steps were still necessary, and we chafed at the delay. At last nailed boots alone were sufficient to grip the flaky surface of the ice. We toiled upwards, breathing hard. The silvery skyline before us sank suddenly below the level of our vision and was replaced by the giant precipices of Kamet. We trod the soft snow of the little plateau forming the summit of the bulge. There we leaned on our ice-axes and panted for breath.

We sat in the snow, untied our rucksacks and rummaged for our lunch. Out came the familiar tin of sardines. As usual, the key that is optimistically supposed to roll back the lid broke. Savagely, I drove my pocket tin-opener into the portrait of the beautiful French lady who, surrounded by many elegant scrolls, ornamented the lid. How good those sardines were ! How well their oil lubricated our parched throats ! And after the sardines, a tin of Californian cling peaches and a cup of tea apiece from a vacuum flask made life seem good.

It was a day of superlative calm ; not a zephyr whispered across the snow; the sun shone hotly from an unclouded sky. The world was at rest and peace ; the smoke from my cigarette rose with scarcely a waver ; not even the growl of an avalanche broke the noonday quietude.

Our languid gaze passed for a few yards across the dazzling snows of the little plateau on which we sat, and then there was nothing—nothing save the depths from which we had emerged, more felt than seen, and beyond, mountains upon mountains, violet-shadowed and remote. Our gaze swept upwards. The sun was declining ; stealthy shadows were stealing down the eastern precipice of Kamet. It is a precipice that might well cause the most hardened mountaineer to shudder. In sunlight it had looked forbidding ; in shadow, it became appalling.

Owing to the recent bad weather, the upper part of

Kamet was plastered with new snow and glazed with ice. We need expect but little more rock climbing between Camp Four and the summit, but this new snow was going to make tracking exceedingly laborious.

We had expected to find smooth, unbroken snow-slopes leading up from Camp Four to Meade's Col, but the slopes before us by no means justified this expectation. Some 500 ft. above us, the slope was riven by huge crevasses and broken up into séracs. The former presented no difficulty so far as we could see, for they were mostly choked with snow, but the latter were composed of ice walls anything up to 100 ft. high. The way through such a maze was by no means obvious, and though the Meade and Kellas expeditions experienced little difficulty in overcoming this portion of the route, conditions might well have changed. Ice conditions vary from year to year, and a glacier slope that is easy one year may be difficult or impassable the next year. In the present instance, the ice-fall could be outflanked, if need be, by an upward traverse across an ice-slope falling from the Eastern Ibi Gamin. This alternative was, however, a disagreeable one, and would necessitate arduous step-cutting.

But, try though I might to concentrate my attention on the problem before us, I soon found myself relapsing into a placid contemplation of the glories about us. We sat upon a promontory of snow and ice, from which the icy billows swept round towards Kamet, a tempestuous yet immobile sea. Green waves of ice, hundreds of feet high, gleaming in the slanting rays of the afternoon sun, lurched outwards over shadowed gulfs. Sometimes there waves break from their bonds, and Kamet shudders as avalanches

CAMP FOUR, 22,000 FT. AND MEADE'S COL. 23,500 FT.

weighing thousands of tons are hurled with dreadful uproar down its flanks.

The precious hours of delightful repose soon passed ; we must return to camp. Sitting we had forgotten that we were 22,000 ft. above the sea, but the effort of rising to our feet set heart and lungs clamouring for oxygen. There was no sign of Birnie and his convoy of porters, and, approaching the edge of the plateau, we shouted down the slope. There was a faint reply, but it came from far below ; evidently, Birnie had not thought it advisable to bring his porters up to the plateau in view of the hard work that would be required of them later.

We took one last glance round. The air about us was still calm, but from the serene skyline of Meade's Col little "snow devils" were rising against the deepening green of the evening sky. Placid weather in the Himalaya is short-lived.

The slopes up which we had come had been in shadow for the past two hours and our steps had frozen into a hard staircase. How easily we descended ! It seemed incredible that it had cost us four days of hard work to make a route up the precipice. Yet, if the fixed ropes had been removed and the precipice reduced to its pristine condition, we should not have been in camp before dark.

Birnie's porters had dumped their loads of provisions on the topmost rocks, and it was only necessary to carry them up the final slope.

It was a perfect evening, and we descended happily, conscious both of physical fitness and ever-increasing acclimatisation to altitude.

At length the last fixed rope was behind and the steep little couloir below it descended. We almost ran down the snow-slopes to the glacier plateau.

That evening in camp we held a council of war. At the Base Camp we had vowed that under no circumstances would we rush Kamet until we were properly acclimatised to altitude, but now, after only ten days on the mountain, some of us at least were so well acclimatised, as had been proved by our ability to work hard from 20,600 ft. to 22,000 ft., that we felt fit enough to make a push for the summit. It remained only to consider the weather—and the weather was good. How long would it remain good? Supposing the monsoon was earlier than usual? If we tarried to acclimatise still more, might we not be asking too much of the weather? If it should break, we should regret ever afterwards that we had made no attempt. Supposing that an immediate push made by those who were best acclimatised failed, those who were now not so well acclimatised should by then be sufficiently acclimatised to make a fresh assault. It is pleasant to record that those who were not yet acclimatised were unanimous in recommending an attempt on the summit by those who were acclimatised.

There was another point to be considered—porterage. Mountain sickness had so reduced our high-camp porters that only ten men were available for carrying loads to Camps Four and Five. To establish Camp Five with equipment and provisions sufficient for an immediate summit attack by the whole party was an impossibility, for it was necessary to provision Camp Five with something more than the bare essentials of existence if an attack on the summit was to be carried out under favourable conditions. Not to provision Camp Five properly would be to court disaster, for even supposing Camp Four was properly provisioned a blizzard might isolate Camp Five.

At the moment Shipton and I were the fittest. Shipton had gone better than anyone and had participated in every climb. I possessed the incalculable mental and physical advantage of having climbed the Jonsong Peak, 24,344 ft., in 1930. Mentally, my starting-point on Kamet was 24,344 ft. Physically, the experience in 1930 was valuable because, once the human body has learned to acclimatise itself to high altitudes, it will acclimatise more quickly and easily when called upon a second time. But, first of all, Camp Four must be established and provisioned. Only when this was done could a final decision as to the summit assault be made.

Thanks to Birnie's organisation and some splendid work by our porters, both on the part of the men working above Camp Two and the men working between the Base Camp and Camps One and Two, Camp Three was now provisioned and fuelled for about a month. We had at least established our Advanced Base Camp, and felt ourselves to be in a strong besieging position. We were even prepared to dig ourselves in, and had all the necessary shovels with which to to do it should the weather deal hardly with us.

June 18 dawned brilliantly fine. Holdsworth, who had completely recovered from his earache, decided to accompany Shipton and myself. Owing to the limited number of porters available, we carried quite 20 lbs. each, ourselves, whilst Holdsworth, in addition to this load, burdened himself with a pair of ski and sticks, as he hoped to be able to ski at least part of the way from Camp Four to Meade's Col.

It was a heavy day. For once we could appreciate the lot of our high-camp porters, even though we carried little more than half their load. Theirs is a heritage of service and hard work of the most exacting description. I cannot believe that it is entirely for pecuniary gain or for self-glorification that these men are prepared to undergo the toils, hardships and dangers that are inseparable from mountaineering on the greatest peaks in the world. I believe that, like their sahibs, they are born with that strange instinct men call " adventure."

At the upper rocks we added to our loads from the dump of provisions left by Birnie's party until we were carrying as much as we could manage. Fortunately, the upper slope was in excellent condition, but the treadmill-like action of stepping from hold to hold with a load on the back, so heavy that it threatened to overbalance one backwards, was fatiguing work, and it was with something more than ordinary relief that we gained the plateau.

The porters were far behind. They were too wise to ascend as quickly as we. Their slowness gave us time to drive an ice-axe deep into the snow and soft ice of the plateau, tie a long length of rope to it, and let the end down the icy upper section of the slope as a hand-rail for the porters. This done, we sprawled in the snow for a delightful siesta. The weather was again perfect, and, in spite of the plateau's exposed position, a lighted match scarcely flickered. Yet, the " snow-devils " were sporting on Meade's Col and Kamet, and their uneasy spirals rose high into the sky.

Presently, we heard voices below, and going to the edge of the plateau looked down and saw the porters coming up. Wisely, they were taking their time and conserving their energy : a few steps, a halt, a few more steps, and another halt to lean on their ice-axes and regain their breath. Yet, their progress, if slow, was inevitable and magnificently steady. On the previous day the local men who had accompanied Birnie had not unnaturally displayed some timidity for the steepness of the climbing—it was outside their experience. But now these same men were ascending with the sure-footed nonchalance of our Darjeeling men. It was a striking proof of their aptitude for mountaineering, for they are born mountaineers, and only experience is necessary to equip them for the most difficult and sensational climbs.

One by one the porters breasted the edge of the plateau and sank down into the snow breathing heavily, then, with broad grins, they set about erecting the tents. They were as pleased as we at the establishment of Camp Four.

The tents pitched, they set off back to Camp Three, leaving only Lewa and Nima Dorje. Holdsworth accompanied them, leaving his ski at the camp. After the work of carrying them up from Camp Three, his enthusiasm deserved to be rewarded above Camp Four.

The day ended cloudlessly, but the wind increased in force : it no longer confined its attentions to Meade's Col and Kamet, but swept down upon our camp. How cold were its gusts ! It was as though Death himself breathed on us.

The sun sank behind Kamet, its red rays lighting the spirals of wind-tossed snow. Almost we could fancy ourselves gazing upon flames, not of heat, but of cold, rising from the cold hell which the Tibetans believe exists for the eternal damnation of the evildoer. A glimpse through my monocular disposed of this vagrant fancy. I could see the loose and powdery snow being torn off Meade's Col and the northern slopes of Kamet, whirled furiously into the air and beaten down on the lee side of the eastern precipice in a furious writhing *tourmente*.

Shuddering with cold, Shipton and I crawled into our little tent and slid into our sleeping-bags. Presently, the grinning countenance of Nima Dorje thrust itself in upon us, accompanied by two plates of steaming soup. We supped well, even luxuriously, rounding off the meal with cups of hot " Ovaltine " that quickened sluggish circulation and wrapped us in a warm glow, then, lying side by side in our sleeping-bags, we smoked and yarned. By the time that sleep claimed us we had come to the conclusion that the affairs of the British Empire should have been entrusted to a cabinet consisting exclusively of ourselves. It was not the first time we had reached such a conclusion.

I think we both slept well, although troubled by the usual worrying dreams. One of the curious facts relevant to high altitudes is that insomnia, so long as it is induced solely by altitude, matters but little. Rest and not sleep is the first essential, and although one may lie awake for hours at a high camp unable to sleep, this does not necessarily induce mental or physical weariness or restlessness. Provided one is warm one lies peaceably, scarcely conscious of the passage of time, and rises next morning feeling fit and refreshed. The reason for this is probably that sleeplessness is induced solely by altitude and not by physical or mental ill-health, as is sleeplessness at low altitudes. Thus subconsciously the mind realising that there is no physical or mental disability does not worry, and the body can rest content. Actually, I cannot remember spending a sleepless night above Camp Two, nor can I find any mention in my diary of having done so, although I remember that on one or two nights sleep must have been hard to woo, but I am quite certain there must have been occasions when I slept intermittently, and the fact that I did not consider these worthy of mention in my diary goes to amplify my previous remarks. At Camp Four we found it necessary to sleep with the head considerably higher than we were normally used to, as this position allowed of easier chest expansion, and aided the flow of oxygen to the lungs. Possibly the greatest bar to sleep is what is known as "Cheyne Stokes breathing," which at sea-level is symptomatic of heart affection. In its effect, it makes the mountaineer at high altitudes take a series of rapid short breaths followed by a deep easing deep breath. As regards dreams, I can only remember one in detail, and this was so ridiculous and absurd that it may possibly be of interest as an example of the type of dream experienced at high altitudes.

I dreamt that I was sitting among the crowd in the pavilion at Lord's on the occasion of a test match between England and Australia. The start of the match was already overdue when, of a sudden, a fat man, came rushing agitatedly down the steps of the pavilion looking to right and left of him. Suddenly, he espied me and jostling his way past the intervening people reached my side. "We're a man short and you've got to play," he whispered urgently.

" But I'm no good at cricket, and I've no clothes or anything," I protested.

" No, no, no ! you must come," he exclaimed, and fairly dragging me from my seat pulled me through the throng of spectators into the pavilion. There I was able to borrow a flannel shirt, but there were no flannel trousers available and only one pad. A few minutes later, the huge crowd were doubtless much edified at perceiving Mr. K. S. Duleepsinhji, correctly clad, and myself, clad in a white flannel shirt and a pair of dark striped morning trousers, on the left leg of which reposed the one dirty pad with which the M.C.C. had been able to provide me, and my feet encased in a pair of Mr. Carter's climbing boots ornamented with grey spats, emerge from the pavilion to open the batting for England. Just as we were about to pass through the pavilion gate, a tall, woebegone man, dressed in black like an undertaker, came up to me and said with a broad Yorkshire accent :

" Remember, laad, ——"—naming a well-known Australian fast bowler—" either bowls at your brains or y' guuts. Keep tha baat straight, and tha end oop."

As my partner and I walked across the expanse of green towards the wickets, we argued fiercely as to who should take the first ball. This was finally settled by our stopping half-way to the wicket and tossing a half-crown. I won and, to my immense relief, did not have to take the first ball.

We arrived at the wicket, but before play could commence, the umpire and I took a boiling-point thermometer-reading. The height above sea-level of Lord's cricket ground having been determined to the satisfaction of the umpire, play was allowed to begin. The bowler, a tall man with arms like flails, retreated to the edge of the ground, then sprang forward in a series of huge leaps towards the wicket, but long before he got to it he swung his arm and delivered the ball. It missed the umpire by a fraction of an inch and struck the wicket at my end. Instantly, a tremendous shout of " How's that ! " went up. " Hout ! " said the umpire laconically. At this there came a savage scream from the pavilion, and I saw a number of old gentlemen wearing public school and college ties leap to their feet, shaking their fists. As I started to walk towards the pavilion, the uproar around the ground increased. Police with drawn truncheons and an armoured car filled with the " Flying Squad " appeared from behind the bowling screen. Then there came a series of staccato reports and I saw the umpire and the players begin to fall one by one upon the turf. Looking up, I perceived that one of the old gentlemen, red-faced, white-moustached, and with an Old Etonian tie, was perched on the pavilion weather-vane, with a Lewis machine-gun with which he was sweeping the ground. I threw myself flat to escape the hail of bullets. Around me the uproar grew and grew and grew . . . and then I woke up. I make psycho-analysts a present of this dream.

The sun found us early next morning, and we breakfasted leisurely in its warm rays. It was delightful knowing that a whole day of ease was before us, whilst our satisfaction was increased by the knowledge that we had earned it. A week's hard labour was behind us. It was on June 13 that we had left Camp Two to prospect the route to the site of Camp Three ; now we were almost within striking distance of the summit.

Lying at our ease on a tarpaulin laid over the snow, we could gaze up at Kamet. To-day it looked almost kind. Its eastern precipice was not shadowed and terrible as it had been the previous afternoon, but its details were revealed by the sun. Our gaze passed up the broken slopes leading towards Meade's Col. Would their jumble of séracs and crevasses present any difficulty ? And what of the final slope of Kamet ? Long we gazed at it. Only the eastern edge of it was visible. Here and there it was broken by ice-walls which we could only hope did not traverse the whole width of the face.

Yet we experienced a feeling of confidence. Up to date everything had gone well. Our plans, which had materialised with scarcely a hitch, seemed but movements in some intricate symphony that would conclude inevitably on a note of triumph. . . . Yet might not Kamet be preparing a furious resistance ? For ought we knew, a blizzard might be gathering its forces in the blue dome of the unclouded sky. Kangchenjunga had taught some bitter lessons. It had taught me that Himalayan weather is fickle, and that Himalayan peaks are ruthless and cunning. It had taught me, paradoxically, always to assume the unexpected. And so as I looked upwards at Kamet shining serenely in the morning sun, my confidence was tortured by devils of doubt and misgiving. Plan an attack on a Himalayan peak with all the experience and skill of mountaineering craft at your disposal, and you still depend on luck. In the pitiless frost of adverse weather conditions the most elaborately organised assault must wither and droop. Should the weather deal hardly with us now, not only should we fail to reach the summit, but we might be hard put to it to retreat to Camp Three. Yet against such forebodings had to be set the fact that so far we had not experienced snowstorms approaching in ferocity and precipitation those that assail Kangchenjunga. Another comforting reflection was that even if we were forced back to Camp Three, such a retreat would not necessarily spell defeat, for Camp Three was so well stocked with food and fuel that it would enable us to lay siege to Kamet.

When the brain is disturbed by such conflicting thoughts it is difficult to resign oneself to a day of inaction, yet inaction was necessary if we were to become acclimatised. For a while impatience predominated, but the brain, realising its futility, presently rejected it. Doubts and fears for the future vanished like wraiths ; we dozed in the sunlight, until the world seemed unreal and unsubstantial, and the peace of the hills embraced us.

Soon after dawn we had espied the remainder of the party setting out from Camp Three, mere specks on the glacier plateau below. Now, towards mid-day, we heard voices, and from the edge of the ice-slope we could see them toiling upwards. The porters were all going well, and the local men in particular had mastered the rhythmical method of progression to which I have previously alluded. One by one they breasted the ice-slope, halted a moment leaning on their ice-axes, breathing heavily the while, then sank down into the snow with guttural grunts of satisfaction. They had done well, and their grins when they had recovered their breath showed that they realised it.

Shipton and I were surprised and delighted to find that Beauman was with the others. When we had left Camp

Three he was still unacclimatised, and we had not expected him to be fit enough to ascend to Camp Four for several days. Recently, Greene had experimented with ammonium chloride, and had administered this to himself and Beauman. The theory underlying this experiment is that ammonium chloride counteracts to some extent the diminution of acidity in the body which results from oxygen lack at high altitudes. Whether or not the experiment had the desired effect of hastening Beauman's acclimatisation must remain non-proven, but in its effects it was at least harmless, and, on the small evidence available, it would appear desirable to experiment further with it. An interesting point is raised by this question of diminution of acidity at high altitudes. It would seem to show that climbers whose tendency at sea level is towards acidosis will do better at high altitudes than those whose tendency is towards alkalosis.

Later in the day, Holdsworth, with his usual energy, ascended on ski the snow-slopes for a few hundred feet above the camp and ran back to the camp as steadily as though he was ski-ing on an Alpine peak and not at 22,000 ft. He found the consistency of the snow to be variable and running difficult, and that, owing to the altitude, swings necessitated a considerable expenditure of energy. The pleasure derived from ski-ing is, of course, inversely proportional to the altitude.

We spent the remainder of the day laying our plans for the morrow. A total of nine porters, including Lewa and Budhibal Gurung, were available. It was arranged that we should split up into two parties. Shipton, Holdsworth and I were to constitute the first party; on the morrow we should establish, if possible, Camp Five on Meade's Col, taking with us the nine porters. Lewa and Nima Dorje were to remain with us at Camp Five, and the seven remaining porters return the same day to Camp Four. The following day the first party were to make an attempt on the summit, weather conditions and their physical fitness permitting.

The same day that the summit attempt was being made, the second party with the seven remaining porters were to ascend to Camp Five with provisions and fuel sufficient for several days.

So much for the plan, simple enough in itself, yet dependent for success on several factors : good weather, reasonably good snow conditions, lack of insuperable difficulties on Kamet, and the fitness of ourselves and our porters.

CHAPTER XIII

CAMP FIVE

I AWOKE early next morning, June 20. It was very cold, and the roof of my tent sparkled with my condensed and frozen breath. Through the little window at the head end of the tent I could see that the sky was brilliantly clear. The dawn was stealing down Kamet, not a lurid dawn of riotous colourings presaging evil, but an ordained and gradual awakening.

Presently the sun's rays warmed the camp, and I arose in the midst of a miniature snowstorm falling from the roof of my tent. A few minutes before, everything had been in the grip of intense cold and now, miraculously, life had returned to the white corpse of the world.

Seated on packing-cases, we crammed food into reluctant stomachs. A few minutes were needed for final preparations and, within an hour after the sun had risen, Shipton, Holdsworth and I with our nine porters were on our way to Meade's Col. We started with the " good lucks " of our friends in our ears.

The surface of the snow-slope immediately above the camp had frozen into a hard crust, and we ascended easily for the first two or three hundred feet, except for Holdsworth, who found it difficult to edge his ski into the crust. But the crust could not long withstand the fierce rays of the sun, which poured upon our backs with a relentless fury that sapped both will-power and energy. We began

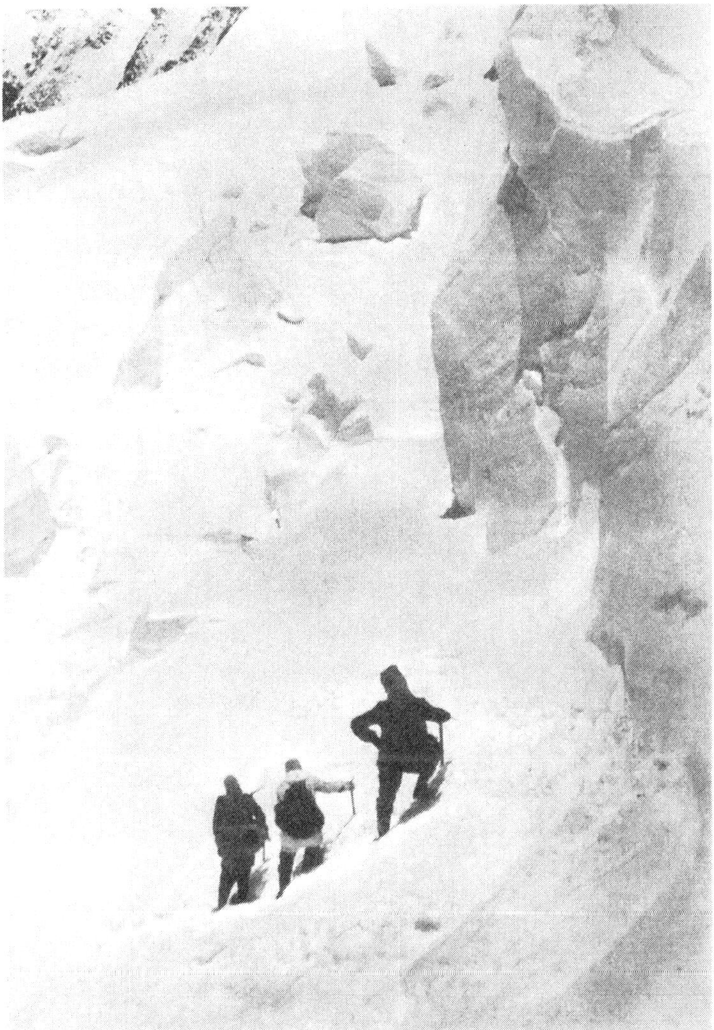

THE ICE WALL BETWEEN CAMPS FOUR AND FIVE

to sink in, at first only an inch or two, and then, as the snow became softer and softer, over the ankle and finally the top of the boot.

Taking it in turns to break the trail for the heavily laden porters, Shipton and I advanced slowly, while Holdsworth zigzagged easily now up the slope. For a man on ski there was no necessity for the rope, but Shipton and I deemed it advisable on account of sundry concealed crevasses. As we trudged upwards, we scanned anxiously the ice-fall ahead of us. Most prominent in our vision was an abrupt wall of ice that appeared to stretch across the whole width of the slope between Kamet's eastern precipice and the Eastern Ibi Gamin. If it extended without a break and was impossible to climb, we should have no option but to outflank it on the steep ice-slopes of the Eastern Ibi Gamin. Such a course would be disagreeable in the extreme, owing to the amount of step-cutting that would be required. Here and there fragments of ice fallen from the séracs above showed through the snow. But we need apprehend no danger from ice avalanches, for the séracs were stable, as evidenced by their smooth facets and clean-cut edges.

The slope steepened and the snow thinned out. Ice supervened. A few steps landed us on to the lower lip of a crevasse twenty yards wide. This crevasse was choked with snow and formed a trough running horizontally across the slope. Its upper lip was formed by the ice-wall we had previously noticed, varying between thirty and fifty feet in height.

Immediately facing us the ice-wall rose vertically, and continued thus without a break across the whole width of the slope to the left, but to the right a portion of the wall had sagged outwards and downwards, forming a projecting bastion. In the angle between the bastion and the wall there was an obvious line of least resistance, for the slope at this point was not vertical, but between 40° and 60° in angle. It was the one breach in the fortification, and had it not existed, we should have had no option but recourse to the long and arduous traverse of the Eastern Ibi Gamin ice-slope.

At the foot of the slope the snow was in good order, and step-kicking only was necessary. Higher up, where the angle of the ice was too great to hold snow *in situ*, steps had to be cut. The ice was not tough and hard as it had been on the precipice below Camp Four, but brittle and flaky. Less than a dozen steps sufficed. Yet the work, if not technically difficult, provided us with a foretaste of what to expect near the summit of Kamet should step-cutting be necessary. Altitude, a blazing sun, and the soft snow-slopes had already sapped our energy, and a few swings of the ice-axe sufficed to set heart galloping and lungs gasping. As I stepped over the top and sank down into the snow, I saw to my great relief that, save for a crevasse or two, gently inclined snow-slopes alone separated us from Meade's Col.

Shipton joined me, and together we sat basking contentedly in the sun. Presently, our peaceful contemplation of our surroundings was interrupted by an exclamation and a slithering sound. We peered over the edge in time to see Holdsworth drop his ski and sticks into the snowy trough of the choked crevasse at the foot of the ice-wall. We felt sorry for him as he descended to collect them, but we could scarcely repress a chuckle at this sudden tumbling of the gods head over heels, as it were, down their own Olympus. The ski were finally hauled up on the end of a rope.

We waited to see the porters safely up the ice-wall, then continued on our way. A few yards above the ice-wall the snow-slopes were split by some crevasses, the largest of which was a huge rift of unknown depth. Fortunately, it was securely bridged with snow and, crossing it, we found ourselves on slopes leading without a break to Meade's Col.

If Shipton and I had found it hard work breaking a trail for the porters on the slopes below the ice-wall, it was even harder work above. The snow became softer and softer, and at times we were sinking in half-way to the knees. In consistency the snow was not powdery, but heavy, wet and soggy. Every few yards it was necessary to halt and kick balled masses of it from the boot. Tricouni nails, excellent in many ways, are at their worst under such snow conditions, for the snow coagulates between them on the sole of the boot and soon forms a heavy and awkward ball.

Slowly we toiled on, taking turns at leading every few minutes. An almost vertical sun blazed down upon us with pitiless intensity. Its glare was reflected from the snow to such an extent that we halted to replace the face-cream washed away by sweat, for without it the skin would have been stripped from our faces like paper. The porters were going very slowly. Even had they been physically capable of ascending more quickly, they were far too experienced in high climbing to do so. They knew that once Camp Five had been established they could return to Camp Four with little effort and in but a fraction of the time they were taking for the ascent.

The slope before us rose gradually to a horizon of snow, beyond which, and invisible, was the crest of Meade's Col. That horizon seemed always as far away. Halts became more and more frequent. It was not enough to lean on the ice-axe and gasp, we had to sit in the snow until strength could be mustered for further advance. Soon after mid-day, a mist formed and swooped down upon us. Detail was obscured, and all we could see before us were a few yards of blinding snow-slope. If this mist had been thick enough, it might have protected us to some degree from the sun, but its effect was to interpose a burning-glass of vapour between us and our tormentor, thus increasing the glare and sapping our remaining dregs of energy.

Perhaps half-way up the slope, Budhibal Gurung found himself unable to carry his load another step. He was not a professional load-carrier like our Darjeeling men and he need not have ascended beyond the Base Camp. It was his own personal enthusiasm and desire to do his bit for the expedition that brought him thus far. Dogged determination and tenacity of purpose had alone kept him going. We found out later that his lack of experience in load-carrying, coupled to an awkward load, had resulted in a badly flayed back, yet he had continued without a word of complaint. It appeared as though his load would have to be temporarily abandoned, but once again Lewa insisted on doing two men's work. *He took on Budhibal Gurung's load in addition to his own.* At that height it was a *superhuman* effort; there is no other word to describe it.

BETWEEN CAMPS FOUR AND FIVE

The slope gradually eased off. So far as we could see between rents in the shifting mists, we were not more than three hundred feet below the crest of Meade's Col. The porters were now far behind, and the afternoon was drawing on. If we continued farther, the porters might not be able to return to Camp Four in daylight, and it was essential that they should return the same day, for there was not enough food to feed them. Close by was a horizontal shelf running across the slope ; on it we decided to pitch Camp Five. This decision made, we flopped down thankfully in the snow to await the porters. They were a long time in coming, but at length they appeared, a straggling line of weary men. Among them, and not behind them, was Lewa. He must have been carrying a load of about 80 lbs. on his back, and that at a height of over 23,000 ft. The men arrived and squatted apathetically in the snow, slipping their heavy loads from their backs and their sweat-soaked head-bands from their foreheads. They had done a splendid day's work, but they were too tired at the moment to realise it. We expressed our admiration for their conduct as well as we could in the limited language at our command. A few minutes' rest served to restore them. An atmosphere of languor was dispelled as usual by Nima Dorje's inevitable grin. They busily set about erecting the tents and cooking some tea for themselves and for us. How good that tea was !

At length the men were ready to return to Camp Four. They swung their empty sacks on to their backs and strode off down the slope, leaving only Lewa and Nima Dorje behind with us.

As the sun swung down, the mists began to melt away. Far up in the gauzy vapours a silvery crest stood out against the dark blue sky—the summit of Kamet. The cool alchemy of evening dissolved the lingering vapours and the white eaves of the world were bathed in the golden radiance of the setting sun.

Above us rose the final slopes to the summit of Kamet. Long we gazed at them. There were two distinct possibilities of making an ascent. Rising directly from Meade's Col was a ridge set at a moderate angle. At a first casual glance, it appeared to afford an easy route to the summit, for it was not broken by any serious gap or obstacle, and its angle, although moderately steep, was not such as to suggest difficult climbing. Yet, when we came to examine it more closely, we saw that there was one fatal objection. For a considerable portion of its length it was heavily iced. The westerly wind which rushes through Meade's Col and across Kamet strikes this ridge before anything else, and it had stripped the loose snow from it, exposing ice, black ice, gleaming evilly. There was no avoiding this ice. The crest of the ridge and the slope on the eastern side of it were both iced, whilst the western side of the ridge was, we judged, in all probability a sheer precipice. Hours of step-cutting would be necessary.

The sole alternative was the slope rising directly above the camp. Here and there, this slope was broken into séracs, which limited the route high up to the eastern flank of the face not far from the edge forming the crest of the eastern precipice.

In form the slope was concave, and, although we were looking at it from a point directly in front where

THE SUMMIT FROM CAMP FIVE SHOWING TRACK OF PARTY

OWING TO FORESHORTENING, THE SLOPE IS MUCH STEEPER THAN IT APPEARS

foreshortening and distortion would tend to make us underestimate its angle, it was apparent that in its upper portion it was very steep—far steeper than the ridge. In the afternoon shadow the last few hundred feet appeared to spring up in an almost sheer wall. Was this final slope possible? Long we scanned it. We could not assume that it was snow but only hope that it was not ice. If it was ice, we should in all probability be forced to establish another camp, and it was doubtful whether any spot could be found on that inhospitable mountain-side on which tents could be pitched.

Another factor to be taken into consideration was the danger of avalanches, but the weather had been fine now for some days, and the wind which we had seen almost every afternoon and evening sweeping the upper slopes of Kamet must have hardened the surface of the snow into a safe crust. The problem boiled down to this: the ridge from Meade's Col was possible, but its ascent would certainly entail another camp; the direct ascent of the face was obviously possible to a point about 400 ft. beneath the summit ridge, but whether or not the summit could be reached in one day from Camp Five depended on the state of the final 400 ft. slope. We decided, therefore, to attack the face in preference to the ridge. Actually, we had left the Base Camp fully prepared to establish a camp above Meade's Col, and our decision to try and reach the summit in one day direct from Camp Five was influenced by unexpected physical fitness and acclimatisation, allied to perfect weather conditions. Another reason was lack of porters. With only the few men available it would take two or three days getting up enough food and fuel for another camp. Supposing that, after this had been done, the weather was to break, we might be robbed of the summit when it was almost within our grasp, and to retreat knowing that we had not seized an opportunity would be a bitter experience. Actually, the decision to go on next day and attempt the summit was an unspoken one. As soon as we had seen that there was no insuperable difficulty, we had tacitly assumed that we were to go on, and it had not been necessary to voice this decision.

If I have gone into some detail as to the pros and the cons of the final problem, it is because I would have the reader form some idea as to the many factors leading up to a decision in Himalayan mountaineering. Those who know mountaineering for the craft it is, know that one false move on a Himalayan peak may result in checkmate, with the mountain as master of the situation. I remember that after the decision was made to push on with the attack, I experienced a strange feeling of confidence and happiness, a feeling, I believe, shared by my companions.

As we packed our rucksacks with food, spare clothing and photographic and cinematographic apparatus in preparation for the morrow, Lewa and Nima Dorje busied themselves with the preparation of our supper : and the hiss of the pressure stove was the only sound in our ears, save for our own laboured breathing and the pumping of our hearts.

The sun slid downwards almost parallel to the crest of the ridge leading from Meade's Col to the summit of Kamet, and its rays lingered long upon us. The shadows lengthened ; dusk stole from the valleys. No longer were the snows harsh, white and glaring, but every undulation was revealed by blue shadows. The beautiful Mana Peak was no longer a brutal fang of blank snow and black rock jagging a brazen sky as it had appeared in the noonday sun, but a queenlike mountain with perfectly proportioned shoulders, rising to a crest so fine and delicate that only the Great Architect Himself could have chiselled it with His instruments of sun and frost. Far beyond, above orderly ranks of lesser ridges, rose Nanda Devi. Seen from this direction, it stands out as a symmetrical pile, not unlike Kamet, and no other peak challenges its sovereignty. Beyond it, huge masses of coppery cumuli towered above the foothills. Our vision swept eastwards, past an isolated and graceful snow-peak, that rose above the mists concealing the valleys of western Nepal, to the snows of Gurla Mandhata, and Kailas, the sacred peak which Hindus believe to be the throne of Siva and the hub of the universe. North-west of Gurla Mandhata the Himalaya fell away in brown waves crested with snow into the golden plains of Tibet, which were just visible beyond a shoulder of the Eastern Ibi Gamin. Were it not for that glimpse of Tibet the mountaineer standing on the slopes of Meade's Col might fancy himself in a world given over to an eternal and awful desolation. Our eyes feasted on that little strip of golden earth as the eyes of a shipwrecked mariner feast on a distant shore. On those plains of Tibet men dwelt and moved ; we were not the sole inhabitants of a frozen planet.

Night welled from the valleys ; the higher peaks stood from it, like fairy isles of rosy coral. The towering cumulus clouds in the far south flared up one by one as though ignited by some huge conflagration sweeping the far-off foothills. The lights died, the peaks sank pallidly into the night, all save Nanda Devi, which, long after other summits were quenched, defied the darkness. The plains of Tibet changed from gold to daffodil, from daffodil to ochre, and from ochre to a weird greenish-blue. A wave of purple lifted itself from the east and swept up the sky, distributing a myriad stars. Lightning began to flicker in the south. From one cloudy turret to another its darting spears were launched, whilst now and again the clouds burst asunder and fountains of mauve fire leapt from their cavernous recesses, illuminating for an instant some citadel of the sky. The snows about us reflected this conflict of the elements like chalk cliffs lit up by the flashes of a nocturnal naval engagement, yet so distant was the storm that no sound reached the ear, and the profound peace of high mountains at eventide was unbroken.

The cold was intense, and we sought refuge from it in our sleeping-bags.

Holdsworth unselfishly occupied a small and uncomfortable Norwegian bivouac tent ; Shipton and I shared a Meade tent. As we slipped into our sleeping-bags, we blessed them for their capaciousness. After hearing tales of mountaineers, who had almost exhausted themselves at high altitudes by having to insinuate themselves inch by inch into tightly fitting bags, I had designed sleeping-bags of generous width. Yet, even so, the slight effort required for settling down and making ourselves comfortable brought about temporary breathlessness.

A final hot drink put us in a warm glow which lasted all night. We did not take off our clothes as we had done in the lower camps, for it was impossible to do so owing to the cold and consequent risk of frostbite. As a rule we took off our clothing and donned pyjamas whenever possible, as heavy clothing at night tends to retard circulation. When sleeping in clothes, therefore, it is advisable to relieve the body of pressure by releasing encumbrances such as braces and undoing buttons, for anything that retards circulation at high altitudes not only makes sleep impossible, but renders the affected portion of the anatomy sensitive to frostbite. Shipton, unfortunately, was not feeling at all well, but such was his enthusiasm for the morrow's task that I believe he already assumed himself as good as on the summit. It is such an assumption, so selfless as to rise superior to bodily infirmity, that will one day take mountaineers to the summit of Everest. I do not think Shipton slept much, but Holdsworth and I both enjoyed a tolerably good night. As I have mentioned before, it matters little whether or not a man sleeps at high altitudes, provided mind and body are untroubled by ill. At frequent intervals during the night I awoke and, lying placidly on my back, stared vacantly at the roof of the tent, taking little account of the passage of time. Now and again the green canvas was lit by distant lightning, and my mind was prodded from its lethargy : I remember thinking that we were sleeping higher that night than any of our fellow-men.

CHAPTER XIV

KAMET CONQUERED

THE NIGHT passed; the lightning became feeble and finally died away; petulant gusts of wind set the frost-stiffened canvas rustling and crackling.

A cold dawn filtered into a cold world. With a conscious effort I heaved myself to my knees. The sleeping-bag cracked sharply; it was sheeted with ice deposited by my congealed breath. With numbed fingers I fumbled at the frozen tapes securing the flaps of the tent and, parting them at last, peered outside. A cloudless sky was shot with green and orange; the peaks stood from the night like pallid statues. I glanced upwards. Dawn was gilding the crest of Kamet. Now was the time to start, but it was too cold—the coldest morning I ever remember in the Himalaya. The world almost creaked in the cold. To have left the comparative shelter of our tents would have meant certain frostbite. It was essential that we should start comfortably, with a hot breakfast inside us, and cooking and eating under such conditions were impossible. I slipped my hands back into my sleeping-bag and busied myself restoring the circulation to my numbed finger-tips. How easily circulation is lost at high altitudes, and how slowly and painfully it returns!

The sun was not long in coming, and we emerged thankfully from our tents into its life-giving rays.

Breakfast was a hurried affair. We craved sugar more

than any other substance, but tinned fruit and sardines also went down well, and so did steaming cups of tea.

We spoke but little ; our minds were busied by thoughts of what the day might bring forth. At 8 a.m. we started off, on our final push for the summit.

We climbed on two ropes, Shipton and Lewa on one, Holdsworth, Nima Dorje and I on the other. We carried rucksacks with food and spare clothes, and Nima Dorje bore a heavy load consisting of some 20 lbs. of cinematograph apparatus.

Between Camp Five and the foot of the northern face of Kamet stretched an almost level expanse of snow. We had hoped against hope that the westerly winds which lash the upper regions of the mountain had hardened the surface of the snow into a crust sufficiently solid to enable us to walk comfortably without having to do anything more than kick steps. Our hopes were not fulfilled ; we had not marched more than a few yards from the camp before we were sinking in boot deep.

The foot of the slope up which we must go was littered with ice-blocks, fallen from a line of séracs 1,000 ft. higher. Fortunately, by keeping well to the left, we were able to avoid the danger zone, and were thus spared the ordeal of having to run the gauntlet of ice avalanches.

But the snow, if disagreeably soft, was at least consistent in its softness ; it was possible to maintain a rhythm. I have already written of the importance of maintaining a rhythm in high-altitude mountaineering. It is better to have moderately soft snow consistent in its softness than a mixture of very soft and very hard snow on which rhythmical movement is impossible. Of course, when very soft snow is encountered, rhythm is equally impossible, owing to the difficulty and effort of lifting the foot, and had the snow between Camp Five and the summit of Kamet been very soft the whole way, there would have been no hope of reaching the summit in one day, and we should have been forced to pitch a higher camp.

Shipton, Holdsworth and I took it in turns to lead. We did about a quarter of an hour each. Had there been only two of us to stamp out the steps the work would have been very exhausting, but the difference between taking a turn every half an hour and taking it every quarter of an hour at such an altitude is enormous.

In its lower portion the slope was between 30° and 40° in angle : it steepened gradually.

We sat down for a rest. As we sat, our thudding hearts and hard-pressed lungs gradually eased to a more normal rhythm. We had climbed the first 500 ft. in an hour and had reason to congratulate ourselves. Immediately below us were Meade's Col and the camp—toylike tents and snow crumpled with footmarks. Only the Eastern Ibi Gamin overlooked us. To the right was the snowy edge of the eastern precipice. Fleecy clouds were beginning to twist up from the valleys. The plains of Tibet were opening out ; their brown and yellow expanses melted into violet distances. Eastwards, Gurla Mandhata rose serenely.

We munched a little chocolate and sipped tea from a Thermos flask. It was gloriously hot in the sun, and as yet no wind had arisen to chill us. Lolling in the snow, I felt languid and sleepy. Further advance seemed unnecessary and even absurd. Why not continue to sit and drowse the day away in the warm sun ? I forced myself to take some

VIEW FROM 25,000 FT. ON KAMET

photographs and change a cinematograph film. It was simple and easy work, yet it involved expenditure of both physical and mental energy.

The few minutes we allowed ourselves soon passed. Shipton and Lewa rose to their feet and started up the slope. It was interesting to watch them. Shipton, a born mountaineer, has acquired to perfection the art of climbing a snow-slope with the minimum of effort. Lewa, on the other hand, is so constituted that he tends to expend more of his magnificent energy than is necessary. So much fire and dash is his to command that he cannot properly control its tumultuous outflow, and his eager jerky movements contrasted oddly with the almost leisurely rhythm of Shipton. As they toiled through the soft snow, I trained the cine-camera on them and "shot" some film. I remember wishing as I did so that I had not burdened myself with the work of taking a film of the expedition, and I vowed that I would never do it again.

Holdsworth, Nima Dorje and I followed. One moment we had been sitting at ease, fully capable of appreciating the glorious panorama spread out before us ; the next moment, almost with a suddenness of a blow, ease had been relegated to the past, and we became once more panting automatons of flesh and blood. Sitting, we had forgotten that we were breathing the thin air of nearly 25,000 ft. but even the effort of rising to our feet served like the touch of a foot on the sensitive throttle of a powerful racing car, to set the machinery of heart and lungs pounding furiously.

The snow worsened. Previously, it had been merely soft, but now we encountered crusted snow of the most malignant type, crust which broke when the whole weight had been transferred to the forward foot, letting us sink helplessly into the soft powdery snow beneath.

Even had we taken snow-raquettes with us they would have been useless—the slope was too steep. Ski also would have been impracticable, for, although the crust was not sufficiently frozen to withstand the weight of a booted man, ski would not have broken it and could not have been edged into it. Rhythmical movement was impossible, and we resigned ourselves to something worse than ordinary toil. Our speed of ascent dropped from 500 ft. to about 300 ft. an hour. From 100 ft. at a stretch by the leader, we were reduced to 50 ft. Jealously we glanced back at the square-topped summit of the Eastern Ibi Gamin, but it was long ere we overtopped it.

Here and there the slope had been riven by crevasses. These were now choked with snow over which we could pass safely, but in some cases the upper edges of the crevasses rose in steep lips, necessitating a few steps being cut. Step-cutting over 24,000 ft. is dreadfully fatiguing work, and every minute or two the leader had to stop and gasp and gasp for oxygen.

Perhaps 1,000 ft. below the summit we encountered plate-like masses of hard snow, resembling shallow mushrooms several yards in diameter, that had been plastered to the slope by the wind. These plates cracked and slithered away when the foot was placed on them, and we sank knee deep into the powdery snow beneath.

During the ascent of the first 500 ft. we had been content to halt only while the lead was being changed, but now, owing to the exhausting nature of the work, the leader found it necessary to sink down into the snow for a rest every few yards, whilst even those behind were glad to follow his example. During these frequent halts we could discern nearly 3,000 ft. beneath us the second party mounting slowly towards Camp Five. If to us they appeared mere dots moving with the slowness of a clock's hour hand, how must we have appeared to them ? It was good to see them, for we knew that they must be watching us, and were with us in spirit urging us on to success.

We arrived at a point where the slope steepened abruptly. Ice-walls and soft snow forced us diagonally to the left towards the edge of the eastern precipice. Now, for the first time since leaving the camp, we could see the final slope separating us from the summit ridge. It was at this slope, 400 ft. high, that we had gazed so doubtfully the evening before. Previous opinion as to its steepness needed no confirmation. From the camp it had looked steep, and we knew now that it *was* steep. Everything depended on its condition. Supposing that the rippled, wind-blown snow covering it concealed hard ice ? If step-cutting was necessary throughout its entire height it would be impossible to overcome it without pitching a higher camp. Time would defeat us ; it would take many hours—a whole day's work at least. And supposing the slope consisted of snow ready to avalanche if disturbed ? There was no avoiding it. Ice-walls barred approach to the right, sheer precipices fell away to the left. Then indeed we should be conclusively beaten. Supposing it proved necessary to pitch a higher camp ; was there a ledge on that inhospitable slope of Kamet where a camp could be pitched ? We could see none. And were the porters capable of carrying up equipment ? It was doubtful ; they were already tired from their exertions between Camps Four and Five.

The edge of the eastern precipice abutted as an ill-defined ridge against the final slope. At the point where the ridge merged into the slope a large boulder of Kamet's reddish granite projected from the ice. It looked a welcome resting-place where we might recoup our energies for the final tussle. Up to it we started to climb. Perhaps 100 ft. below the boulder, our feet struck ice beneath the snow. The snow thinned until it was no longer deep enough to hold the foot securely to the ice. Step-cutting became necessary. The leader braced himself to the task. The axe swung back and leapt forward, meeting the ice with a dull thud.

In the Alps, the ringing thud of the axe and the swish and tinkle of dislodged fragments are music in my ears. The confident raising of the body from step to step, by limbs untired and in perfect training, brings happiness and contentment. But cutting steps in ice at 25,000 ft. is a very different matter. The ice-slope is not to be welcomed as providing a test of skill ; it is an implacable enemy, mute yet savage, passive yet resistant. It hates.

Thud, thud, thud. A step is made. The foot lifts slowly ; the nailed boot grinds into the ice.

Thud, thud, thud. There is a duller, less confident ring in the sound of the axe striking the ice. The work stops. Heart and lungs are striving desperately for oxygen ; the snow-slope swims uncertainly before the eyes of the exhausted mountaineer. He doubles up, and gasps, and gasps, and gasps.

Presently, his body ceases its clamouring for oxygen. He

braces his tired and quivering muscles, grasps his axe, and swings it forward again into the green face of the ice.

Thud, thud, thud.

And so it goes on.

One hundred feet—an hour's unremitting toil. We approached the red boulder and, glancing gratefully at it, promised ourselves a long rest on its sun-warmed surface. But as we cut steps up the ice by the side of it our premature gratitude changed to disgust. The boulder was smooth and sloping and there was no place on it where we could sit. But, in one respect at least, fate was kind ; the snow above the boulder lay a foot deep on the ice. One by one, we sank down into it.

Nima Dorje was last on the rope. He was going badly. His feet were slipping from the ice steps and he was using the rope as a hand-hold, a sure sign of exhaustion. As he approached, I could see that his eyes were dull and had lost their animation. His thick lips were parted widely and his lower jaw hung down. It was no surprise to us when, on joining us, he sank into the snow gasping out that he was finished, and could go on no farther. He had bravely done his best and had carried a load of cinematograph apparatus weighing 20 lbs. on his back to a height of over 25,000 ft. He soon recovered from his temporary exhaustion, and although it was impossible for him to continue, he was able to return alone safely, for the route was devoid of danger so long as he kept to the uphill track, and a slip on the ice-slope could be attended with no worse consequences than a slide into the soft snow beneath.

It was now 2 p.m. Six hours had passed since we had left Camp Five. The first 500 ft. had been climbed in about an hour, but the last 1,300 ft. had taken five hours, an average speed of well under 300 ft. an hour. This slow rate of progress had been due to the terrible snow and the time spent hewing steps in the ice-slope below the boulder. Anxiously we stared at the slope above us. There was no deception as to its steepness. Its average angle was well over 50°—an angle at least as steep as that of the ice-slopes on the Brenva face of Mont Blanc. Everything depended on the condition of the snow. Had the slope been pure ice from top to bottom there would have been no alternative but to retreat and devote our energies during the next two or three days to the difficult task of establishing a higher camp, or possibly of attempting the alternative route from Meade's Col.

As far as the boulder, a slip could not have mattered, but the final slope overlooked the great eastern precipice of Kamet, and a slip on it was not to be thought of. Heaving ourselves wearily to our feet, we recommenced the ascent. Again we found ourselves on disagreeable mushroom-like plates of snow, but on the whole firmer snow than we had encountered lower down. Between these plates there was powder snow, and the foot sank into it encountering ice. Here step-cutting was necessary. To do it we had to summon up the whole of our mental determination as well as our physical energy, and both were now dulled by fatigue and altitude. The temptation was to kick steps and trust to the snow holding. Luck had been with us so far, and we could scarcely afford to abuse it now. In places steps were necessary for safety, and I am glad to be able to record that those steps were cut.

The slope steepened until it was practically a wall. We

THE SUMMIT RIDGE

advanced in turn. A few feet at a time was enough, and we would then stop to gasp for oxygen and renewed energy.

I remember that on these occasions, as I leaned forward to rest on my in-driven ice-axe, I could see my feet, a few yards of wind-caked snow-slope, and then the East Kamet Glacier, nearly 7,000 ft. beneath. By the boulder sat the solitary figure of Nima Dorje. The sun was still shining on him, but already we were in chill shadow.

In with the ice-axe and on. The plates of hard snow swished away into the abyss, a gentle sibilant whisper. When I was leading, there was naught but the blank slope before me. When my companions were leading, my vision was limited to their feet. I remember once experiencing a ridiculous feeling of annoyance at the sight of Holdsworth's boot, breaking away one of the evil snow-slabs. I thought savagely to myself, Why can't he kick a better step—why fiddle and fumble in that ridiculous manner? But, when my turn came to lead, my feet kicked just as clumsily. Directly above us the declining sun illuminated a small flake of snow projecting from the summit ridge with a calm gleam. The flake seemed always as far away. Then suddenly, to my surprise I could touch it. Driving my ice-axe in before me, I hauled myself up on both arms, crushing the flake beneath me. I found myself sprawling, exhausted with the effort, face downwards, across the summit ridge. My head was in the sun, my feet in the shadow. Huge columns of cloud were rising djinn-like from the blue depths into which I gazed. They swayed unsubstantially for a moment as I fought for oxygen. For perhaps a minute I lay gasping like a stranded fish, then, pulling myself together, swung astride the sharp roof-like ridge and began taking in Holdsworth's rope round the ice-axe. Presently, we were all congregated on the ridge.

We had hoped to find ourselves on the summit, or within a few yards of it, but we saw immediately that we were separated from it by a knife-like crest of snow. As we gazed along the narrow path we must tread, we experienced a pang of apprehension. Some thirty yards distant the ridge rose up into a sharp point. Beyond this nothing was to be seen, but we realised instinctively that the point was not the summit. Slopes of rock and snow, which we could see sloping up beyond it, indicated something higher. Had Kamet a surprise in store for us? What if there was an impracticable cleft in the ridge between us and the summit? We would have given much for a rest, but to rest was impossible, until we had stood upon the point and seen what lay beyond.

We started to toil along the ridge. It was nearly horizontal and exceedingly sharp. On either hand the slopes fell away with great steepness; it seemed incredible that we could have ascended from those shadowy abysses to the right of us. I remember trampling and crushing the delicate snow edge with a careful yet savage deliberation. There must be no mistake now. On the slope below we had been mere automatons—toiling atoms incapable almost of reasoned and coherent thought—but now we were thinking men again, capable of realising our amazing position on this snowy edge of the world. Tiredness was replaced by a fierce exhilaration. The numbed brain leapt into renewed activity. The summit was almost within our grasp; surely it could not escape us now? We gained the point and gazed over and beyond it. At our feet the ridge

VIEW FROM SUMMIT, LOOKING SOUTH-EAST

HOLDSWORTH ON SUMMIT

SHIPTON ON SUMMIT

Photographs, E. E. Shipton

sank down to a shallow gap. Beyond the gap it merged gently into a small cone of snow—the summit !

We seized hold of Lewa and shoved him on in front of us. As I clutched hold of him I could hear the breath jerking from him in wheezy gasps. I do not think that he quite understood what we were doing. And so he was first to tread the summit. It was the least compliment we could pay to those splendid men, our porters, to whom we owed the success of our expedition.

As we reached the summit we saw that there was another equally high summit a few yards away, so, to be quite sure, we trudged across to it. Nothing further disputed us and for the last time we sank down into the snow.

With numbed and fumbling hands, I manipulated my camera and cine-camera, photographing and filming the party, the view from the summit, and the summit itself from the range of a few yards. By the time I had finished, my fingers were stiff, white and dead. Fearing frostbite, I beat my hands together. Circulation returned sluggishly and so painfully that I could barely refrain from groaning.

We left Camp Five at 8 a.m. and arrived on the summit at 4.30 p.m. ; eight and a half hours work for about 2,300 ft. of ascent. As the first 500 ft. had been climbed in a little over an hour, the ascent of the last 1,500 ft. had taken no less than 7½ hours—an average climbing speed of little more than 200 ft. an hour. Snow conditions, rather than altitude, had been responsible for this funereal rate of progress. As we lay in the snow, Holdsworth smoked half a pipe. We had often chaffed him for his devotion to his pipe, but we could scarcely do so after this. Whether or not he *enjoyed* smoking a pipe at 25,447 ft. is another matter. At all events, this offering to the Goddess Nicotine deserves to be recorded.

The view? It is difficult to render any account of it. We were too far above the world. Our gaze passed almost contemptuously over mighty range upon mighty range, to seek repose in the violet hazes of illimitable horizons. Huge clouds, sun-crested above, purple-shadowed below, stood out from the valleys, but their topmost turrets could not attain to our level. The breeze fanning us was deathly cold, the silence and sense of isolation almost terrible. There were no green valleys to be seen; all about us were peaks of black rock and glaring ice and snow, frozen outposts of the infinite. Thousands of feet beneath curved the glacier flowing south-westwards of Kamet, ribbed and girded with moraines like some monstrous dragon crawling from one cloudy cavern to another. Our sole link with the world was the camp we had left, now a mere blob on the snow of Meade's Col. Perhaps our friends there were regarding us. We rose to our feet, waved ice-axes, and let out a gasping shout. But our voices sounded pitifully weak through the thin air, and there came no response from the dotted tents.

In the far south, anvil-shaped plumes of coppery nimbus stood out from the foothills. Nanda Devi was buried in clouds and there was naught to challenge Kamet with the exception of Gurla Mandhata's glorious *massif*, 110 miles away. I have a dim recollection of a range on the extreme north-western horizon. Was it the eastern wing of the Karakorams? If so, it was 280 miles distant. Only in the north was relief to be found from a savage mountain world:

EAST KAMET GLACIER FROM SUMMIT OF KAMET

there, barren hills, streaked untidily in snow, fell away into the golden plains of Tibet, tessellated with blue cloud shadows.

It was 5 p.m., time was vital ; in less than three hours we should be overtaken by night. We rose wearily and stiffly to our feet, and tramped back along the summit ridge.

When we came to the point where we had gained the ridge we halted a few instants. At our feet we could see the East Kamet Glacier curving in a serene arc through its gorge of peaks. I looked for Camp Two, but could not distinguish it. My vision swept upwards and over the ranges to the cloud-girdled south, where tall cumulus clouds passed, like ethereal ghosts, along the foothills of the Himalaya. The declining sun caressed us in its kindly glow.

We grasped our ice-axes in a firmer grip, and one by one stepped from the ridge. Next instant the shadow of Kamet's northern face had engulfed us.

Now that the job was done, we began to realise how tired we were. It is at such times of mountaineering anticlimax that accidents occur. The oncoming of night, cold, fatigue and desire to return as quickly as possible to the comparative comfort of Camp Five all combined to tempt us to rush down the upper slope. To have done so would have been mountaineering folly of the most elementary character. Steadiness was imperative ; impatience had to be curbed. We progressed slowly, rope length by rope length. How slow it was ! Impatience and resignation flared up alternately. It seemed as though we were doomed for ever to cling and crawl like snails to this snowy flank of Kamet.

We descended in two parties, as on the ascent, but found it quicker to take separate lines rather than for both parties to descend the upward track, even though occasional step-cutting was necessary. Yet, if progress was slow, it was also certain and efficient. In drove the ice-axe into the snow until it struck the ice beneath ; the rope was hitched around it, and down went the first man as quickly as possible, until the whole length of the rope was out ; then he in turn anchored himself firmly, and took in the rope of the last man as he descended. In the Alps such tactics are seldom necessary even on the steepest snow-slope, but we were not in the Alps ; we were tired men at a height of 25,000 ft., and a slip must be expected at any moment.

Fortunately, we did not find it essential to adhere to our uphill tracks owing to the improved quality of the snow, and by keeping more to the west were able to make a route that in its lower portion did not overlook the eastern precipice.

At the foot of the final slope Holdsworth and I halted to await Shipton and Lewa. The latter was moving very slowly and was obviously distressed. His face was greenish in hue, his eyes rigid and staring from exhaustion. He groaned out that he was in great pain, and pointed to his stomach. There was nothing we could do for him save to encourage him to continued effort and to relieve him of his load. As I lifted the rucksack with its 20 lbs. or more of film apparatus, I was forcibly reminded of the amount of energy Nima Dorje and Lewa had expended getting it to the summit. Swinging it on to my back overbalanced me, and my tired legs almost collapsed beneath me. Yet, even at that moment, I said to myself that as the " damned thing" had been got to the summit, it somehow had to be got down again.[1]

On the ice-slopes below the boulder it was necessary to go carefully, for the rough surface of the ice was frozen so hard that an uncontrolled slide would have stripped a man's skin from him like paper.

Below the ice-slope we unroped. We had hoped to descend the lower slopes quickly and easily, but the soft snow had frozen into a vicious breakable crust, and the hard snow had frozen into icy boards. In some places our feet broke through the crust into the powdery snow beneath, and had to be dragged out again ; in other places we slithered unpleasantly. Once or twice we tried to glissade, but this proved impossible on the breakable crust or dangerously uncontrollable on the harder and icier slopes.

Slowly the Eastern Ibi Gamin rose to the level of our vision. The camp below, a single blob when seen from the summit, resolved itself into the separate specks of our tents.

About 1,000 ft. from the camp I decided to abandon the load of cinematograph apparatus, as its weight was delaying me, whilst the difficult snow made it an exhausting load to carry. At all events, it was left within range of the camp and could be recovered next day.

The cold became more severe, and the coldness of high altitudes is akin to the coldness of space itself.

The sun's last flare lit peak and snowfield. Night, a vast

[1] To those explorers and mountaineers who may be contemplating a cinematograph record of their achievements I can only say that they must remember that, if their picture is to be a success with the film magnates and the film-going public, they must contrive to include incidents faked or authentic at least as revolting as those that delighted the audiences of the Colosseum at Rome. The mentality that can tolerate pictures such as the Akron airship disaster when men were photographed falling to their death must be fed on lust and horror.

phalanx of purple, rushed up the sky. The slanting rays of the setting sun flooded the Tibetan plains, throwing into sharp relief numberless little crags and hills, that stood out like the fantastic buildings of some demon city.

Day drained quickly from the peaks. A cold pallor invested the world. And now we witnessed a strange spectacle. As the sun sank in the west another sun rose to rival it in the east, but a sun with rays, not of light, but of darkness, that radiated upward to the zenith of the evening sky. It was the parallel shadows of the peaks in the west cast by the real sun across the sky to such a distance, that they appeared to converge in a point above the eastern horizon.

I do not remember feeling exhausted, yet I do remember that my knees were so curiously weak that a stumble in the crusted snow or a slither on the hard crust was difficult to correct without falling.

Figures detached themselves from the camp beneath and came slowly through the dusk to meet us. A few minutes later I was grasping Birnie's hand and drinking hot liquid from a vacuum flask which he had thoughtfully brought with him. A glowing warmth spread through my tired limbs ; a profound contentment permeated my whole being. A hundred yards more and the tents of Camp Five loomed up before us. The afterglow of a cloudless sunset saw us stumbling into camp.

We had not escaped scatheless. Intense cold during the descent had wreaked its will upon us. Poor Lewa was so exhausted that he could scarcely stagger. The removal of his boots and stockings revealed feet frozen and immovable, the whiteness of which was already changing to a dark purple. Men were immediately set to work to try to restore their circulation, but though they massaged for an hour or more his feet were far beyond the initial stages of frostbite, and circulation would not return. Holdsworth's right big toe was also frostbitten and Shipton's toe-tips were slightly affected. I was the only one to escape, and I attribute my immunity, not to an exceptionally good circulation, but to the fact that when mountaineering and ski-ing in the Alps I have made it my invariable practice to keep my toes moving in my boots by bunching them up and straightening them out at periodical intervals throughout a cold day. This had become so much of a habit that, though I cannot remember doing so, I feel certain that I kept it up on Kamet.

Supper went down well that night, although we were too tired to eat much. Tinned beans and tinned fruit, followed by a jorum of hot rum, set us in a warm glow that lasted throughout a cold night. For some time Shipton and I lay cosily side by side in our sleeping-bags, recalling the events of the day. Already they seemed a past chapter of life, and, as drowsiness gradually overcame me, they receded farther and farther into the forgotten. Quietness fell upon the camp. In the south, lightning winked and glimmered ceaselessly over the foothills.

CHAPTER XV

THE SECOND ASCENT

THE SECOND party decided not to climb Kamet the day after the first party, but to spend a day at Camp Five acclimatising, and, if weather conditions permitted, ascend on the following day. Another reason for this postponement was Lewa. His feet were so seriously frostbitten that the sooner he was sent down to the Base Camp the better. Greene said that he would not be answerable for the consequences if this was not done : in the denser air of lower altitudes and increased oxygenation of the blood lay the only chance of saving his feet.

During the day three local porters arrived with a mail, surely the highest postal delivery ever made? One of these men, Kesar Singh, was retained, and Budhibal Gurung was put in charge of the party detailed off to take Lewa from camp to camp down the mountain. We had already seen enough of him to know that he was to be relied upon absolutely. Another piece of work that had to be done was the recovery of the abandoned cinematograph apparatus. To begin with, not a Darjeeling man would volunteer for this. Superstition was rife among them, and they would not stir. According to the second party, Nima Dorje had returned to camp in a hysterical condition and babbling of gods and devils whom he affirmed had taken all the air away. And now the all-powerful god of Kamet had burnt Lewa's feet. At last Birnie managed to prevail upon his own servant, Dorje, to brave, for a consideration, the wrath of this outraged god and ascend to recover the apparatus.

The day was not a pleasurable one. Holdsworth, Shipton and I were experiencing a certain physical and mental reaction. The air was not so still as it had been previously, and the gentlest breeze at 23,300 ft. is sufficient to send the mountaineer shivering into his sleeping-bag. The weather appeared to be deteriorating, and leaden clouds massing in the south boded ill. In spite of these omens, the morning of June 23 dawned fine, except that the loose powdery snow was streaming in twisting clouds from Meade's Col and the final slopes of Kamet, whilst even Camp Five was not immune from the wind's hateful activity.

To the great regret of all, Beauman decided that he would not accompany the second party. He had not yet acclimatised properly, and he doubted his ability to reach the summit. Unselfishly, therefore, he decided not to imperil the safety or success of his companions by risking exhaustion or collapse. It was a wise decision, and one made in accordance with the best traditions of mountaineering. How much disappointment it meant, I do not think any of us realised until afterwards. I am confident that, had it been possible for him to have spent another day or two at Camp Five, he would have acclimatised sufficiently to have made the ascent.

The second party were not burdened with cinematograph apparatus, but they decided to take a porter to carry their odds and ends, their clothes and food, etc. But a porter was not easy to obtain. Not a Darjeeling man would go. Nima Dorje had shaken them profoundly; Lewa's feet had demoralised them. To them Lewa was something more than a sirdar; he was a strong man, one whom the gods had endowed bountifully with strength far in excess of their own; if the gods had treated him thus, how should they escape even worse consequences for invading their sanctuaries of snow? And, after all, had not Kamet been ascended by the sahibs? Why worry, why risk life and limb by making a second ascent? Such were their arguments and convictions, and not even Birnie could shake them. It was indeed strange and pathetic to see these hardened veterans of Everest and Kangchenjunga, the prey to superstitious fears, crouched cowering in their tents.

But the Bhotias of Niti and Mana were not cursed by such fears and superstitions. Among them, Kesar Singh appeared to regard the expedition as one huge and continual joke, and not even the thin air and cold of 23,300 ft. had shrivelled his grin or quenched his natural cheerfulness. Gods and devils meant nothing to him. Of course, it was quite on the cards that there might be a few odd ones knocking about on the summit of Kamet. Was there not supposed to be a golden palace there, tenanted by a powerful god? Yet here he was, only a short distance from the summit, and there was no sign of any such thing. Women's tales! The imagination of fakirs, who had never seen Kamet, but who terrorised for their own pecuniary ends the villagers in the Alaknanda Valley. And it would be something to have seen England from the summit. Had not the Gurkha soldier with Longstaff Sahib said that it was visible? What a triumph it would be! He would be king of his village, of his valley. The village elders would sit at his feet in respectful admiration, and he would say, " I, Kesar Singh, have been up with the sahibs to the palace of the gods. The sahibs singled me out from among many as being the strongest and best. Even their own Darjeeling wallahs would not go, and without me they could not have got to the summit of Kamet. Behold those whom the sahibs and gods favour," etc., etc., etc. Thus Kesar Singh, a plausible and likeable rascal, and one with the lust for adventure in his veins. There are more of his type in the valleys of northern Garhwal, and, given the same opportunities as the Darjeeling men, they would, I am convinced, develop into even finer mountaineers, finer at all events in that they would not be cursed on a mountain with unnerving superstitions.

Kesar Singh had been equipped with the same clothing and boots as had the Darjeeling men and other local high-climbing porters. He was thankful enough of the former, but refused to wear the latter. He preferred to don the local footwear, and wrapped layer after layer of sacking and cloth round his feet. It hardly seemed suitable footgear for 25,000 ft., but he so evidently preferred it to boots that he was allowed to wear it.

The second party started at 6.45 a.m. June 23—more than an hour earlier than the first party, for the morning was not so cold as on June 21. Yet, an hour later, when the sun's warmth tempted us from our tents, they seemed to have covered but a short distance and were still near the camp.

Watching them, we could realise how slow our own progress must have been. There they were, mere dots fastened to the vast slopes of Kamet. We would go into our tents and spend an hour or two in our sleeping-bags and come out again : there they were, the same place as before ; no, just a little higher. As the morning wore on, one black dot detached itself from the other two and was left behind. We wondered whether it was Kesar Singh, but when the dot moved on again in determined pursuit of the first two dots we knew it must be either Birnie or Greene, for if Kesar Singh had been left behind he would hardly have had the initiative to try and catch up again.

As the day wore on the dots crept up the mountain-side. The sun passed westwards, shadows engulfed them, and they were lost to view.

It had been our intention to climb, if possible, the Eastern Ibi Gamin. Beauman suggested the ascent, but I fear that Holdsworth, Shipton and I did not greet the suggestion with the enthusiasm it deserved. It was not that we were lazy, but that we were tired. Lost energy is difficult to recoup at high altitudes. Holdsworth, however, despite his frostbitten big toe, visited Meade's Col on ski, 23,500 ft., the highest point to which ski have ever been taken. He reported on his return that the slopes fell sheer on the other side of the col and the ridge leading to Kamet, which we had first thought to be the easiest route to the summit. We realised now that, had we attempted to climb the ridge, it would have been impossible to have deviated from its crest on to its western side, and that the ice-slopes would have had to be cut up.

During the afternoon, gusts of cold wind kept us in our sleeping-bags most of the time, and in our brief excursions outside our tents we saw that clouds of snow were blowing off

HOLDSWORTH RETURNING FROM MEADE'S COL, 23,500 FT.

BELOW CAMP FIVE

AT CAMP FIVE

the summit of Kamet. Towards evening the wind dropped. We scanned the slope anxiously for signs of the returning party. At length we spotted them, and Holdsworth and I set out to meet them, carrying food and drink. Night was falling as we toiled up the snow-slopes towards them.

Before proceeding further, I will quote Captain Birnie's own account written to *The Times*.

"After collecting raisins and chocolates for lunch, we roped and started at 6.45 a.m. We followed the tracks of the former party, Greene leading at a rhythmical pace which kept us going for long periods without need for a rest.

"After two hours the lead was changed. This may have been a mistake, for after a further hour's work Greene feared the possibility of his not reaching the summit, and insisted on my continuing with Kesar Singh without him, saying he would rest and follow if he felt like it.

"After another hour's climbing we decided to abandon rucksacks and rope, in order to lighten ourselves to the minimum. This was a big mistake, due to my not realising the steepness of the snow and ice-slope to the summit ridge.

"Our route continued up very steep snow, ice steps, cut by the former party, proving very welcome and greatly accelerating our progress. From time to time we saw Greene following half an hour behind.

"As we rose, a magnificent view appeared. To the south and east only peaks over 20,000 ft. broke through an ocean of white cloud. To the north the vast brown plateaux of Tibet stood out in contrast to the snow-clad peaks to the south, dominated by Nanda Devi. Far away to the north-west, a magnificent range of mountains must surely have been the Karakoram, over 250 miles away. Our immediate object was a big rock, 300 ft. below the summit ridge, which we hoped to reach in two hours, but actually took three.

" Progress was now extremely difficult. Looking down from the rock, we saw Greene still coming up, a splendid effort, as he was not feeling fit from the start. After a rest we began the final 300 ft. to the summit ridge. This proved very hazardous, as the angle increased considerably, and the slope consisted of ice thinly covered with snow. Traces of Smythe's party had been completely spoiled by their downward tracks. This necessitated a long session of step-cutting. Kesar Singh assisted splendidly, holding my feet to the slope while fresh steps were cut. Almost unconsciously the work continued, a feeling of despondency dominating everybody, a feeling that the summit would never be reached.

" Greene was still following, and now called to me. It was heartening to hear him, and I shouted, ' The summit's quite close,' though actually despairing of ever reaching it.

" Suddenly the ridge appeared six feet above. We were there ! We climbed the distance in as many seconds, and gazed for the first time south from Kamet's ridge. But we were not yet on the summit, though only 150 yds. from it. We walked along the knife-like edge until we reached the two rounded domes which form the summit of Kamet. The wind was bitterly cold, so we dropped down the mountain to the south for protection. Shortly afterwards Greene arrived, having made a splendid effort. We wasted no time on the summit owing to the cold.

" On starting to descend, Kesar Singh for the first time

demurred, saying that his cloth boots would not hold on the steps. Here was where my fault in leaving the rope behind was accentuated. We laughed him out of his temporary fright, Greene leading down the mountain. I came next, Kesar Singh following close behind. I ordered him to use me as a brake, which he did half-a-dozen times before the rock was reached, 300 ft. below the summit. Thence he held the steps very well. Above the camp we were met by Smythe and Holdsworth, with rum and chocolate, a most welcome reviver, for we were all very tired and not at all ashamed to allow the offered arms to support us into camp. So ended an arduous climb—made pleasant by the wonderful attention of those in camp on our return."

Like the first party, the second party did not escape scatheless. Kesar Singh, thanks presumably to his cloth boots, escaped frostbite, but Birnie had a little toe badly frostbitten, and Greene's finger-tips were slightly affected. He told me afterwards that he had removed his gloves for a few seconds to take a photograph, and in that few seconds the cold and wind had numbed and frost-bitten his fingers. The mountaineer who climbs to such heights is made to realise that he is approaching that outside limit of the earth beyond which life cannot exist save under artificial conditions.

CHAPTER XVI

THE DESCENT

JUNE 24 dawned evilly. The clouds that had been massing in the south for the past few days had now spread a menacing pall across the zenith, and the summit of Kamet was smoking a wrathful pipe of wind driven snow. There was no question of remaining longer to climb the Eastern Ibi Gamin. Provisions were running low, bad weather was impending, and the party, both sahibs and porters, were tired from their efforts of the past few days. Our thoughts turned not to further conquests but to rest and warmth. The Base Camp ! The very words had a homely ring.

With fingers frozen by vicious flurries of wind-driven snow, we packed our tents. We turned to go. The scene was inexpressibly desolate. Fugitive patches of wan sunlight were chasing affrightedly across the upper slopes of Kamet. Through rifts in the massing clouds sawed menacing fangs of rock and ice. From above came a dull sound, more felt than heard—the orchestra of the storm.

The porters squatted down on their haunches, slipped their head-bands over their foreheads, heaved themselves to their feet, wriggled and shifted their loads into a position of comfort, and lumbered off in their ungainly way down the snow-slopes.

Empty food tins, scraps of paper, and odds and ends were all that remained of our highest camp. There is no anti-litter league on Kamet ; nature is an efficient scavenger. Soon the débris would be covered, the trampled snow smoothed, and again Kamet would know peace.

Save that our legs were still a trifle tired, it was an easy matter walking downhill, and we descended at an Alpine pace. Holdsworth ran down on ski in a series of long, clean traverses and Christianias which even his frostbitten toe did not prevent him from executing. Birnie, however, found that his little toe had swollen to such an extent that he could only limp slowly and painfully. The wind rushed at us spitefully as we stood on the crest of the ice-wall. Wind is always unpleasant on any mountain, but at high altitudes it is imbued with a quality of devilishness which must be experienced to be appreciated. It does not blow constantly nor even from the same direction, but thrusts venomously at the mountaineer just when he is congratulating himself on having escaped its attentions.

We hurried down the slopes beneath the ice-wall and gained Camp Four, where all six of us somehow managed to squeeze into the Meade tent standing there and eat some lunch in its shelter, while the porters pitched another tent and crammed themselves into it.

We had managed to bring all our equipment and remaining stores down from Camp Five, but as there were not enough porters to carry the spare tent, provisions and equipment remaining at Camp Four, we decided to cast two or three loads down the precipices to the glacier plateau.

The falling loads afforded a horrid spectacle. In the way the bundles of tents and sleeping-bags fell they might have been human. They slid sedately yet helplessly for the first few yards down the smooth ice-slope. In a second or two their pace increased, they turned over, and commenced to roll. The rolling became faster and faster, increasing to such a fearful velocity that we could hear the rush and the wind of them. They struck the rocks at the foot of the snow and ice-slopes hundreds of feet lower, leapt insanely into the air, and, turning over and over, disappeared into the depths. I could scarcely repress a shudder as I watched. Supposing they had been human bodies ! I descended to Camp Three with something more than ordinary caution.

We had intended to unloose the fixed ropes during our descent, but the cold wind made us shun this task. We had plenty of rope to spare, and were not likely to require fixed ropes on other mountains.

A dull afternoon was lapsing into a dismal evening as we tramped across the well-remembered snow plateau to Camp Three. The jettisoned loads had arrived safely on the plateau, albeit torn and battered, and we were able to congratulate ourselves on having evacuated Camps Four and Five without abandoning anything of importance. The worst that could now befall us was a snowfall deep enough to render the upper part of the gully leading down to Camp Two dangerous. But the weather, if unpleasant, did not appear to have the heart to summon up a snowstorm.

At Camp Five, we had sent off Budhibal Gurung with a telegram telling of our successful assault on Kamet, but owing to the strain and difficulty of getting Lewa down, our Gurkha had forgotten it, and we had found it in the tent at Camp Four. Holdsworth, however, volunteered to take it from Camp Three to the Base Camp in one day on ski. Next morning, therefore, he started before the rest of

HOW THE YAKS CROSSED THE DHAOLI RIVER

us, and accomplished this journey successfully. It was a long hard day, which none of us on foot would have cared to have faced, and demonstrated the utility of ski. As regards the rest of the party, it was arranged that Beauman and Shipton with two men should take Lewa from Camp Two, which he had reached on the day that we had descended from Camp Five to Camp Three, whilst Birnie, Greene and I stayed at Camp Two to supervise the bringing down of the remaining loads from Camp Three.

Descending from Camp Three, we were reminded of the recent fine weather and the approach of the monsoon. Rocks were peeping through the snow where formerly none were to be seen, but now the peaks were shrouded in sluggish mists, and desultory snowflakes told of bad weather above us.

The bed of the gully leading down to Camp Two and the East Kamet Glacier had been considerably altered by the sun, and it was possible to descend on broken rocks by the side of it for some distance. Falling stones had worn out a deep runnel in the snow of the gully. Porters who had ascended or descended it almost every day since we arrived at Camp Three must have narrowly escaped being hit, but as they seldom worry about anything until it actually happens, and none of them *had* been hit, we had heard nothing about it. Theirs is a fatalistic philosophy.

As we descended the steep upper pitch of the gully there came a sudden clatter. I glanced hurriedly upwards, but before I had time to move there was a whirr and a whizz, followed by several dull thuds, as the stones plunged into the soft snow. I never saw the stones—they were moving too quickly to be visible. I shouted up to Randhoj Kan, who was behind me, to hurry up. My words had no effect, and the little Gurkha descended nonchalantly, with a broad grin ; obviously he considered falling stones a huge joke and an occurrence calculated to add zest to an otherwise dull descent.

The East Kamet Glacier had changed considerably in appearance. When we ascended to Camp Two it had stretched white and unbroken ; now it was split by crevasses and strewn by boulders as large as cottages.

It was extraordinarily warm, and the soft, moisture-charged airs and roof of grey fish-bellied clouds betokened the onset of the monsoon. I descended in my shirt-sleeves, and the sweat dripped from me.

We trod the glacier and zigzagged between the crevasses. In one place a snow bridge over a crevasse had given way, and an ominous black hole suggested that someone had made an intimate acquaintance with the depths of the glacier. We learnt later that this investigator of subglacial regions was none other than the Old Soldier. Fortunately, however, he had been pulled out again by a rope uninjured.

As we approached Camp Two, the tents of which straggled between the boulders and crevasses, we saw a number of local porters, who had come up that day, seated smoking their usual villainous mixture of yak dung and charcoal. In the middle of the camp was a solitary figure.

It was Budhibal Gurung. He was standing at attention, as rigid and erect as a ramrod. His head was up-tilted, his chin thrust forward, and his eyes fixed unblinkingly on the infinite. I greeted him in English, but he did not answer, and remained standing stiffly at attention. I could not understand what was the matter with him until I suddenly realised the meaning of his strange behaviour. He had remembered his oversight in leaving the summit telegram at Camp Four, and this was his way of doing penance, a self-imposed fatigue drill for neglecting to carry out an order. It was not until Birnie had arrived and "dismissed" him that he allowed himself to execute an "about turn" and march off to his tent.

Lewa was at the camp. He had refused to go any farther as he wanted to wait for us. His feet were a dreadful sight, and it was obvious that if they were to be saved he had to be got down to lower levels without delay. Mentally and physically he was a different man. Lying helpless, with his fierce impetuous spirit chained to a disabled body, unable to give orders, and forced to watch the inefficiency of his fellows without being able to intervene, was gall and wormwood to him. From Camp Five, he had been able to walk down most if not all of the way, but further walking was out of the question. Frostbite in its worst form is cumulative in its effects. To begin with, the part affected is frozen and it is only after it has thawed that the real trouble begins. The tissues have been destroyed, the corpuscles of the blood killed. Gangrene sets in and destroys the affected part. Fortunately, unlike other forms of gangrene, it is local and cannot spread provided sepsis does not supervene, and those portions of the limb or extremities capable of recovering recover, but cause great pain to the patient in so doing. Transportation of badly frostbitten men is no easy matter. Four men under the charge of Beauman and Shipton were detailed off for the work of carrying Lewa to Camp One. Where the East Kamet Glacier was snow-covered and reasonably smooth, he could be dragged along, seated on a blanket, but this was only possible for the first mile and he had to be carried the remaining four miles. It was a long job, and it took them seven weary hours to Camp One.

It had taken us little more than an hour to descend from Camp Three to Camp Two, and, as the day was before us as many porters as could be mustered were sent back to Camp Three to fetch down the remainder of the loads. These men went under the command of the Old Soldier, who, as temporary sirdar in place of Lewa, exhibited commendable alacrity in getting them together. They returned the same evening with all the loads.

The following day, June 26, Birnie, Greene and I set off to the Base Camp, taking with us all the porters. We had to leave some half-dozen loads, but these could easily be retrieved later by the local men. It was a dismal morning, and mists shrouding the peaks drooped down almost to the level of the East Kamet Glacier. For a while the sun shone feebly, then, giving up an unequal contest, disappeared.

As we trudged down the glacier into the jaws of its great gorge, the mountain walls on either side, concealed behind leaden mists, seemed full of an indescribable menace. If we could not see, we could at least visualise the hanging glaciers above us with their unstable walls of ice, waiting only for the monsoon's warmest breath to sweep the glacier in cataclysmic avalanches. I could not help thinking, that here was Kamet's last chance for revenge. For a while we walked downhill in mist, then, emerging from the mist, found ourselves on the level plain where the glacier bends round a corner before rising steeply towards Camp Two. On the way up to Camp Two we had kept as far as possible to the northern edge of this plain, but the local men who had been working between Camps One and Two had had no thought but to spare themselves work; they had ascended by the easiest route, and this lay across the middle of the plain. It showed their complete ignorance of mountaineering principles or contempt for danger, for the plain was strewn with blocks of ice, many of them weighing tons, which had recently fallen from the hanging glaciers perched thousands of feet above on the side of the Mana Peak. We wasted no time hereabouts, and, hurrying across the dangerous area, gained the crest of the big side moraine running along the northern bank of the glacier, where we could breathe more freely.

The gloom increased. Snow began to fall, at first in desultory flakes, then in a heavy storm. We ate a cold, uncomfortable lunch in the lee of a boulder. We were no longer in the danger zone, and, as though to emphasise our safe deliverance, the clouds parted and pools of sunlight fell upon the glacier. By the time we were abreast of Camp One we were warm and dry.

There was no need to visit Camp One, and we cut across to the southern side of the glacier, having to make many toilsome ascents over moraine mounds in the process. On the way up we had borne patiently with these, but now they exasperated us. Our thoughts were concentrated, not on the beauties and grandeurs about us, but on the sumptuous meal we were going to have at the Base Camp, and of how long and comfortably we would sleep.

At last we turned the corner under the little peak at

the junction of the East Kamet and Raikana Glaciers. I said to myself, " In another twenty minutes we shall be there." It was more like two hours. Landmarks as we had known them had disappeared. The snow partially filling the hollows between the moraine mounds had melted. We wandered wearily and fretfully in a stony maze, soon losing touch with one another and taking different routes, each man convinced that his was the best route.

Evening was drawing on apace, and I was beginning to wonder whether we should find the Base Camp at all that day, and was thinking with a certain grim humour that it would be somewhat of a joke to have to bivouac on that vile moraine probably within a few hundred yards of it, when of a sudden there came a distant shout, and I perceived a figure standing on the summit of one of the moraine mounds. It waved an arm and disappeared like a jack-in-the-box. A minute or two later it reappeared, this time on the summit of a nearer moraine mound. After this process had been repeated a number of times, the sheep-like face of Alam Singh, carved into a broad smile of welcome, suddenly shot up over the crest of a neighbouring stone ridge a few yards away. He pointed in the direction I must go, then went off to round up my companions. Even so it was difficult to find the Base Camp amid such a bewildering labyrinth of stony mounds. Once I saw its green tents, seemingly only 100 yds. or so away, but when, after toiling up to the crest of the next ridge the tents had mysteriously vanished, I began almost to imagine myself moving aimlessly about in some " Looking-glass " land, and I should scarcely have been surprised had I seen the grim-visaged Red Queen stumping towards me over the stones. And then, suddenly, I heard voices. I could sniff the familiar odour of burning juniper. There was the Base Camp below me not 20 yds. away !

The porters did not turn up until after dark. They had wisely chosen a more circuitous but easier route from Camp One, which had been carefully cairned while we were on the mountain. Short cuts on a mountain seldom pay a dividend of saved time.

At the Base Camp we learnt that Beauman and Shipton had experienced considerable difficulty in getting Lewa down from Camp One. The local men had refused to carry him and had started up the East Kamet Glacier towards Camp Two, saying that they would rather bring down the remainder of the loads. Nima had been sent after them to expostulate with them and bring them back. There had never existed any particular love or sympathy between the local men and the Darjeeling men, and words had run high. Finally, Nima received somebody's fist in his eye. However, enough men were got together to carry Lewa. Apart from the natural antipathy liable to flare up at any moment between the local men and the Darjeeling men, the attitude adopted by the former towards Lewa was undoubtedly due to the treatment he had meted out to them in the first place. Driving-power, and not tact, was Lewa's strong suit.

It was a happy party that sat down to supper in the mess tent that evening. Not even a return to Achung could dim our cheerfulness. Even soup tasting of juniper and greasy dish-cloths could be forgiven and forgotten when our last bottle of brandy went the round and when pipes and cigarettes had filled the little mess tent with a blue haze. Then Shipton got out the gramophone and records from the packing-case where they had lain during our sojourn on Kamet with the tenderness of a mother raising her child from its cot ; and once more Frank Crumit, Gracie Fields, Caruso, Paul Robeson, Kreisler, and other well-tried favourites made their bow to an uncritical assembly. Between whiles we yarned ; yarned of incidents already almost forgotten, of delights and difficulties, of humours and hardships. Of what we had done and what we might have done, of Piccadilly and Camp Five, of our favourite grill-room and the cooking of Nima Dorje. We were not the only ones to make merry. From the direction of the porters' quarters came a constant chatter of voices, punctuated with guttural laughs—the care-free laughs of men who had found happiness in the knowledge of work accomplished.

It was late when we turned in. The snow-charged clouds of the day had long relinquished their burden and melted away. The moon rode high ; glacier, peak and snowfield were bathed in her radiance. No lightning flickered to disturb the serenity of the night. Remote from the world, the moonlit summit of Kamet was hung from the stars.

CHAPTER XVII

TO GAMSALI

THE WEATHER, after harrying us during the descent, regained its former tranquillity. We spent three days resting. During that period the sun shone from cloudless skies and we basked in its rays. But on the peaks there was evidence of bad weather. The smoke from our cigarettes scarcely wavered in the still air, but we could see the banners of wind-blown snow streaming from Kamet. Peaceful days they were except for me, for I had to spend many hours every day chained mentally to a typewriter, thumping out a full account of our doings.

While we rested, the last loads came down from Camps One and Two and the yaks came up from the pastures where they had been grazing. On June 29 we packed up preparatory to descending to Niti and Gamsali.

On June 30 we left the Base Camp. On the way up to it we had trudged over snow for the last mile, but now, save for scattered drifts, it had melted. Stones and grass had taken its place, and many little brooks had been born that babbled over the red pebbles or paused to repose themselves in quiet pools which mirrored the peaks around. A soft moisture-charged breeze brought a fragrance of flowers. Between the boulders were little alps set green and level, like elfin bowling-grounds. Here perhaps the snow-maidens join hands with the " Lordly Ones " of the pastures. The shush of the wind in the grasses might almost have been their impish whisperings.

The yaks, after a long sojourn on the pastures and a life of luxury and ease, made it plain that they resented a renewal of work. Off went their loads one after another amid curses and entreaties from their drivers, but presently they resigned themselves grumpily to their task.

We lounged downhill to the plain at the confluence of the Raikana and Dhaoli Rivers. Ascending, we had crossed the Dhaoli River by a snow bridge of avalanche débris, but the bridge had long since melted or been swept away and we found ourselves confronting an unfordable, raging torrent. Fortunately, it was possible for an active man to cross the torrent higher up, but this involved rock climbing and did not appear a feasible route for laden men. It seemed best to span the torrent by a rope bridge stretched between two large boulders that stood opposite to one another on either bank. Our local men were fully equal to such an emergency, and promised us that they would soon make the bridge. As it was already late in the afternoon and it would take many hours for ourselves and our loads to cross the torrent, we decided to camp.

Growing near the camp were spring onions, which made a welcome addition to the cooking-pot. The evening was wonderfully warm, and even night chilled the air but little; evidently, the monsoon was close at hand.

Early next morning a rope of five strands of alpine line was securely stretched between the two boulders. A sturdy V-shaped juniper root was trimmed and whittled until its surface offered the minimum of friction to the rope; this was placed inverted over the rope, and from it, suspended by various odd bits of rope, another root which had to bear the load or man. The contraption was then hauled along the rope across the torrent. It was a primitive form of the rope and breeches buoy arrangement by means of which shipwrecked mariners are rescued. Alam Singh stood on one side of the stream and screamed instructions ; Natar Singh stood on the other side and screamed back ; the men, taking no notice of either of their sirdars, pulled the loads one by one across the stream.

But if the contraption was able to transport men and loads, it was scarcely able to cope with a yak. The yaks, however, were fully capable of crossing the torrent without extraneous aid. Unladen, they were driven in a herd to the edge of the torrent at a point where it curved slightly, and with yells, shouts, imprecations, sticks and stones from the porters, urged into its raging waters. For a few seconds they struggled ineffectually to keep their feet—then they were swept helplessly away. It seemed as though some at least must perish in the turmoil of water, but all the time their sturdy feet were pawing at the bed of the torrent, and so, helped both by their own efforts and the bend in the torrent, they heaved themselves ponderously on to the other bank none the worse for their adventure. The only yak to require assistance was a half-grown one which for a while resolutely refused to enter the river, but, when a rope had been fixed to it as a safeguard, it seemed to realise that it must follow its elders, and set out resolutely for the opposite bank, which it reached without misadventure. In such a torrent a man would have been swept instantly from his feet and smashed to pulp on the boulders. The same fate would, in all probability, overtake a horse, but a yak, despite its ungainly appearance and ponderous body, is endowed with enormous strength, whilst its centre of gravity is so low that it cannot be capsized easily.

As to our own crossing of the river, if not as dangerous as the journey by lorry from Ranikhet to Baijnath it was at least as terrifying. The rope bridge sagged in the middle, so that the legs, and even the nether garments of the heavier members of the expedition, were immersed in the stream. It was an instance where the light-weights, Beauman, Birnie, Shipton and myself, scored over the heavy-weights, Holdsworth and Greene. It took many hours to get all the loads across, but the crossing was effected without casualty, save that a valuable camera outfit of Birnie's broke away from its securing strap and was lost in the torrent.

We camped at Goting in drizzling rain, and next day, July 2, set out for Gamsali. It was a damp, hot day, with heavy clouds gathering in the south. On the way Budhibal Gurung managed to shoot two bharhal. As it was impossible to carry them down, the choicest and tenderest portions were separated and added to the loads.

Our porters were in great spirits, and I noticed that most of the Darjeeling men deviated from the path in order to visit Niti. Below the village we found Miss Benham encamped on the same spot where she had been when we left Niti. Local information had it that some English people were coming up the valley and were camped close at hand. As we saw some tents on the hillside we took these to be their camp, and were not a little disgusted when, on

ROPE BRIDGE

toiling up to them, we found that they were the tents of some nomadic Bhotias.

As we passed along the path through the Niti Gorge we endeavoured to cheer up Lewa. We had managed to procure a pony for him at Niti, and on it he now sat bowed and huddled like a dispirited Napoleon returning from Moscow. The tears were streaming down his cheeks, and he was sobbing bitterly, not, I believe, so much from pain as from what he felt to be an undignified position and thoughts of the future. He was but a shadow of his former self, and we could not help but perceive in his moral breakdown and distress the essential difference between the European and the native. Had one of us been seriously frostbitten he would at least have *tried* to bear his misfortune with stoical calm and fortitude. But a native cannot control his feelings ; he is a child ; his mind cannot master pain or mental depression ; he seeks not to know the whys and wherefores of a physical infirmity—he only knows that he is hurt or ill, that something is wrong with him, and that is sufficient to cause a moral breakdown which is all the more pitiful when it happens in the case of an otherwise strong man.

As Greene and I walked along the path we noticed one of our porters ahead of us. As we approached him we saw that his walking, both in execution and direction, was decidedly erratic. We watched him a trifle anxiously, for the edge of the path was unprotected and there was a sheer precipice of several hundred feet into the Dhaoli River. As we passed him, we received a foolish grin. It was Passang. And a Passang who had partaken of spirituous liquor. Passang, the stolid, the sober, the respectable, was drunk !

Now we knew why our porters had visited Niti. Passang was not the only one. As we neared the camping-ground at Gamsali we heard an uproar of angry voices. The bone of contention—and it was literally a bone—was the leg of one of the bharhal shot by Budhibal Gurung. Two or three Darjeeling men had hold of one end of it and two or three local men the other. It was a fine tug of war, and we only arrived in time to prevent an affray in which kukris might have done serious injury. The dispute was easily settled—if the porters could not decide whose property it was, the sahibs would have it. There were no more arguments as to the ownership of the meat. There were also some empty packing-cases which were coveted by the local men. As we had no further use for them, we were disposed to give them away to the more deserving. As, however, the local men refused for some time to set about their task of collecting firewood, orders were given for the destruction of the boxes to start a fire. This brought the malcontents to their senses and they implored us to spare the boxes. It was the only occasion on which trouble occurred among our porters, and it was the result simply and solely of the local firewater, which fanned into flame the smouldering jealousy existing between the Darjeeling men and the local men. Order was soon restored, and the men set about erecting our tents. Passang hitting his thumb with the mallet in mistake for the tent peg, and the Old Soldier, always preternaturally solemn when under the influence of alcohol, entangled in the guy-ropes of my tent were not the least amusing incidents of the day.

Apart from the necessity for a rest at a reasonable altitude in order to recoup strength and allow enlarged hearts to return to their normal size, it was necessary to reorganise our porterage and overhaul our stores. Men had to be engaged in place of yaks, and in this sparsely populated district they were not easy to find. Food was lasting out well. As however we were short of sugar and jam, a message was sent to Captain Clarke at Ranikhet asking him to send up to Badrinath a load of provisions including these commodities, and also golden syrup, the omission of which from our original stores was a grievous mistake, and had been often bemoaned.

Our next objective was Badrinath. The easiest and longest route was down the Dhaoli Valley to Joshimath, and then up the ordinary pilgrim route. We had resolved, however, to cross the Zaskar Range to the south of Kamet. Only one pass, the Bhyundar Kanta, 16,700 ft., had been made across the watershed of this range. The date on which it was first traversed is not known, but it is known to have been crossed in 1862 by Colonel Edmund Smyth, who reopened it when it had been disused and forgotten for many years. His Bhotia porters lost their way and he had to bivouac in the open on the pass. This pass leads into the fertile Bhyundar Valley, which joins the Alaknanda Valley some five miles north of Joshimath and ten miles south of Badrinath. When Doctor Longstaff's party crossed the pass in 1907, local information had it that a descent of the lower part of the Bhyundar Valley was impossible owing to steep and narrow gorges. He, therefore, climbed out of the Bhyundar Valley at the point where it bends in a southerly direction, and, crossing the easy grass pass of the Khanta Khal, 14,750 ft., descended to Hanuman Chatti, some five miles south of Badrinath, on the pilgrim route. Another route between the Alaknanda and Dhaoli Valleys was that made by Meade from Mana by the Kuhlia Ganga and Bhyundar Kanta Passes. A way has now been trodden up the gorge of the Bhyundar Valley by shepherds and their flocks, and it is no longer necessary to traverse the Khanta Khal Pass in order to reach the Alaknanda Valley. Our object was to cross the range north of these passes and make as direct a line as possible between Gamsali and Badrinath and Mana. Doctor Longstaff mentioned that the late A. L. Mumm found unexpected indications of a pass at the head of the Banke Glacier which fills the upper part of the Gamsali Valley. These indications were not, however, followed up.[1] We intended to act on this information and make a new and more direct route to Badrinath and Mana from the head of the Banke Glacier. We hoped also to examine Kamet's southerly outpost, the Mana Peak, 23,862 ft., with a view to attempting an ascent. Further, the head of the Banke Glacier and its tributary glaciers should repay exploration.

With these objects in view we decided to send our heavy luggage round by the lower route via Joshimath to Badrinath under the charge of Alam Singh, and proceed as a light mobile party across the Zaskar Range with a limited number of porters carrying only a small amount of food and light equipment. Lewa was to accompany the heavy baggage party to Joshimath, where there is a hospital at which his frostbitten feet could be looked after.

The monsoon had now arrived, and during the three days that we were at Gamsali warm drizzling rain alternated

[1] *Alpine Journal*, vol. xxiv pp. 127-9.

VILLAGE SCHOOL

with sunny periods, and woolly grey clouds, hanging low on the peaks, seemed an earnest of worse weather to come.

One afternoon we spent visiting the village of Gamsali. It is a quaint little place, and its primitive houses are almost indistinguishable from the huge grey boulders among which they cluster. Like other villages in this part of the world, it is built anywhere and anyhow, and its streets, if such a name can be applied to the refuse-stinking channels between the houses, run in any and every direction. Yet, even this remote corner of the British Empire possesses its social amenities. There is a school, a collection of ragged little urchins every whit as impudent and potentially intelligent as their East End prototypes, ruled by a headmaster even more ragged and disreputable in appearance than they are. His shirt was torn, tattered and filthy, his trousers beyond repair, sacking in lieu of boots encased his feet, and his long melancholy face wore an expression of patient martyrdom. There was also a tailor who was the proud possessor of an aged sewing-machine.

A mob of curious children followed us round. We were invited by the head man to partake of tea with him, but had not the courage to enter his filthy-looking abode. The inhabitants were mostly Hindu-Bhotias, Hinduism being evidenced by the number of girls and women with rings piercing their nostrils. Unlike the sullen-faced, suspicious Hindus of the plains, these Bhotias are a friendly, cheerful and happy-go-lucky people, reflecting in their broad grins and graceful salutations the freedom and *camaraderie* of the hills. Of a very different type was the itinerant fakir who visited our camp. He was on a pilgrimage, so he said, to the sacred peak of Kailas, though I suspect, like many others of his type, his pilgrimage was merely an excuse for beggary and extortion, on religious grounds, from the villages along his route. Never have I gazed upon a more evil countenance; it made us shudder, and his fixed automatic smile could not disguise the calculating evil of his cruel eyes. He was a gymnast, and for the sum of one rupee stood on his head on the top of a large boulder and contorted himself into various attitudes, principal among which was a lithesome locking of the legs. He knew four words of English, one, two, three and four, and shouted these out like a sergeant-major at every kick of the legs. We were not sorry to see the last of him, for he was the incarnation of evil and vice.

At length, on July 4, the loads had been made up by Shipton and Beauman, who sorted out from among a mountain of provisions the quantity required for the crossing of the range. The only commodity in which we were seriously short was sugar. We had left Ranikhet with 100 lbs. of it, and it had melted away like snow, for, as I have previously explained, sugar is the fuel on which the body works at high altitudes. Admittedly the amount was a miscalculation, but, even so, it had disappeared in an extraordinary way, and there is no doubt that the Sherpas' and Bhotias' predilection for anything sweet was in part responsible. Expeditions would do well to note this point, and to divide their sugar supply among small sealed and numbered bags, which can be easily checked. Fortunately, as a substitute we had the native goa, a coarse brown sugar both palatable and nourishing, which is sold in large lumps the size of a man's head, wrapped around with leaves as a protection from dirt.

At length all was ready, and we bade farewell to poor Lewa and, leaving Birnie behind us for an extra day to complete the arrangements for the porterage of our heavy luggage, set off on July 5 up the Banke Valley.

CHAPTER XVIII

THE BHYUNDAR PASS AND THE VALLEY OF FLOWERS

JULY 5 had dawned fine. It was a morning charged with a joyous freshness, and only gossamer remnants of the monsoon mists clung to the peaks, or explored, like tiny yachts, the deep blue ocean of the sky. From every hollow in the hillsides jaunty brooks poured, to add their quota to the thundering torrent from the Banke Glacier. The moist turf gave springily beneath our tread. Shining drops of water hung from every flower, as though numberless elfin glass-blowers were practising their craft.

Doctor Longstaff compared the Banke Valley to " the vale of Lauterbrunnen carved on a sublime scale, but without the forests." It does indeed bear a striking similarity to the great Oberland trench. Stern precipices hemmed us in on either side ; the eye passed almost giddily up their sweeps to a skyline of jagged rock peaks around which the morning mists wove patterns of light and shadow. From the cavernous recesses of deep gullies the melted snow-waters boomed sullenly. Here and there, where hollows permitted, rested small glaciers, the green tongues of which licked downwards towards the valley.

The Vale of Lauterbrunnen encloses the traveller between its limestone walls ; it is gloomy and depressing at the best of times. The Banke Valley is wider and sunnier. It is open to the breezes that blow from the snows, it possesses the subtle charm of the little known. We could gaze up its cliffs and reflect that they do not serve as rubbish-chutes to hotels. There was no shriek of funicular, no honk of motor-horn, no hum of power-station. Peaks unnamed and unclimbed stand watch over pastures where the stolid brown-eyed yaks graze, and the ragged weather-beaten shepherds make music on their flutes.

For a while we traversed the southern slopes of the valley, then, crossing the stream where it was securely bridged by avalanche snow, gained an alp of luscious grass where the shepherds of Gamsali and Bampa graze their flocks. For nearly four miles above this alp the valley floor is almost level. We could just perceive the stone-covered snout of the Banke Glacier curving round a corner. The view up the valley was dominated by a beautiful peak. It is one of the few peaks that has been triangulated in this district, and its height is given as 19,815 ft. In shape it reminded me strongly of the Oberland Bietschhorn, for it has the same graceful shoulders supporting a delicately soaring peak. Shipton was particularly attracted by it, and I saw his eyes wandering over it with the speculative predatory gleam of the mountaineer who sights a foe worthy of his steel.

We ambled along the valley, passing, here and there, rude encampments of piled-up stones beneath which the shepherds shelter when minding their flocks.

We camped on a level meadow by a brook. This camping-ground is named Thur Udiar, and Doctor Longstaff's party camped there in 1907. It is 12,000 ft., but the evening was so warm that we did not have to don extra clothing, and sat in comfort around the camp fire.

The following day, July 6, we continued on our way. After clambering over slopes of boulders forming the terminal moraine of the Banke Glacier, we gained the crest of that glacier's northerly side moraine, which afforded an easy and convenient route. This was the only day of the expedition which I did not in some measure enjoy. I was afflicted with a raging toothache. For a week or two past I had been forced to eat sugary substances and drink hot and cold liquids with circumspection, but now the tooth needed no such stimulant—it ached continuously —and not even the arrival of the mail by a runner, and the fact that it was my birthday, could alleviate my sufferings.

We camped on the grassy shelf a few feet above the glacier, known as " Eri Udiar " (" Cold Cave "). There, screwing up my courage to sticking-point, I asked Greene with a wan smile to remove the offending tooth.

" Certainly," replied Greene, with a broad grin and offensive cheerfulness. " But I'm afraid I've no cocaine or chloroform. It's gone round to Badrinath with the heavy luggage."

A good many people are cowards where their teeth are concerned—I am one of them. Before the discovery of anæsthetics patients about to undergo an operation were wont to fortify themselves with rum. Our limited supply of rum had of necessity to be rationed sparingly. On this occasion, however, my companions generously offered no objections to my partaking of an extra ration of it. I must, however, question their veracity when they say that I lowered three-quarters of a bottle. I must also question another statement which they are strangely unanimous in making. They said that before the rum I pointed up the

Banke Glacier to a fine ice-peak that rises from the head of it and said, " Look at that peak up there, typically Himalayan, hopelessly inaccessible. No one will ever climb those terrific ice-ridges." But after the rum I said : " Look at that peak up there ! Anyone could climb *that*." My recollection is that I was stabbed in the chest with a morphia syringe, a gag artfully carved from a piece of juniper root was thrust between my teeth and then . . . The tooth came out, removed with skill and dispatch by Greene. I remember nothing more until I awoke in my tent feeling somewhat the worse for wear. Rum and morphia do not go well together.

Three months later, after Greene had assisted in the removal of some more of my teeth under a general anæsthetic in London, he said that it was fortunate that the tooth he pulled out at Eri Udiar was not like the others, the pulling of which added considerably to the muscular development of the dentist's biceps.

The following morning, July 7, Shipton and Holdsworth set out at dawn to attempt the conquest of the 19,815 ft. peak. During the day Birnie arrived with the good news that the heavy luggage had gone off safely under the charge of Alam Singh and our two Gurkhas, of whom Randhoj Kan was to remain at Joshimath to look after some baggage which was to be left there, and Budhibal Gurung accompany Alam Singh with the remaining baggage to Mana.

Shipton and Holdsworth did not return until dusk. They had got within 300 ft. of the top of their peak after a long and difficult climb, involving both ice and rock-work, and then had been forced to turn back owing to lack of time in which to complete the ascent. They were confident, however, now that the route had been worked out, that the peak could be climbed directly from the camp. As Eri Udiar is only 14,690 ft., to reach the summit in one day meant a climb of 5,125 ft.—a formidable day at such an altitude.

As Shipton was bent on completing the ascent, he and Nima set out again next morning. Unfortunately, Holdsworth was experiencing trouble with his frostbitten big toe and was unable to accompany them. This time the summit was reached, after a climb that Shipton described as being equal in difficulty to a Cumberland " severe." That rocks of such difficulty were climbed at a height of nearly 20,000 ft. was indicative both of acclimatisation and freedom from deterioration. Kamet, instead of weakening us had raised us to the pinnacle of fitness. There is no doubt that many Himalayan peaks now thought to be inaccessible will be proved accessible in the future by acclimatised men in the zenith of their powers.[1]

Shipton reported that the view had been obscured for the most part by clouds. Nima, he said, had climbed splendidly ; it proved again that the best of the Darjeeling Sherpas and Bhotias are fit to accompany Europeans on the most difficult and exacting climbs.

The same day that Shipton and Nima ascended the 19,815 ft. peak, Beauman and Greene explored the head of the Banke Glacier with a view to ascertaining whether a practicable pass existed across the range to Badrinath and Mana. They returned with the depressing news that the Banke Glacier was hemmed in by a wall of peaks across which there was no practicable route, at all events

[1] Immense difficulties were overcome by the Bavarians on Kangchenjunga in 1929 and 1931 at a height of over 23,000 ft.

for laden porters. We had hoped that a pass might be found across the ridge to the north of a measured peak of 21,198 ft. and between it and an unmeasured ice peak, as this was, presumably, where Mumm had noticed indications of a pass, but the face of the ridge, on this its eastern side, presents a sheer wall of ice, plastered above and below with hanging glaciers that constantly discharge avalanches. One look had been sufficient. From their farthest point they had gazed northwards into a cirque of peaks, some of which presented pinnacles and faces comparable in sharpness and steepness to the Aiguilles of Mont Blanc. The Mana Peak, they declared, was hopeless to attempt by its southern side or south-eastern face. If another reason was wanted for not attempting the difficult or impossible, it was the avalanches which were being detached by the monsoon from every peak. Throughout the day they roared and thundered like heavy guns—not only avalanches of ice, but avalanches of snow, for so warm was the weather that masses of old and consolidated snow were slipping periodically from every steep snow-slope. Thus, we had no alternative but to abandon our scheme and revert to the easy route across the range by the Bhyundar Kanta and Khanta Khal Passes.

On June 9 we packed up and set off from Eri Udiar for the Bhyundar Kanta Pass. It was a dull morning, and heavy mists blanketed the peaks. From Eri Udiar the route to the pass is by no means obvious. The Banke Glacier is bounded on its south-western side by a ridge from which spring two great peaks, Rataban, 21,198 ft., and a nameless peak to the north-west of Rataban, which, according to the map, is precisely the same altitude ! Between these two peaks lies the pass, which is 16,700 ft. high according to the measurement of Doctor Longstaff. Two glaciers lead up towards the pass, and the westerly of these appeared to us the one to follow. Our local porters, however, assured us that the proper route ascended the easterly glacier under the northern precipices of Rataban. They were so positive that we must follow this glacier that for once we decided that local advice must be trusted.

To cross the Banke Glacier meant the usual tedious ups and downs and détours which are such an annoying feature of Himalayan glacier travelling. By the side moraine of the glacier was a small lake. In its icy waters Greene had mortified his flesh the previous day. The lake was over 15,000 ft. above the sea. Few people can have bathed at such an altitude, whilst the number of people who want to bathe at such an altitude must be even more limited. The " fine frenzy " that induces a human being to break the ice of the Serpentine before breakfast, or to jump into a glacier lake is self-inflicted castigation akin to the religious craziness that causes Indians to slash themselves with knives, or Burmese to suspend themselves in mid air from meat-hooks.

A well-defined moraine led us easily up the small side glacier towards our pass. As we trudged uphill, the heavy mists drooped still lower and rain began to fall, a cold, penetrating rain that soaked through our climbing clothes to our skin. Now and again, between sombre mists we saw the northern precipices of Rataban, grooved with couloirs that swept up to the green lips of hanging glaciers. Once or twice our feet struck blocks of ice beneath the snow—we were just within range of the ice artillery.

After the brilliant weather to which we had become accustomed, such a day seemed unreasonably depressing, yet to appreciate mountains they must be seen in gloom as well as sun. When only the black ribs of the peaks glare through the mists, when the snow-slopes are blank and shadowless and not even the deadly ripple of the masked crevasse is visible, the mountaineer feels himself to be encompassed about by the forces of death, and the awful solemnity and majesty of his surroundings strikes at his very soul.

By keeping to the northern side of the glacier we were able to avoid the danger zone of ice avalanches from the cliffs of Rataban. The porters were going badly. They had not fully recovered from the effects of the local alcoholic poisons they had imbibed at Gamsali and Niti. As we rose, the rain changed to sleet, which was lashed into our faces by a biting wind. It was impossible to see more than a few yards ahead. More by luck than judgment we hit off the lowest and easiest point on the ridge forming the Bhyundar Kanta Pass. We huddled shivering under the lee of a boulder and ate a little chocolate. We waited perhaps half an hour for Birnie and Beauman, who were a long way behind, and then, half frozen by the wind and soaked to the skin, started to descend the other side of the pass. This was a piece of neglect on my part, for however numbed and cold I was, I should have remained on the pass to see all the porters safely across it.

We knew from Doctor Longstaff's account that we had to slant diagonally downwards in a westerly direction. Owing to the mist, visibility was limited, but not sufficiently so to prevent us from glissading long and easy slopes of snow. As we descended, we left the wind behind us, and entered a region of calm. We sat down on the wet rocks to await the others. As we did so we saw that we had entered the Kingdom of Flowers. Barrenness was replaced by beauty. Our misery was forgotten as we gazed upon little clusters of light blue primulas, peeping from ledges and crannies, watered by melting snows. Presently we heard voices, and, traversing across the hillside, joined Birnie and Beauman, who had with them some of the porters.

No difficulty in descending was experienced, and soon we were treading the stone-strewn surface of what we took to be the Bhyundar Glacier, but which subsequently proved to be a tributary of that glacier which is not marked in the map. For a mile or so we tramped down through wet mists. A side moraine loomed out of the mist, and we climbed to the crest of it in search of a camping-site. When the moraine petered out into the hillside, we took to the latter. The mist thinned ; the rain now was light and warm, like the rain of a spring day in a Devon combe. Lower down we entered what I can only describe as an Eden of flowers.[1] Growing among the rocks was the tiny stemless *Primula reptans* ; the flowers of the commoner but beautiful *Primula denticulata* covered the hillside, and above the glacier were three varieties of androsace. Between clumps of creamy dwarf rhododendrons, the ground was purple with dwarf irises, and blue and yellow with pansies and fritillaries. As the track descended we came upon the most beautiful of all Himalayan flowers, the mecanopsis (blue poppy). Its petals are as blue as a glacier lake, and its stamens as golden as the sunset glow on the great peaks beneath which it grows.

[1] I am indebted to Holdsworth for the following names.

BHYUNDAR VALLEY

We camped on a small grassy shelf, gay with flowers. At the entrance to our tents grew creamy anemones, homely blue forget-me-nots, golden, white and red potentillas, purple primulas, androsace, blue and pink geraniums, and many other plants. The pipes of Pan could scarcely have surprised us here.

The porters arrived with disturbing news. One local man recently recruited had been taken mountain-sick and, abandoning his load, had returned to Eri Udiar. It was difficult to understand how a man used to spending the majority of his life at an altitude of 10,000 ft. or more should be afflicted with mountain sickness on a pass of 16,700 ft. He was not the only one : three more men had not turned up, and it was to be presumed had bivouacked on the slopes below the pass. It had not been a heavy day —indeed an easy one—and our Darjeeling men were frankly scornful of our latest recruits. We could only presume them to be exceptionally poor specimens of Bhotias, or else soft from easy living and indulgence in the aforementioned spirituous poisons. Natar Singh, who had been appointed sirdar over the local men, was ordered to send some men back immediately. This was done despite grumblings and protestations. The men returned in the last daylight, declaring that their comrades were quite safe, though I suspected that this statement was prompted by imagination rather than observation.

Next morning a strong body of men was sent out to bring in the errant ones and their loads, and also to recover the abandoned load on the far side of the pass. This was successfully accomplished, some men returning with the news that the man who had abandoned his load had descended safely to Eri Udiar and Gamsali, whilst others brought down the loads of the three who had bivouacked out. The latter appeared to have had a comfortable night despite a lack of shelter. Bhotias of Garhwal think nothing of spending a night out in bad weather at 15,000 ft. or more under conditions which would make a European quail.

The same afternoon we decided to move our camp farther down the Bhyundar Valley in order to shorten the march over the Khanta Khal Pass. The weather was mending. Shafts of sunlight piercing clouds lower down the valley disclosed green pastures and a dark wash of pine forest. Through rifts in the monsoon mists the dark bastions of Gauri Parbat stood out like the blunt rams of some mid-aerial battle-fleet.

As we descended, the flora became more and more luscious, until we were wading knee deep through an ocean of flowers, ranging in colour from the sky blue of the poppies to the deep wine red of the potentillas. We filled our buttonholes and adorned our hats. A stranger had he seen us might have mistaken us—at a distance—for a bevy of sylphs and nymphs. But had he taken a closer look he would have seen, beneath a canopy of flowers, beards sprouting from countenances browned, scorched and cracked by glacier suns. Nor are tricouni-nailed climbing boots an appropriate footwear for sylphs and nymphs.

Leaving the untidy, rubble-strewn Bhyundar Glacier behind us, we strolled on across the meadows until at length we discovered an ideal camping-ground of dry sandy soil near a clear-running brook.

To us the Bhyundar Valley will always remain the Valley of Flowers. It is a place of escape for those wearied

THE VALLEY OF FLOWERS

of modern civilisation. The means of sustenance are to be found there. Rhubarb grows abundantly, an edible second only to eggs in Shipton's estimation, but one for which Holdsworth evidenced a strong dislike. Sheep are driven up to graze, and doubtless bharhal and other game are to be shot. It would be easily possible to secure an abundant supply of provisions from the Alaknanda Valley. True, it would be necessary to descend in the winter to warmer and less snowy levels, but for half a year the lover of beauty and solitude could find peace in the Valley of Flowers. He would discover joy and laughter in the meadows ; the stars would be his nightly canopy ; he would watch the slow passing of the clouds ; he would share the sunset and the dawn with God.

Beyond the hills, nations might fly at one another's throats ; Mussolinis rise and fall ; anarchy and revolution rot the nations ; but in the Valley of Flowers the only strife would be that of the elements, the only sounds the wind in the flowers, the voice of the stream, and the rumble of the avalanche.

Towards evening, the sluggish monsoon mists drifted asunder. Summits peered through from immeasurable heights. Far up the valley the crest of Gauri Parbat glowed in the declining sun. Day's cold fires were drawn by the dark stokers of night.

Peace and contentment were ours as we sat around the camp fire. Felt rather than seen were the peaks about us. A million stars eyed us. The voice of the mountain torrent lulled us to sleep.

CHAPTER XIX

TO MANA

THE FOLLOWING morning dawned brilliantly, but soon soft grey clouds began to poke their noses up from the south. At breakfast, there was the usual rhubarb grouse, excluding of course Shipton, yet, when wild rhubarb was so plentiful, what could we do but eat it, for it is valuable as an anti-scorbutic.

From our camping-place we could see the route to the Khanta Khal Pass. From the Bhyundar Valley the way lay up a secondary valley and then over a grassy skyline cloaked in monsoon clouds. To enter this secondary valley covering we had to walk across meadows the flora covering which was the most luxuriant that I have seen. The hillsides were snowy with anemones ; potentillas lifted delicate petals of deep wine and yellow ; nomicharis mingled with crimson orchids. We saw pale blue borage, mauve polemonium, rosy-petalled cypripedium, dwarf larkspur, clumps of superb purple asters, and clustered primulas of the deepest purple. Fat bumble-bees satiated with honey buzzed languidly ; fritillary butterflies, red brown and mother-of-pearl, fluttered from flower to flower ; small birds raised a gay song ; a gentle intermittent breeze, stirring the flowers, wafted their fragrance abroad.

We encountered a flock of sheep. There evidently exists a well-trodden path up which the shepherds drive their flocks from the Alaknanda Valley to the rich upper pastures. The shepherds eyed us curiously. They were hardy, weather-beaten men with sinewy frames, and their far-seeing, deep-set eyes reflected the quietude and immensity of the mountains among which they spend their lives. They paused to bid us cheery *salaams*, and passed on their way, walking with a loose-limbed shambling gait.

Where the side valley debouches into the Bhyundar Valley it is narrow and steep, and the smoke-like spray of its falling torrent issued from between the silver birches lining its rocky banks.

A slope ablaze with flowers took us quickly uphill. Gradually, the valley opened out into rock-strewn slopes set at a lesser angle. Dirty masses of avalanche snow cluttered the way ; between were little lawns of bright green grass ; golden kingcups lined the streams. Once or twice we saw the blue poppy peeping out shyly from beneath overhanging boulders. The monsoon brought a warm, thin rain. Now and again the mists, sundered by vagrant winds, revealed snowy summits.

We came to the verge of a small rubble-strewn glacier ; above it through the shifting mists a hanging glacier loomed. We did not linger within range of its missiles, but, turning to the left, mounted grassy slopes towards our pass. It was an easy ascent, yet some of the local porters complained of the weight of their loads. Possibly, they thought they could hold us up for an increase of pay. Again, they may have resented the nonchalant and even swaggering manner in which our Darjeeling men, now tough and perfectly trained, carried their loads. They had no cause to complain, for, owing to the food that we had eaten, they were carrying lighter loads than those they had shouldered originally at Gamsali. We determined to dismiss most, if not all of them, at Mana, for many of them were fit only to cross easy grass passes and were obviously incapable of sustained exertion at higher altitudes.

We reached the pass bathed in the perspiration we had learnt to associate with monsoon weather even at 15,000 ft. Mists prevented us from seeing Nilkanta, but it was pleasant reclining on a soft couch of flowering turf, watching the play of light and shadow on the nearer peaks.

Scattered about on the grassy crest of the pass were some crooked whitish objects. These our porters pounced upon eagerly, declaring that they were the antlers of fairy deer which bring luck to the finder if they are burnt as incense to the gods. It was a charming thought, and the objects in question, which are probably some species of fungoid growth, do resemble minute antlers. Scarcely less eagerly did Holdsworth pounce upon yet another variety of primula, the ninth species that he had discovered since descending into the Bhyundar Valley.

The mists obstinately refusing to lift, we started to descend. For such an easy pass as is the Khanta Khal the descent is a steep one. The difference in height between the summit of the pass and Hanuman Chatti, in the Alaknanda Valley, is no less than 6,500 ft., and this in a horizontal distance of a little over two miles. Long glissades in snow-filled gullies took us expeditiously down the first 2,000 ft. The snow petered out, and we continued the descent on steep vegetation-masked hillsides, following a rude track. Doctor Longstaff reached

Hanuman Chatti in three hours from the pass. This was exceptionally fast going, and, although we were not set on emulating him, we were congratulating ourselves at being as good as in the Alaknanda Valley when the track almost disappeared beneath vegetation including dense thickets of bamboos, and, to cap its wilfulness, zigzagged sharply uphill.

The evening was hot, close, and thunderous, and sweat poured from us as we forced a way through the bushes.

At length the apology for a track became horizontal, and even began to descend slightly. We rounded a corner, and found ourselves forced to traverse a cliff face set at a formidable angle. Here the track had collapsed or been washed away, and considerable time was lost in negotiating a slimy outward-sloping slab.

By the time gentler slopes had been reached night was falling swiftly, and we had no option but to camp. Fortunately, we were able to find a grassy shelf on which to pitch our tents.

It was not a pleasant spot. The moist monsoon air was tainted with tropical odours—the stench of rotting undergrowth, rank grasses and shrubs. The vast vegetation-cloaked valleys of the Himalaya come as a strange anticlimax after the snows, and their fœtid airs reek of disease and death.

We were glad to get on the move again next morning. As we descended we congratulated ourselves that we had camped where we did and not tried to force our way down to the Alaknanda Valley the previous evening. Had we attempted this, we should most certainly have been benighted on precipitous slopes overgrown with dense vegetation. Conditions must have changed greatly since Doctor Longstaff descended by this route, for the vestige of a path we had been following now disappeared completely beneath a tangle of undergrowth and bamboos, and it was only with difficulty that we were able to force our way downhill. The porter carrying the ski had a sorry time of it here.

We crossed the valley torrent with some difficulty, and after traversing some loose and unpleasant slopes of detritus found that no further difficulties separated us from the floor of the Alaknanda Valley. Once I heard the thin piping of a marmot and saw the quaint little beast scurry under a boulder. Looking under the boulder, I saw it sitting there eyeing me fearfully. Next moment it rushed out again and sought a more secure refuge beneath another boulder.

We reached the end of the valley, where are some primitive huts, the inhabitants of which eke out a precarious existence from little fields of grain between the boulders. A horde of children eyed us shyly, energetically sucking their thumbs the while, and a ragged fellow whose clothes were not worth an anna grinned cheerily at us, and gabbled unintelligibly. We passed a natural stone basin in a boulder filled with water from the overflow of the stream, where the women of the village were washing clothes. The only laundering known to them is to soak their garments in the water and beat them energetically against a neighbouring slab, worn and polished by centuries of washerwomen.

We found ourselves at last on the pilgrim route to Badrinath. The first objects that attracted our attention were the telegraph-poles that bear a solitary wire from Chamoli to the telegraph office at Badrinath. Possibly, I ought here to pay a compliment to the Indian Posts and Telegraphs for their enterprise in carrying a line into this remote corner of the Himalaya, especially as the expedition was not slow to take advantage of the facilities afforded thereby ; but we had come from the Valley of Flowers, and at first sight this evidence of civilisation grated horribly. As I gazed upon the ugly line of poles topped by white insulators gleaming like soulless eyes, my predominant thought was that soon we must follow them back to civilisation. It was a comfort to think that for a time at least we might turn our backs on the lower valleys from which the telegraph-poles straggled, and adventure once more among the snows.

The pilgrim path is so broad that a baby motor-car might be driven along it for miles on end, but Heaven forbid that these solitudes of Himalaya should suffer such a fate : let civilisation cherish its noise and Himalaya its quietude.

Below the path rushed the Alaknanda River, its turbulence and volume reflecting the power and majesty of the peaks that gave it birth. At this season of the year, when warm monsoon airs are melting the snows on the highest peaks, the Alaknanda is in spate. A man who fell into it would be smashed to pulp in a few seconds. See how the great boulders in the bed of the torrent appear one moment and disappear the next beneath a furious gush of grey glacial water. It is almost as though the heart of the river responds tempestuously to the caress of the summer sun.

The pilgrim way was impregnated with what I can only describe as an odour of sanctity. It was not like other smells that I have smelt, but a special Eastern smell that includes in it an odour of spices, exhalations from unwashed bodies, and other things too unpleasant to enumerate.

Pilgrims, old and young, were toiling up the path. Maharajahs and Maharanees visit Badrinath and its sister pilgrim city Kedarnath, so also do miscreants who seek to escape from the law, and the filthiest beggars, odorous, unwashed, ragged, and whining for alms, who batten on the charity of the villages through which they pass. Educated Indians with university education and the lowliest "untouchables" from Calcutta, Madras and Bombay toil through the humid tropical heat of the lower valleys, braving cholera, dysentery, typhoid, malaria and other tropical diseases in order to pay their respects to the holy snows of Himachal, to see the sacred image of Vishnu in the temple at Badrinath, bathe in the sacred hot spring there, and cleanse soul and body in the icy waters of the Alaknanda. Some of the more fanatical seek to expiate their sins by falling on their faces, stretching out their arms before them, drawing a chalk line; standing on it and falling again. Such take many months to accomplish their pilgrimage. To Western ideas there is something inexplicable and almost terrible in such immolation. To appreciate political motives in India it is necessary to delve deep down to the basic root of all things, and that is religion. Europeans who listen with languid boredom to sermons preached on Sundays cannot understand how great are the powers of religion in India for good or evil.

PILGRIMS AT HANUMAN CHATTI

Fanaticisms and hatreds are always simmering, like a molten, subterranean lava lake, and it is only the firm rock of British rule that prevents explosion. Here and there they find a peaceable outlet for their turbulence, and the pilgrimage to Badrinath and Kedarnath is one, but once allow those imprisoning walls to collapse and India would become an unimaginable shambles. The law abiding Hindus toiling up the path to Badrinath would become fiends incarnate, seeking to tear the Moslem population of India limb from limb, sparing neither man, woman nor child ; and down upon this shambles would come the tribesmen from the north-west, and the Gurkhas from Nepal, to carve their way through what was left of India.

India is not, and cannot be for centuries, fit to rule herself, and to abandon her would be equivalent to putting all the animals of the Zoo in one cage. The strong would survive, but the agonies of the weak would be too terrible to contemplate. With India would fall the British Empire. Let us, in the interests of humanity, maintain a just balance in that most complicated and passionate of lands.

We came to the little village of Hanuman Chatti, which, like other villages along the pilgrim route, consists largely of pilgrim rest-houses. These are reminiscent of a hop-picker's temporary abode, but they are infinitely dirtier. There are a few straw-thatched shops which sell their wares to the pilgrims. Earlier in the expedition we should have turned with disgust from the dainties these displayed, if only on account of the flies that swarmed about them, but weeks of Achung's cooking had hardened us body and soul. I have heard it said that, in nine cases out of ten, no one would again visit a restaurant in London if he could peep behind the scenes. The same applies with tenfold force in India, but Achung had long since eliminated any scruples we might have possessed, and we turned with relish to food not cooked by him. And the food we got at Hanuman Chatti was surprisingly good. There were chupatties, warm, greasy and savoury, and sweets—the coarse local goa disguised in various ways. Of the latter, the ones which we most favoured were tapered masses of brown sugar speckled on the outside with "hundreds and thousands." In the back of each tumbledown shop the shopkeeper squatted, cross-legged, with a small charcoal fire before him, over which, in pans black with age and dirt, he prepared his delicacies.

We continued on our way, forging through the village in as few breaths as possible. The pilgrims huddled in the shade eyed us apathetically ; most of them appeared worn out by travelling and privation, and exhibited no elation at being so near to their goal. One old man, clad only in a loin-cloth, with stick-like arms and legs, and wild unkempt beard, rushed out in the middle of the street and, crouching there, raised trembling suppliant hands. He was, probably, one of the professional beggars who infest the pilgrim route. We emerged from the village with relief. It is strange that man, an intellectual superior to animals, can surround himself with filth that most animals would instinctively reject.

The Alaknanda Valley is worthy of the torrent that rages down it. Its precipitous sides spring up on either hand for thousands of feet. Cliffs, black and dripping with moisture lurch threateningly over the traveller; rocky pinnacles cleave the sky thousands of feet above him. It is a fitting pathway to Himachal and the foot of Vishnu.

In places the path disappeared beneath the dissolving and dirty remnants of spring snow-avalanches that had swept down gullies in the hillside. Some of these avalanches still spanned the Alaknanda with their débris. During the winter months Badrinath is snowed up and deserted, and its inhabitants retire to the lower and warmer valleys.

We lunched in the shade. Pilgrims passed us, ascending or descending the path, some with their wives and some without, the wealthier, the aged and infirm, being borne in palanquins by sweating bearers. The wives it was who carried the family goods and chattels, toiling in the wake of their husbands, who had nothing more to do than concentrate their thoughts on the sanctity of their pilgrimage and the absolution of their sins.

In the early afternoon we reached Badrinath. The first thing we saw was the ugly red corrugated iron roof of a bungalow that might have graced a south coast " resort." The second thing was an Indian gentleman clad in a saucy pullover and a pair of Oxford flannel trousers. He passed us without a salutation. Possibly he was a Congress wallah detailed off to spread the germ of unrest in this peaceful corner of the world. Another shock in store for us was an iron bridge, in the process of building, intended to span the Alaknanda River. As it was not yet completed, we had to cross by the existing bridge a short distance higher up the river. Whether, owing to the building of an improved bridge, this had been allowed to fall into disrepair, or whether the state in which we found it was its normal state, I am not prepared to say, but Mr. Heath Robinson in one of his lighter moments could scarcely have designed a more intriguing structure.

Theoretically, it was a suspension bridge ; practically, it was an intricate network of wires, ropes and odd bits of cord and string overlaid with rotting wooden planks. Portions weary of cohesion had already collapsed, and hung from the underside of the bridge like seaweed from a pier. Even the Indians, whose casualness in such matters is usually beyond the comprehension of Europeans, had erected a notice advising a maximum load of four people. My own peace of mind was seriously disturbed by Holdsworth, who trod the bridge behind me so heavily and unexpectedly that the crazy structure trembled and swayed like an aspen-leaf in a gale.

Having safely crossed the bridge, we entered the main street of Badrinath. We were surprised to find ourselves passing between reputable-looking shops—book-shops and trinket-shops, tailors, fruiterers, grocers and so on. There was even a local photographer, whilst one member of the expedition was able to purchase a tube of toothpaste at a price far below that charged in the plains of India. Many shops advertised a drug known as Shilkret. Neither vendors nor manufacturers of this drug have anything to learn from Western advertising methods. Shilkret is the panacea for all ills, the elixir of youth, the essence of the gods ; it will make the old young, and the weak strong ; the germs of cholera, dysentery, typhoid and malaria wilt and die at sight of it. From rabies to housemaid's knee, there is nothing it cannot cure.

A large crowd soon collected around us, and we elbowed

THE RAWAL OF BADRINATH

THE BRIDGE AT BADRINATH

our way towards the temple through a throng of pilgrims, shopkeepers, loungers and scroungers.

The temple is not the imposing affair that might be imagined, and compared to the magnificent edifices of the plains is a humble building. Inside it is a shrine dedicated to the sacred image of Vishnu.

The Rawal is the high-priest, and his house stands between the temple and the Alaknanda River. To reach it, we had to descend a flight of stone steps. These steps, worn and polished by the tread of countless pilgrims, offered but a little friction to tricouni bootnails, and first one member and then another of the expedition came a cropper down them. As conquerors of Kamet we can hardly have impressed the bystanders. Presently, the Rawal came out from a dark passage-way to greet us. He was short of stature, and a typical plainsman in appearance. He had come from Madras, and, to judge from the heavy European overcoat he was wearing, found it chilly living so close to the snows. He is the keeper of the temple and temporal ruler of the Badrinath district. He greeted us shyly and eyed us a trifle askance, and small wonder, for our appearance was positively terrifying. I saw his dark eyes fix themselves fascinatedly on Birnie's red beard. However, in a minute or two he appeared to realise that we were not quite so villainous as our appearance warranted, and invested us with garlands of flowers which had been awaiting our arrival. After thanking him for helping arrange our porters' food, we continued on our way to Mana, where we intended to pitch our camp, accompanied by two of his servants in scarlet sashes with large gilt buckles.

As we neared Mana we became aware of a confused medley of sound, and saw a procession wind down a steep path to the Alaknanda River, cross a crazy wooden bridge, and approach us to the accompaniment of much drum-beating. The village had put itself *en fête*, but whether this was in honour of our advent, or whether it was merely a feast-day in honour of some deity, we could not imagine.

The procession approached us, drumming furiously and waving brightly coloured banners in the air. In the middle of it was carried a long and gaudily painted wooden idol. It was an attenuated and ill-nourished object; possibly, therefore, the proceedings were intended to propitiate the god of Famine who stalks occasionally through these valleys.

Mana is a Bhotia village, and the broad and cheery grins of its inhabitants vouched for the fact. The local Mr. Jack Hylton and his orchestra passed us, and, stationing themselves on the hillside above the Alaknanda, beat furiously on their drums. We were glad to cross the crazy bridge and leave the din behind us.

As we breasted the little plateau on which stands Mana, Alam Singh hurried to greet us, radiating huge grins and gabbling out many expressions of welcome, whilst Budhibal Gurung in the background clicked his heels together and drew himself rigidly to attention. From them we learnt that Lewa's feet were so bad that the doctor at Joshimath had insisted that he must remain there to be treated, and not continue to Ranikhet. All the heavy luggage had come safely round by the lower route, and Randhoj Kan was satisfactorily posted in charge of the luggage we no longer needed, at Joshimath.

We pitched our tents on a grassy shelf, well away from the village hovels and their attendant garbage. Huge boulders, fallen in some catastrophic landslide, surrounded us. A few minutes after our arrival, a messenger from the Rawal arrived, bearing the following delightful missive.

" From His Holiness the Rawal Sahib.
" Temple—Sri Badrinath.

" DEAR SIR,

" I and the public of Badrinath greatly admires and congratulates you on your brilliant victory in having succeeded in climbing the reknowned Kamet peak for the first time in history.

" I am therefore proposing to accord you and the party a most loyal welcome in a public meeting and to hear from you the romantic and heroic description of your expedition.

" Would you therefore please accept this humble request and inform us the date and time for the purpose convenient to you. Further we will be highly interested to witness an expedition of the connected goods and implements with their use that you carried with you for helping in the achievement of your expedition, if you can possibly arrange it to be done side by side as well without any great inconvenience to you.

" Thanking you in anticipation,
" Yours sincerely,
" (*Signed*) THE RAWAL."

Who could refuse such a charming request ? Birnie was the only one among us who could speak Hindustani, and it was arranged, therefore, that he should give the Rawal and the public of Badrinath a lecture on the expedition after our return from our proposed explorations in the Badrinath Range.

As Shipton was again suffering from one of his attacks of egg-fever, a man was dispatched post haste to Badrinath with orders to go through that town with a small comb and bring back with him every egg he could find, irrespective of age or quality. Alas ! his efforts were unsuccessful, but at least we were able to indulge in an orgy of mangoes : they were poor, small, coarse fruit, but to men who had been pining for fruit for weeks they seemed delicious.

Our tents pitched, and our goods unpacked, we could look about us. The scene suggested the stony savagery of the Dauphiny. We gazed into the heart of the Badrinath peaks through a portal of splendid precipices from which issued the turbulent glacier waters of the Alaknanda. Perhaps fifteen miles away. Somewhere near the head of the Bhagat Kharak glacier, two beautiful ice-draped peaks over 22,000 ft. high were visible. In the sky eagles wheeled, mere specks that emphasised by their smallness the vast scale of the precipices on which they dwell.

Evening brought another messenger from the Rawal bearing a generous gift of mangoes, nuts, onions and goa.

Mana is 10,000 ft. above sea-level, but the night was remarkably warm, and numberless small moths and other insects fluttered about us as we sat over our dinner in the mess tent. Our minds were occupied no longer with thoughts of the morrow and what the morrow might bring—on Kamet. The bogey of altitude had been laid, the problem solved ; we could go on our way unmolested by doubt. The mountains about us were friendly mountains.

I was awakened in the night by the dull thumping of drums, accompanied by the plaintive wail of some primitive instrument and voices raised in tuneless song—our porters were making merry in Mana. Just as I was dropping off to sleep again I heard someone blundering about among the tents and voices raised in drunken argument—an argument brought to a premature conclusion by a fluent and pungent flow of Hindustani from Birnie's tent. After that, quiet settled down on the camp.

CHAPTER XX

THE ARWA VALLEY

NEXT morning, when I looked out of my tent, the first object I saw was the Old Soldier. He was seated on the ground, his head buried in his hands. A minute or two later he rose slowly, and with an obvious effort, to his feet and, tottering to the brook that ran down past the camp, immersed his head therein. Obviously, he was unfit to minister to my personal needs ; this was done by Nima Dorje, who materialised from the direction of the cook-house with a broad grin and a cup of hot tea. " Nima Tendrup no good, sir," he informed me confidentially. Then, pointing to his forehead and stomach in turn, he explained significantly, " Drink plenty chang, sir. Very strong, sir." I was well able to appreciate the last part of this statement, for I knew from experience that the Old Soldier was usually impervious to the effects of local firewater. Others among our porters were in an even worse state, and Nima waited upon us at breakfast with a fixed, vacant and bloodshot glare in his eyes that was painful to see.

We decided to stay two whole days at Mana, as this would enable us to reorganise our porterage and plan our expedition into the Badrinath Range. As was usual on " rest days," so called, Birnie worked hard arranging details of our porterage, paying off porters, paying advances to new porters, and arranging for porters' food, while

I had to hammer away on a typewriter at a dispatch to *The Times* and answer dozens of letters and telegrams. These proceedings were enlivened by funeral processions that passed and repassed the camp. Whether they were the outcome of last night's dissipation in the village I cannot say. As they were composed exclusively of drummers and wailing women and children, possibly they were professional mourners, but there was nothing professional about the drumming, which resounded from the village at all hours of the day, in an uproar indicative rather of the personal feelings of each drummer than of any attempt at timing or rhythm.

Moist grey clouds stole up from the south, but seemed incapable of precipitating anything more than an occasional drizzle of rain—they had vented their spleen on the foothills, and the Mana. Villagers told us that only ten or twelve days of rain need be expected during the height of the monsoon season.

Our plan was to cross the Badrinath Range, the watershed of the Alaknanda and Gangotri Rivers. As mentioned already, Meade had explored the Bhagat Kharak and Satopanth Glaciers and visited passes from them that appeared to lead across the range. We preferred not to follow in his footsteps, but to explore the next glacier valley to the north and parallel to the Upper Alaknanda Valley and Bhagat Kharak Glacier system, and try to find a pass from it leading to the Gangotri Glacier system. This is the Arwa Valley, and it is marked in the Indian Survey map as containing a glacier some twelve miles in length, extending to within three miles of the Sarsuti Valley, which runs northwards from its junction with the

Alaknanda Valley at Mana, to the Mana Pass, 17,890 ft. A certain vagueness in the map's delineation of the glaciers flowing into the Arwa Valley suggested that the northern end of the Badrinath Range would repay exploration. While criticising the existing map of this district I should like to make it plain that the survey work was done in the 'seventies and is not to be compared to the excellent work done by the Indian Survey in other Himalayan districts. According to an old report, surveyors in Garhwal were ordered not to waste time on uninhabited districts, but to devote their energies to mapping the inhabited valleys and main lines of communication. Their triangulation of such is reliable, but the existing map of the Badrinath Range is not a topographical survey, and all that the surveyors did was to sketch in what they could see without ascending to the snow and glacier level. Thus is it hardly fair to criticise the crude delineation of the Badrinath Range. Perhaps the only justifiable criticism of the existing map is that it would have been wiser to have left unexplored districts a blank and not to have sketched in ridges and glaciers that do not exist, just to " complete " the map.

Owing to the stupidity of the dak wallah (postman), we nearly lost our mail while staying at Mana. Before he started from Badrinath he was told by the postmaster that we had already left Mana and gone up the Sarsuti Valley. He had seen our camp at Mana, and even spoken to one of our men, but in spite of this a misplaced devotion to duty had taken him many miles up the Sarsuti Valley toward the Tibetan frontier. It took all the eloquence of the man we sent after him to persuade him that we were still at Mana, and that an artfully prepared trap was not being laid for his destruction and the theft of the mail. His devotion to duty was praiseworthy, but, as Birnie said, he was a "poggle admi," which is a phonetically descriptive expression in Hindustani meaning fool or madman.

We were not sorry to see the last of the Gamsali men; neither in stamina nor morale were they the equal of the Mana men whom we enrolled in their stead. We retained, of course, the six Niti high-camp men, for these were all first-rate porters, and also Natar Singh; he and the easy-going Alam Singh were poor substitutes for Lewa, but at least they did their best, and their cheerfulness was an asset. As far as possible we reduced baggage to a minimum and left a large dump of surplus stores and equipment at Mana under the charge of Alam Singh, who by virtue of being an inhabitant of the village could be expected to look after it.

On July 15 we left Mana, with 30 porters and food for two weeks. Little trading is carried on nowadays between Garhwal and Tibet over the Mana Pass, but we found the path along the Sarsuti Valley in good condition. Above Mana the Valley rises abruptly in a pitch nearly 1,000 ft. high, in which the Sarsuti River has carved out an amazing slit-like gorge, so narrow that boulders fallen from the peaks above are wedged across its jaws. It is a fearful sight to see the torrent tear downwards a sheer two hundred feet into the gorge, where, strangled by the rocks, it roars and rages like a mad beast. Beneath a stone slab wedged across the gorge that does duty as a bridge the smooth water-worn rocks curve into unseen depths like cyclopian boiler-plates. Shouts and jeers, moans and thunderings, come from far below; the ground shakes to the tempestuous fury of the imprisoned waters. I could almost imagine myself standing on the brink of some watery hell, and it needed no imagination to picture the fate of anyone who fell from the unprotected bridge into the gorge. Gusts of spray, beating up like smoke from subterranean explosions, were lit by the sun until a fugitive rainbow danced and quivered on the brink of this awesome rift.

Above the gorge, the Sarsuti Valley is featureless and dull. Its stony hillsides were blanketed in mist from which swept down spasmodic showers of drenching rain. Presently the mists thinned, there was a sudden gleam, and we gazed astonished at a distant lake of blue sky, flooding the far-off foothills. Obviously we were experiencing, not monsoon rain, but merely local rain, for it was to the south that the monsoon should have been most in evidence.

The mists shrank into a peaceful evening. Unsuspected beauties were revealed by the declining sun; wine-coloured potentillas lined the way and small rock-plants lifted rain-bedewed petals.

It was a longer march than we had anticipated to the pasture at the junction of the Arwa and Sarsuti Valleys, marked on the map at Ghastoli, and the porters began to grumble that there was no wood there, but we had heard this plaint before and disregarded it.

We camped on a gently sloping lawn a mile from the entrance to the Arwa Valley. Juniper bushes were growing abundantly in the vicinity, and in a few minutes the porters had collected plenty of fuel. The evening was a calm one and the last tendrils of mist melted into a sky of deepest green. Our camp was in shadow, but from the other side of the valley rose a ridge of barren and stony peaks which reflected the crimson of the setting sun so brilliantly that each man's face glowed as he moved about the camp. Some miles down the valley and above Mana rose a delicately shaped snow-peak, the ridges of which met in a sharp point of pure snow. Long after the glow had left the rock peaks across the valley, this peak declined the night.

An easy walk next morning brought us to the entrance of the Arwa Valley. Potentillas formed a golden carpet on the floor of the valley, and we almost wished that we were not leaving such a joyful place for the sterility of the high peaks. Across the meadows meandered a brook of crystal purity. The source of which was a pool that might have been used as a mirror by the mountain elves. Greene bathed in it ; it was gaspingly cold, and one plunge was sufficient. The porters were greatly impressed by his performance and there was no doubt that his stock rose several points in their estimation.

Two miles above its junction with the main valley the Arwa Valley is almost blocked by a moraine. According to the map, this was the terminal moraine of a glacier some twelve miles long flowing down the main valley, but as we neared it we saw that it was the terminal moraine of a side glacier descending from the south into the valley. To avoid it it was necessary to contour round the base of it directly under the snout of the glacier, which was about 500 ft. high. There was no difficulty in doing this, but many large boulders, some the size of cottages, perched on the very edge of the dirt-riddled ice above, warranted a sharp look-out. It was no place to linger. The unstable boulders over which we scrambled were pock-marked and scarred, and now and again crashes from above, accompanied by puffs of rock dust, betokened fresh falls of boulders from the glacier snout. Boulders fall erratically down such a slope, and are deflected from rock to rock, so that it is impossible to anticipate the way they are coming until the last moment, and then they may be going so fast as to be difficult to dodge. We were lucky, but one mass of rock, weighing several hundredweight, came perilously near to Shipton. The side glacier from which they fell appears to be advancing and pushing its snout farther and farther across the Arwa Valley. It needs to advance but three or four hundred yards farther to dam the valley, with a wall of ice and stones several hundred feet high. If the stream was unable to percolate or force a passage through the barrier, a lake would form. As the Arwa Valley is practically flat for two or three miles above this point, the lake would be a large one. Should the dam holding it burst, ruin, in all probability on an even greater scale than that caused by the bursting of the Gohna dam in 1895, would overtake the Sarsuti and Alaknanda Valleys. This glacier should be periodically examined, for although it is unlikely to advance much farther, it is always the unexpected that happens in the Himalaya, and catastrophes brought about in such a way are by no means uncommon.

As there was no sign of any main valley glacier above the side glacier, we could only conclude that the surveyors had not ascended the Arwa Valley, but, seeing the terminal moraine of the side glacier apparently blocking the valley, had jumped to the conclusion that it was the terminal moraine of a main valley glacier. In this connection it is interesting to note that the height of insignificant points opposite to side valleys debouching into the Sarsuti and Alaknanda Valleys are usually given in the map, so that it would appear that the surveyors merely *looked up* the branch valleys from these points and made their sketches and deductions from what they saw.

Whether or not any European before us had been far up the Arwa Valley is a matter for speculation, but one of our local porters informed us that his brother had accompanied a Mr. Pigott or Bigott up the valley some twenty years previously, and had visited a pass at its head without, however, crossing the Badrinath Range to the Gangotri Glacier.

We lunched on a flowering slope and drank our fill from a brawling brook that emptied its clear water into the mud-fouled valley river. The weather was ideal, and we lay watching the white clouds trailing leisurely from the red rock peaks lining the valley.

Above our lunching-place the ground became stonier and stonier and walking correspondingly slow and laborious. Beauman seemed to bear a special grudge against the stones, and his epithets relating to them were almost as numerous as the stones themselves. He said they reminded him of the Dauphiny. I could only sympathise with him and register a mental vow to avoid the Dauphiny.

We crossed the valley torrent by a bridge of avalanche débris and proceeded along its northern bank. Dank evening mists were veiling the hillsides as we pitched our tents near the last scattered clumps of dwarf juniper. A day's marching had sufficed to bring us but six miles up the stony valley. Though we had passed two or three other side glaciers, there were still no signs of any main valley glacier.

Contrary to their usual custom, the mists refused to dissolve at nightfall and discharged their moisture in a drizzle of rain that lasted well into the next morning.

In moist, enervating warmth we set out once more, and, negotiating an abominable slope composed of earth in which were lodged unstable boulders like plums in a Christmas pudding, gained the almost level floor of the valley. Still no signs of a main valley glacier could we see as we trudged over the never-ending fields of stones.

Gradually, the mists dissolved in the sunlight, and several glaciers flowing into the main Arwa Valley became visible.

The valley floor had been silted up by floods and moraine débris and was nearly level. The stream rushing down it was a strong one, and there was no possibility that we could see of fording it ; there was no possibility either of our postman getting across to us. He had come up the valley the previous evening from Mana carrying some mail. He had missed the snowbridge by which we had crossed the stream below our camp and, being unable to ford the latter, had tied the mail-bag to a stone and flung it across the stream. He was now wandering disconsolately up the other side of the stream. It seemed probable that he would not be able to join us until we came to the glacier whence issued the stream, and we were surprised therefore to see him an hour or two later on our side of the stream. Doubtless, his native cunning had found him a place where it could be safely forded. The stream was a nuisance, and where a sheer cliff fell into it we were forced to make a toilsome ascent and traverse.

We lunched on a patch of moss and turf gay with flowers,

set like a little park amidst a city of grey boulders. Above this point the main valley forks into two. The south branch contained a glacier covered in rusty red moraines suggesting ironstone. Occasionally, through rifts in the clouds, we discerned ice-clad peaks hemming in the head of this valley. The west branch, which bent round in a northerly direction, was the more important of the two and we determined to follow it.

We turned a corner and saw that the west valley branch was sub-divided into two more glacier-filled valleys. We had marched for only three hours when we decided to camp near the junction of these valleys. During the afternoon grey wreaths of monsoon mist concealed the peaks, and a slight drizzle of rain fell. We turned into our sleeping-bags resolved to learn something on the morrow of the country we were in before pushing forward another camp towards the watershed of the range.

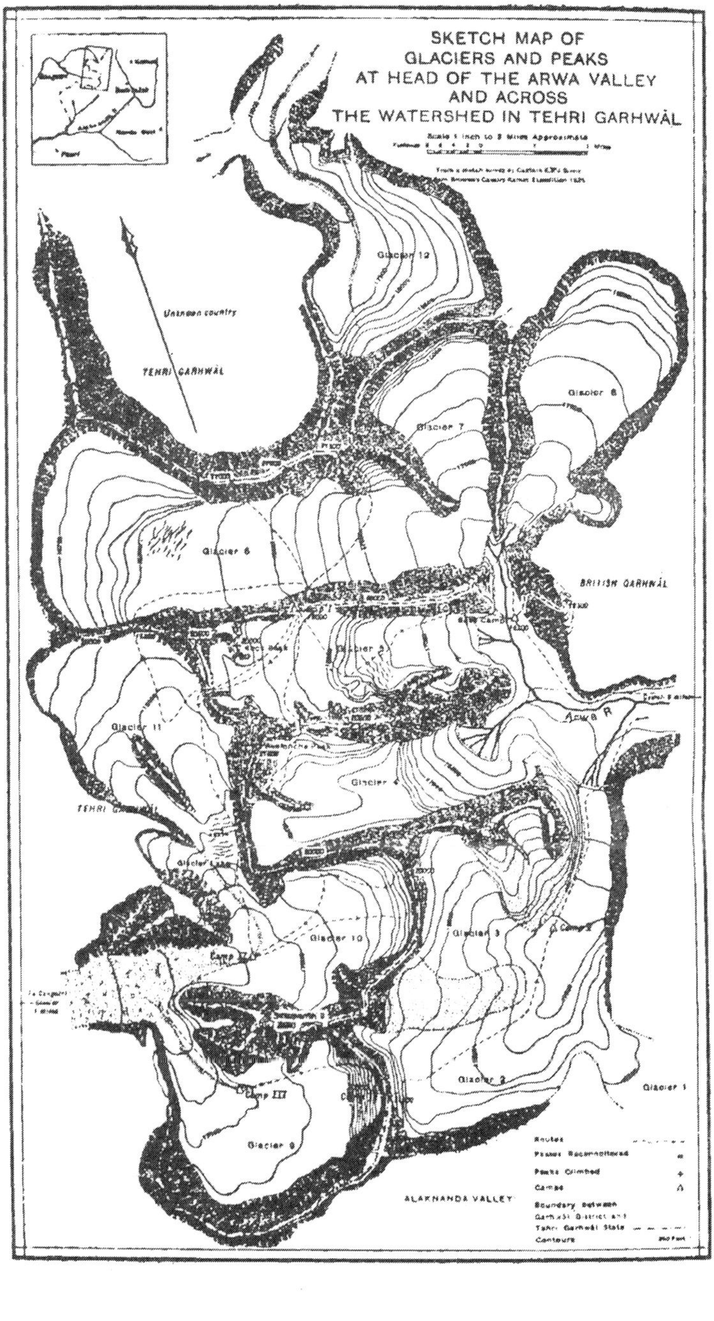
SKETCH MAP OF
GLACIERS AND PEAKS
AT HEAD OF THE ARWA VALLEY
AND ACROSS
THE WATERSHED IN TEHRI GARHWĀL
Unseen country
TEHRI GARHWĀL
Glacier 12
Glacier 8
Glacier 7
Glacier 6
BRITISH GARHWĀL
Glacier 5
Arwa R
Glacier 11
Glacier 4
TEHRI GARHWĀL
Glacier 10
Glacier 3
Glacier 2
Glacier 1
Camp III
Glacier 9
ALAKNANDA VALLEY
Routes
Peaks Reconnoitered
Peaks Climbed
Camps
Boundary between
Garhwāl District and
Tehri Garhwāl State
Contours

CHAPTER XXI

THE TWENTY-THOUSAND-FEET PASS

NIGHT scavenged the mists from the sky, and the following morning dawned frostily clear. The sun was gilding the peaks as Greene, Shipton, Nima Dorje and I left the camp. Our plan was to ascend a peak and take stock of our position. Short of fording the ugly-looking glacier torrent, there was only one peak within easy reach—the one at the foot of which was pitched our camp. The steep mountainside was covered in loose boulders, and, to avoid accidents, we divided into two parties and ascended by separate routes. As we climbed we passed clumps of edelweiss growing in crannies of the rocks. Their altitude was fully 17,000 ft., and with the exception of lichens and mosses I have not seen flowers growing elsewhere at this height. We were at the top of our form and able to climb at the rate of 1,500 ft. an hour. Such a pace is not to be despised in the Alps, and over 17,000 ft. is indicative of perfect acclimatisation and physical condition. So far we had experienced little of the baneful effects of high altitude deterioration. We did not long to return to civilisation, but were anxious to remain in this magnificent district and accomplish as much exploration and mountaineering as possible in the limited time at our disposal.

We did not rest until we were within a few hundred feet of the summit, for already the monsoon mists were gathering in the Arwa Valley. We had expected an interesting view, but the panorama exceeded our expectations. We gazed over a troublous sea of peaks, ridges and glaciers: peaks of ice and snow; rock peaks; aiguilles of splintered granite, spiking the blue sky; peaks possible, peaks impossible, and peaks at which even the hardened mountaineer might shudder on the threshold of his imagination; vast elevated snowfields, over which cloud shadows moved in slow procession; torrential glaciers crushed between rocky walls sinking green-lipped into the monsoon mists.

It was some time before we could sort out this complex and bewildering jumble of mountains, snowfields and glaciers into its individual components. When we were able to do so, we saw that the two valleys at the junction of which was pitched our camp contained snow-covered glaciers[1] of considerable size, enclosed by peaks and ridges exceeding 22,000 ft. These two glaciers were separated by a ridge of approximately the same elevation as the peak we were on. As regards the watershed of the Gangotri and Alaknanda Rivers, it was, unfortunately, impossible to determine whether or not the ridges bounding the heads of these two glaciers formed this, and we were not high enough to see over them and beyond. The most striking peak of all those arrayed before us was an extraordinary fang of ice and snow rising beyond the limiting ridges of the two glacier systems. This peak must be 23,000 ft. high. Although a towering landmark, it was not marked in the map; we had, however, already come to the conclusion that the map was useless to us.

In the south and south-east were a number of high wall-sided peaks rising from glaciers that debouched into the Arwa Valley below our camp, whilst eastwards of these

[1] Glaciers 5 and 6—see map page.

were several needle-like summits, grouped like the aiguilles of Mont Blanc round a massive rock mountain of savage steepness. We spent half an hour roughly sketching in the main features of the country and making prismatic compass bearings and panoramic photographs, and then continued on our way.

The mountain we were on was devoid of difficulty, and after scrambling over some boulders and toiling up a slope of soft snow we gained the summit ridge. The summit was separated from us by a snowridge, but as there was no particular hurry to reach it we sat for a long time on a rocky shelf and basked in the sun. The temperature for such an altitude was unusually high, and we found it unnecessary to don our spare clothing. Later we tramped leisurely up to the snowy summit, which the aneroid gave as 19,300 ft. The mists had risen, spoiling the view to the south and west, but we were rewarded by seeing some additional peaks to the north and north-west and a glacier,[1] some six miles in length, that flowed into the valley a mile above our camp. I do not know how long we spent basking in the sun, but it cannot have been less than three hours. Some imagine that Himalayan mountaineering is one continuous round of hardship and discomfort. So it is above 23,000 ft., for climbing at extreme altitudes is something more than toilsome ; if he would enjoy himself, the Himalayan mountaineer should limit himself to peaks less than 23,000 ft. ; then sometimes he will be able to sit on his conquered summits, in the sun, heedless of the passing hours and mindful only of the beauties and grandeurs about him.

[1] Glacier 8.

We descended leisurely until we reached a snow-filled gully that connected with the northerly glacier which we had noted from the summit. The snow was in perfect order, and we glissaded 1,500 ft. in a minute or two.

On arriving back at the camp, we found that Beauman, Birnie and Holdsworth had also been busy. They had ascended the south valley fork[1] to about 19,000 ft. and had found a camping-site on the ridge separating the two glacier systems. Like us, however, they had been unable to come to any definite conclusion as to which ridge constituted the watershed of the range. The only thing to be done was to establish a camp on the proposed site and explore the heads of the glaciers on both sides of it with a view to ascertaining whether any of the ridges bounding them formed the watershed of the range.

On the following day we set off to establish the new camp. Beauman, Birnie and Holdsworth had been forced to make a toilsome détour in order to cross the glacier torrent, but we discovered that it was fordable near the camp and, once a safety hand-rail of rope had been stretched across it, the porters were able to carry ourselves and the loads across on their backs. It was amusing to stand on the bank and watch Greene, almost completely enveloping the squat Passang, and Holdsworth, his inevitable pipe fixed firmly in his teeth, seated pick-a-back on his diminutive little Sherpa servant, Ang Nerbu, make the passage of the torrent.

With the exception of Holdsworth, who wanted to use his ski, and the porters, the remaining members of the party decided to reach the camping-site by traversing the

[1] Glacier 5.

FORDING THE ARWA TORRENT

ridge between the two glaciers. It was a delightful day ; the weather was fine, there was no hurry, and we lounged along the ridge enjoying beautiful views. We came to the highest point, 19,000 ft., and, distributing ourselves on warm rock slabs, soaked in the sun.

Below, on the glacier, were our porters, a tiny string of specks toiling slowly upwards to the camping-site. Beween the shifting mists opposite to us on the other side of the glacier rose a peak of about 22,000 ft.[1] It was the most graceful mountain in the vicinity of the camp, and we determined if possible to force a way to its summit. We could have stayed for hours on the ridge, regardless of time, watching nature's scene-shifters of light and shadow going about their tasks, but it was necessary to establish the camp, so we plunged downwards through sun-sodden snow, gained the glacier, and plodded uphill to the site of it.

It was not an ideal spot on which to camp, and platforms had to be engineered for the tents between slabs of granite. We ate our evening meal in the rays of the declining sun. There was not a breath of wind. All nature was hushed, as though expectant of some calamity. Above us, the monsoon mists dissolved like foam into the deep green sea of the evening sky. Eastwards, between horizontal layers of cloud, the pyramidal summit of Kamet stood out like a geometrical proposition set by some heavenly Pythagoras.

The sun dipped behind the ranges. The peaks about us stood cold and immutable as marble, and only Kamet continued to glow between long wreaths of ashen clouds. As we watched, mindless of the increasing cold, vast

[1] Avalanche Peak—21,600 ft.

fingers of darkness reached out of the east. It was the same phenomenon as we had witnessed when descending to Camp Five on Kamet, the parallel shadows of peaks in the west, thrown hundreds of miles across the sky by the setting sun, seeming to unite in the east.

In the south rose a huge solitary pillar of thundercloud. Its foundations were sunk deeply into the foothill valleys; higher, it was livid and threatening; on its topmost minarets the day had spilt its wine. The lightning flickered about it, darting like serpents from one cloudy abyss to another or bursting upwards in fountains of mauve fire, but so distant was it that the silence remained unbroken by the faintest grumble of thunder.

For a while time stood still. The World was beautiful; her hair was spun from the golden clouds, her eyes were violet shadows, her breasts of purest snow. And Night, seeing her beauty, rushed eagerly from the east and threw his dark mantle at her feet. But beauty faded quickly from the World, and Night was left with a cold, dead thing in his arms.

A sickle moon shed a soft radiance upon the snows; near the moon blazed a great star. In the south, lightning quivered ceaselessly, and now and again, like the firing of some mine, there was an explosion that reached from the deepest chasms to the topmost pinnacles of the piled-up cumuli, so that their vaporous folds stood out from the night like the dun-coloured smoke of some bloody engagement raging over the plains of India.

Once I awoke in the night and, parting my frozen tent-flaps, peered outside. The moon was declining and the camp was in deepest shadow. Eastwards, Kamet slept between two shawls of mist. The lightning had expended its energy and the pillared thunder-clouds supported the starry arch of heaven.

We had previously decided to ascend the glacier above the camp and explore the ridge bounding the head of it in search of a pass leading over the watershed on to the Gangotri Glacier system. We rose early, but the monsoon mists rose earlier still from the southern valleys, and by the time we had started to trudge up the glacier they were pouring over the ridge we hoped to explore.

The morning was a warm one, and, although the sun seldom appeared, its rays poured down upon us through the blanketing mists with ferocious intensity. The snow was soft and laborious, but we marched steadily uphill, and in less than an hour gained the foot of the slope leading up to the crest of the ridge, which at this point rose 300 ft. from the glacier. The slope was steep, but ribs of broken rock and screes led easily upwards. The ascent was not without its dramatic interest. We experienced a subtle thrill. We were about to see over an edge into new country. What were we going to see over that edge? Only snow and mountains, but snow and mountains never before seen by human eyes. We toiled upwards. A small cornice curled over the crest of the ridge. We advanced cautiously, driving ice-axes deeply into the snow. A rock projected from the crest of the ridge—we made for it. One by one we gained the rock and halted there, gazing silently. At our feet, the ridge fell away in slopes of snow, ice and rocks—a steep slope, but in height no greater than the slope we had just ascended—and below, dimly seen through rifts in the surging mists, sun-chequered and mysterious, was a great glacier,[1] curving downwards in a westerly direction. It could only flow into the Gangotri Glacier. The problem was solved—we were standing on the watershed of the Alaknanda and Gangotri Rivers. Had we been devout Hindus, we should no doubt have fallen on our faces and made obeisance to the gods. As it was, we sat down and devoured a tin of sardines.

Our height was 20,000 ft. by aneroid. The ridge on which we sat ran approximately due north-west and south-east. South-east of us it continued horizontally for some distance, then rose to the crest of a minor rock peak, fell again to a col, and finally merged into the snowy breast of the peak opposite to our camp. North-westwards, the ridge rose abruptly to the crest of a peak, the rocky summit of which was less than 1,000 ft. above us. Two days previously, during the reconnaissance to the site of the 19,000 ft. camp, Holdsworth had noticed an apparent pass from the head of the glacier[2] to the north of the 19,000 ft. camp that appeared to lead over the ridge bounding that glacier. We decided, therefore, to continue with our exploration. Birnie and his servant, Dorje, were to descend the steep slope to the glacier on the far side of the watershed ridge and investigate Holdsworth's proposed pass. Shipton and I were to ascend the peak immediately to the north of the pass we were on. Holdsworth preferred to descend to his ski, which he had left at the foot of the ridge, and run back to camp on them.

Shipton and I were the first away, but as we scrambled along the ridge we saw Birnie and Dorje starting to descend the precipitous face of the ridge to the glacier. Mist

[1] Glacier 11. [2] Glacier 6.

descended, blocking them from our view, but once or twice we heard the thudding of their ice-axes. Evidently the slope was hard and step-cutting necessary. The ridge Shipton and I were on, although steep and requiring care, offered no difficulty. We were climbing between 20,000 and 21,000 ft., yet we progressed as rapidly and easily as though we were on an Alpine peak of but half the height. In less than an hour we gained the summit, where we sat down on the piled-up boulders, warm and glowing from our exertions.

The weather appeared none too promising. Mists enveloped us, and particles of snow began to fall. The warmth was almost unnatural, and we should scarcely have been surprised had we heard the bellow of thunder. We occupied ourselves in building a large cairn, and then sat down hoping that the mists would clear. Our patience was rewarded ; the mists drifted apart for a few instants. A peak was revealed, the same matchless fang of ice and snow we had seen from the 19,300 ft. peak two days previously. It is, as I remarked to Shipton, worth an expedition to climb. As though to emphasise the majesty of this splendid mountain and our own insignificance, the window in the mists lengthened and we saw the figures of Birnie and Dorje on the glacier at our feet. So minute they seemed—a snowflake might have covered them.

Snow was falling heavily as we descended, and visibility on the glacier above the camp was limited to a few yards. We experienced some misgivings as to Birnie and Dorje. From our peak we had seen the pass they hoped to cross. The descent on the Arwa side of the watershed did not look easy, and the route was liable to bombardment from hanging glaciers. It was a relief when, soon after reaching camp, the snowstorm abated and visibility improved. Later, we saw Birnie and Dorje descending the glacier[1] to the north of the camp. In order to reach the ridge on which was the camp they were forced to climb up a steep slope of snow, rocks and screes about 1,000 ft. high, which must have come as a trying finish to a long day's work. As Shipton and I had suspected, the route was a dangerous one, and Birnie described how, when the mist and snow cleared for a few instants, he had seen huge walls of ice threatening them.

During our absence, the porters had erected several large cairns about the camp, on the summits of which they had placed rags as peace-offerings to the gods, an adornment calculated no doubt to inspire the deities with feelings of benevolence towards the expedition. Unfortunately, however, one of these cairns had been built on the ridge directly above the camp. It was a rickety structure with a pronounced lean towards the camp, and apparently needed but a zephyr of wind to ensure its destruction. I gave orders for its removal, and Ondi, who was both its architect and builder, reluctantly took it to pieces. One could only hope that the mountain deities would not regard this demolition as a disrespect and disbelief in their powers. Whether or not the little incident two days later that I have yet to describe had any bearing on the matter I cannot say, but I suspect that our superstitious porters regarded it as a retribution for the insult tendered to the gods.

[1] Glacier 6.

CHAPTER XXII

THE AVALANCHE PEAK

On July 21, Shipton and I set out to attempt the peak opposite to the camp, taking with us Nima as porter. The weather boded ill, and scarcely had the sun flared up behind Kamet when it was extinguished by leaden clouds. The snow on the glacier was in an abominable state. It bore our weight for two or three steps, then its crust collapsed, letting us sink deeply into the soft snow beneath. The most promising route up the mountain was an upward traverse across the east face to the south-east ridge. We had noted this route from the 19,000 ft. peak near the camp. To reach the northern end of the traverse meant a steep climb of 600 ft. to a well-defined col in the north-east ridge of the peak. This slope was some 50° in angle, and at the foot of it was a berg-schrund half choked with avalanche débris. The slope had been worn into a series of parallel runnels, scooped out by sliding snow. It is these runnels that lend the beautiful fluted appearance to Himalayan snow-slopes, and their formation is due to the heat of the sun and minor avalanches of soddened snow. In the Alps a slope of such steepness and continuity as that confronting us would almost certainly have been ice, but while we were in the Badrinath Himalaya we saw but few bare ice-slopes, although, of course, there were plenty of hanging glaciers forming ice-walls.

The snow on the slope was in good order, and step-cutting

was unnecessary. We mounted quickly. The crest of the col was corniced, and some minutes were spent in hacking a way through the eave of overhanging snow. The weather meanwhile had been steadily deteriorating. As we put our heads over the lip of the col we were met by a biting wind and a scud of whirling snowflakes. On the slope we had been sheltered and warm, but as we stood on the col the wind blew the warmth out of us as a man blows the warmth out of a spoonful of soup. We sought shelter in the lea of a boulder. It was a dismal situation. We banged our gloved hands together and between whiles munched chocolate. We waited thus for fully three-quarters of an hour hoping for an improvement. But the sky darkened until the snows were dead white and lustreless. The wind growled past our rock, and snow began to fall heavily. Damp and shivering, we decided to retreat, and an hour later were imbibing some of Achung's choicest tea, a brew combining the flavours of tea-leaves cooked to destruction, tin, juniper smoke, paraffin, and greasy dish-cloths. It had one virtue—it was hot. Achung was in a bad way, and suffering from his abnormally high blood-pressure. Cause is allied to effect, and the badness of Achung's cooking was directly proportioned to the pressure of Achung's blood. It did not need Greene to tell us that Achung was afflicted by an abnormally high blood-pressure even at the lowest elevation.

The day waned dismally, and snow fell intermittently till evening, when cooler and dryer airs mopped up the clouds. I lay in my tent reading my last mail over and over again. I read the newspapers until I knew all about bears, bulls and other commercial jargon. I became well versed in the latest divorces and murders, the probable winner of the three-thirty, and the reason why county cricket was dull. Later, when the snows were pallid in the after-glow of sunset, and frost had snuffed the warmth from the world, I remember wishing that a certain director of cinema films who had begged me to think out and engineer a " plot " during the expedition had been with us up there. I fear that he would have shivered, but he would have seen the universe's greatest plot, a plot hatched between day and night, enthralling sky and earth with its majesty and beauty.

Half the fun in mountaineering lies in being beaten or in the risk of being beaten. Not only does the mountaineer conceive an increased respect for his adversary, but he returns to the attack with a new zest. Should the citadel fall to his next assault he accepts its surrender not arrogantly, but humbly, for only by humility can the precious moments on the high hills be captured for ever.

Despondence predominated as Shipton, Nima and I trudged once more across the softening snow of the glacier ; already the morning sun was dulled by oily mists slinking up from the south.

The weather was warmer and the snow softer than it had been yesterday, and everything pointed to a renewal of disappointment. Even our previous track could not support us, and we floundered deeply into the snow.

We gained the col. Sunlight glanced on the snow-slopes we must traverse, seeming to beckon us onwards, and so we continued, hoping that the weather might hold.

We found to our disgust that a descent of over 200 ft. was necessary before we could start ascending again. The snow on this descent was the worst we had yet encountered, unless it was some of that on the final slopes of Kamet. We sank in knee deep, and I reflected grimly that we should have to retrace our steps up that slope towards the end of the day. But no one who climbs with Shipton can remain pessimistic, for he imparts an imperturbability and confidence into a day's work on a mountain that are in themselves a guarantee of success.

We took turns at track-making. A quarter of an hour at a time was long enough, for the snow was that exasperating snow the mountaineer must expect to find during the monsoon season. Two or three steps are taken, the snow holds—will it hold another step ? Apparently it will. The foot swings forward and the weight is gingerly transferred. Good ! It holds. The other foot is swung forward, then—crunch ! For apparently no reason save a certain innate cussedness, the crust has given way. The rear foot sinks deeply. Balance is regained only after an effort. Rhythm is lost. Mind and muscles must be braced anew. Imagine the same series of disappointments and mental and muscular recoveries repeated a thousand times at a height of 21,000 ft. and the sum becomes a weary one.

Mists closed down upon us, the sun piercing them exacted its own toll of energy. Difficulty there was none, and even when the snow steepened into an abrupt slope 200 ft. high, leading to the crest of the north-east ridge, we had nothing to do but continue an unrhythmical, treadmill-like trudge which had now lasted for such a length of time that it seemed to me that my whole life had been spent in sinking into soft snow at a height of 21,000 ft.

We sat down gratefully on the crest of the south-east

ridge. Surely now the worst was behind us? Even if the ridge to the summit should prove difficult, we reflected that climbing difficulty was, up to a point, infinitely to be preferred, even at high altitudes, than the slavery imposed by crusted snow.

Our gaze passed along the ridge ; it curved up into the mists like an icy scimitar ; it was sharp and it was steep. If it was iced from top to bottom, we were likely to be defeated, for in that case many hours of step-cutting would be necessary. There is one virtue in high-altitude mountaineering—little things may irritate and annoy to an extraordinary degree, but the big things do not matter until afterwards. They are accepted with an automatic resignation, partly owing to the numbing effect of high altitudes, which makes the brain incapable of appreciating them, and partly to the immensity of nature, for the forces among which the mountaineer moves are too vast to be translated into terms of temperament and temper. And so we sat in the snow, more concerned with the problem of opening a sardine tin than we were with the problem of ascending a peak on which we had set our hearts.

The day was a warm one—we were able to sit and eat our lunch in comfort ; it was also depressing. The air was devoid of that essential *joie de vivre* that transmutes hard work on a mountain into joy of existence. It was heavy, stagnant, dead ; it reeked of the humid far-off plains of India. The mists rolled sluggishly about us. Now and again they were parted by desultory airs. Peaks, ridges and glaciers were revealed, dim, almost unsubstantial, like phantasms in the steam from a witch's cauldron. The sun seemed to weigh on our eyelids, so that we found it difficult to interest ourselves in the scene about us. There was a glacier at our feet, bounded by a rocky ridge nicked by a well-defined col.[1] Beyond was a high peak, terraced with lateral bands of rock, wall-sided and massive. It appeared over 23,000 ft. high, and was probably the peak marked in the map as 23,240 ft.—the only measured point in this district.

Restlessness beset us, a restlessness forbidding long repose until the summit was reached. Time had slipped away and an hour had passed vengefully. Toil was renewed, but it was toil of a different nature from that necessitated by the wearisome snow-slopes below. We had to climb a ridge, always a more interesting job than climbing a snow slope. A ridge, like virtue, is a narrow path, and virtue in this case is more interesting and amusing than the vice of wandering at will on a snow slope. But even the strait and narrow path has its pitfalls. The ridge was corniced. To avoid the cornices, we were forced off its crest on to the eastern face of the mountain. But luck was with us ; what should have been a bare ice-slope was conveniently crusted with snow. Yet, the slope was exceedingly steep and the snow covering the ice but a few inches deep, sometimes only an inch or so. We climbed carefully; a slip on the part of the leader would have meant disaster, for it was impossible to drive the ice-axe into the ice and a fall would have been down the whole western face of the peak—1,500 ft. of ice precipices.

Altitude began to tell. We experienced the same old feeling that the body was a pump worked harder than it

[1] Col 20,000 ft, between glaciers 4 and 10, visited subsequently by Birnie.

liked or was used to. Yet, we climbed that slope at a greater speed than I have climbed the last 1,000 ft. of Mont Blanc.

The slope eased off and merged imperceptibly into a broad and comfortable ridge. The ridge swept upwards into the mists. We passed easily along it, until presently it stretched away before us no longer, but fell away abruptly into nothingness. We had reached the summit.[1]

For a moment we felt no elation. As we gazed vacantly into the murk, dim shapes appeared like the shadowy manifestations of television. The mists were dragged aside. We saw the north-west ridge of our peak sweeping away beneath us in a series of sharp ice-ridges. Some giant had bitten the ridge, and the weather had piled ice and snow on to the bitten-out sections which had been chiselled and moulded by frost into parabolas with edges of delicate acuteness.

Sunbeams glanced through the shifting mists, illuminating glaciers and snowfields, peaks and valleys. Shadows chased across the snows like guilty consciences. There was much that was vague and little that was definite. We tried to disentangle the scene, but it was useless, and we resigned ourselves for a few minutes of quiet gazing, conscious only that we were on the summit of a great peak far removed from the world of men.

We might have stopped there a long time, for the weather was warm, but at the back of our minds was the uneasy thought that perhaps the crust of hard snow on the ice might melt, and we should have to cut many steps. Our

[1] The height by aneroid was 21,800 ft. but in the map Birnie estimates it at 21,600 ft. Actually, I believe that both these are under estimates and that 22,000 ft. is a closer approximation. The ascent from the camp was actually 3,000 ft.

fears were not entirely groundless. The snow-crust still held as we descended, but not so well as it had done during the ascent. The utmost care was imperative, and we moved one at a time, rope length by rope length. Birnie and his servant Dorje were awaiting us on the col, having left the camp an hour or so after we, and, on hearing how the snow was deteriorating, commenced to ascend. They disappeared into the mist, but as we sat on the col we heard the thud, thud, thud of their ice-axes and knew that, unlike us, they were having to cut steps in some places for safety's sake. We waited some time for them, and only turned to go when we began to feel cold.

The descent was easy but unpleasant, and we fairly floundered in the abominable snow. The ascent to the lower col was fatiguing and we were glad to plunge through the cornice on the crest of the col and start down the steep slope to the main glacier. The snow on this slope was slightly crusted, for the sun had disappeared behind mists, and frost had frozen the surface of the snow.

We decided to glissade down the slope. I started off in a sitting position. Shipton and Nima Dorje followed some distance behind me. This was a mistake ; all three of us should have taken separate lines, not followed one another.

As I shot down the slope the snow banked rapidly in front of me and spread out on either side in a small wedge-shaped avalanche, with myself as the apex of the wedge. This was nothing, for it often happens that a glissader down wet snow in the late afternoon pushes a small avalanche in front of him. In a few seconds, however, the avalanche in front of me attained formidable dimensions. There was no danger whatever, as I was above the avalanche, but

AVALANCHE PEAK

FROM 19,000 FT. PEAK. NOTE PORTERS ON GLACIER

+ + MARKS SCENE OF AVALANCHE

I judged it advisable to stop. This I did without any difficulty by driving my ice-axe into the snow. I had just brought myself to a standstill, and was watching the avalanche I had started careering away beneath me, when there came a sudden swish from behind, and a mass of sliding snow struck me and carried me helplessly down the slope. I realised at once what had happened. Shipton, behind me, had started to glissade and detached an avalanche on his own account. It was not a large avalanche, but it was a heavy one, composed of masses and lumps of sodden snow. My first feeling was one of annoyance—the annoyance of a man in a crowd who is carried by a press of people in the opposite direction to that in which he wants to go. Lying on my back, I drove my ice-axe into the snow with all the force I could muster. For a moment I almost stopped, but then the weight of the snow piling up behind me shoved me brutally down the slope. It was that sudden brutal and irresistible force that caused mere annoyance to be replaced by apprehension. And then I remembered the bergschrund at the foot of the slope. We had crossed it without difficulty at a point where it was choked with former avalanche débris, but here and there it was not choked, and gaped widely. With desperate energy I drove my ice-axe again and again into the firm snow beneath the avalanche. I could not stop myself, but I managed to slow myself down and allow a considerable quantity or the sliding snow to precede me. Had the slope been longer, I might have stopped myself altogether, for the avalanche was not more than a few yards in width. But it was too late. I saw the sliding snow in front of me shoot downwards and outwards over the upper lip of the bergschrund, with the lazy grace of water curving over a weir. Everything seemed to take place with incredible slowness. I remember no sensation of falling, no shock, but I found myself on the slope below the bergschrund. Then, without a pause, I was shot forward and downward again. I heard behind me a dull, heavy thudding as the tail of the avalanche continued to pour over the bergschrund. It was still pouring when the van of the avalanche stopped. My position now was that of a passenger in a telescoping train. My head and shoulders were free, but the lower portion of my body was in the avalanche. The sodden snow compacted. I experienced a terrible pressure—I thought my ribs were going to be crushed in like an eggshell—then, abruptly, the pressure ceased.

There was silence save for a slight hissing of laggard snow on the lip of the bergschrund. I struggled to free myself, and was able to do this without much difficulty. I stood up and gazed at the bergschrund. The difference in height between its upper and lower lips was fully fifteen feet, and such was the impetus of the avalanche that it shot clean over the crevasse beneath, which at this point was two or three yards wide. Had the avalanche slid slowly, or had the upper lip been less high, my grave would have been in the depths of the glacier, buried beneath tons of avalanche snow. I suddenly saw Nima gaily glissading, with a broad grin on his face, straight down the track left by the avalanche. With my remaining breath I shouted out a warning to him to go to the right, where the bergschrund was completely choked with snow, and then, feeling winded and a trifle sick, sat down. My hands were white and dead with cold and the numbing effect of driving them into the avalanche. Shipton and Nima massaged them, and circulation returned gradually and painfully.

It had been a narrow escape, and it was an example of how easily an accident may occur on a mountain. It was entirely my own fault. There would have been no danger if I had glissaded with caution, but I had not glissaded with caution, I had shot off down the slope without a thought as to whether Shipton and Nima were near to me or not. Actually, they had not started until some time after me, and the avalanche they detached had attained considerable volume and momentum by the time it reached me. As an avalanche it was so small as to be scarcely worthy of the name, yet it had carried me helplessly down the slope, and, had the fates not been kind, would have killed me. It is not the spectacular snow avalanche weighing tens of thousands of tons that causes mountaineering disasters, but the small, apparently inoffensive slide, that buries the mountaineer in the depths of a crevasse or casts him over a precipice.

There were two interesting features about this accident. The first was the condition of the snow. It had a slight yet definite crust on its surface, formed by frost during the hour or so we had been descending the mountain. I have never seen wet well-crusted snow in the Alps slide,[1] and in the present instance sliding was not spontaneous, but due to our own sliding bodies forcing the snow apart and shoving it down in front of us as well as the sodden condition of the snow, which rendered it so heavy that the slight crust on its surface was unable to prevent its sliding when

[1] Crusted or caked snow (wind slab) consisting of dry frozen snow can be exceedingly dangerous.

disturbed. The second interesting point is that it was not new snow that slid, but old snow. In the Himalaya during the monsoon season, so intense is the heat that snow becomes saturated with water, for perhaps the first foot or so of its depth, and these saturated layers periodically avalanche. It was an avalanche of this nature that carried down Doctor Longstaff and his Alpine guides on Gurla Mandhata. To climb safely the mountaineer must approach the Himalaya with an open mind prepared to amend preconceived Alpine notions. Many conditions are similar, but others are dissimilar, and the possibility of old snow sliding away in large avalanches every day or two is a condition that seldom obtains in the Alps. Experience on a mountain is too often bought dearly ; in the present instance it was bought with unusual cheapness.

It was a miserable trudge back to camp across the glacier. My body was aching from the crushing it had undergone, and every breath was an effort. If the snow on the glacier was soft in the morning, it was now a morass. We sank in half way to the knee at every other step. When at last we reached the camp, Greene diagnosed a broken rib. It was a simple and unimportant fracture, but it shows how near I came to being crushed in the avalanche.

Birnie and Dorje arrived an hour or so after us. They had reached the summit only after some heavy step-cutting, for the thin crust that had so assisted us had melted too much to allow of safe footholds without a step being cut in the ice beneath.

While Shipton, Birnie and I were engaged in climbing the Avalanche Peak, as we dubbed the 21,800 ft. peak,

Beauman and Greene had ascended a rock peak of 20,000 ft. to the south-west of the camp which stands out, boldly, from the glacier. This peak presented no great difficulty, but they had enjoyed a pleasant day's climbing.

The day ended in a snowstorm. Snow fell heavily on June 23, and visibility was too poor for topographical work or for mountaineering.

During our forced inaction we made plans for the week that remained. In order to accomplish the maximum amount of work in that week we decided to split up into three parties. Birnie and I were to cross the 20,000 ft. pass and explore the glaciers on the Gangotri side of the watershed, returning, if possible, across the range by another pass. Shipton and Holdsworth were to make ascents from the 19,000 ft. camp, whilst Beauman and Greene were to descend to Mana and make a reconnaissance up the Alaknanda Valley to the source of the Alaknanda River.

July 24 dawned depressingly—the slate-grey clouds were full of snow. My rib was not worrying me, but my bruised chest hampered my breathing to some extent. It would have been wiser to have remained at the camp, but I decided to accompany Birnie as arranged. If the weather was kind to us, it might be possible to return over the range via the Gangotri Glacier and a pass at the head of the Bhagat Kharak Glacier into the Alaknanda Valley.

Ten porters were selected to accompany us. We left the camp in drizzling snow. The snow on the glacier was in wretched condition, and we sank in deeply at every step. Almost at once I began to experience difficulty in expanding my lungs, owing to my bruised chest. As we slowly gained height, I found it harder and harder to breathe, and presently began to feel sick. I was suffering from an artificially induced anoxæmia.[1] I struggled on for an hour, but then could not advance another step. There was nothing for it but to return to camp. Although it was now snowing heavily, Birnie decided to cross the pass, taking with him seven porters. The remaining three porters started back with me to camp. It was a miserable descent—to be thwarted thus from fulfilling a cherished ambition was maddening. But soon I felt too ill to worry about anything. My legs would scarcely support me, my chest felt as though an iron band was being drawn more and more tightly about it. Once I dropped down into the snow exhausted and half fainting. For the latter part of the descent the porters helped me along, and I was very glad to have them to lean upon. I arrived at the camp scarcely able to place one foot in front of the other. As I stumbled over the rocks near the cooking-tent, I saw something white in front of me. Thinking it to be a patch of snow, I was about to step on it when there was a cry from the cook. I paused—just in time to prevent myself stepping into the middle of an enormous number of eggs laid out in brave array on a slab of rock !

Later, as I lay in my tent feeling much better—for it was only exertion that produced a temporary anoxæmia—Shipton gloatingly told me about the eggs. He recalled to my mind how, before leaving Mana, we had detailed an old man, who was ever afterwards known as the "Egg-wallah," to search for eggs. This search he had conducted with such energy that he had collected no less than a hundred eggs. To do this he must have scoured a considerable

[1] An effect produced by shortage of oxygen.

portion of the Central Himalaya. He had also found two chickens. One was dead—it had flown into a glacier torrent and been drowned. The other was looking none too happy. Apparently, like me, it was suffering from anoxæmia. The Egg-wallah had not known our route up from the Base Camp, and had ascended by a new and difficult route of his own from the glacier[1] north of the camp, yet, notwithstanding, he had delivered his precious burden intact. Perhaps the most charitable thing I can say about the eggs is that they varied from newly laid to nearly hatched. We ate them all, excluding of course those in the latter category, in exactly four meals, which works out at roughly six per man per meal.

Beauman and Greene had already descended to the Base Camp in the Arwa Valley, and had missed the Egg-wallah. It was arranged, therefore, that their share and my share of the eggs should be sent down with me. Four porters were detailed off for the task of helping me down. Although I felt perfectly well lying in my tent, I was still unable to imbibe enough oxygen when walking. It was necessary for four stalwart porters to half-carry and half-drag me down the glacier. The lower I got the better I felt, as, owing to the difference in altitude, the same limited expansion of the lungs would allow me to imbibe more oxygen. By the time I reached the Base Camp I was feeling almost fit again. This incident goes to prove how necessary is a good lung capacity for high-altitude mountaineering. Undoubtedly, there is no finer training for high altitudes than deep breathing exercises, as these expand the lungs and tend to help deep breathing to become automatic at

[1] Glacier 6.

high altitudes. Forcing oneself to breathe deeply at high altitudes is much more tiring than breathing deeply and naturally. That evening we feasted on eggs and eggs and then eggs.

Next morning we were delayed by the slowness of the porters bringing down loads from the upper camp and it was not until late in the afternoon that we set off down the Arwa Valley. The amount of snow that had melted in the past few days was amazing, and the whole appearance of the valley had changed. On the way we met the Dak-wallah with our mail, which included a large bundle of newspapers with little in them besides Indian troubles and financial crises. The world awaiting us was a gloomy one.

All next day we stumbled over stones, and it was not until late in the afternoon that we hurried across the dangerous terminal moraine. Barely had we passed the danger-zone when some boulders thundered right across our track, leaving clouds of sulphurous dust in their wake.

It was good to exchange the blinding glare of the upper snows, and suns that seemed to wither the flesh, for flowering meadows and soft moisture-charged breezes impregnated with the sweet scents of turf and flowers. The walk to Mana on July 27 was a delightful one. Our way was carpeted with flowers. Since we had ascended the Arwa Valley, hosts of little white "everlastings" had arisen, whilst every emerald patch between the grey rocks was gay with red, yellow and white potentillas. We strolled into Mana in the golden calm of a perfect evening.

CHAPTER XXIII

SOURCES OF THE GANGES

BEAUMAN decided to remain at Mana, but Greene and I were anxious to ascend the Alaknanda Valley and visit the source of the Alaknanda. We hoped, if there was time, to ascend some distance up the Bhagat Kharak Glacier and look for possible passes from its head into the Gangotri Glacier. It was scarcely probable that Birnie would attempt to cross one of these passes from the Gangotri side, for weather conditions, although good at Mana, were not good on the high mountains, but if he did we might meet him.

It was misty morning as we walked up the Alaknanda Valley. The summits were concealed yet we could appreciate the magnificence of the portal of granite precipices through which we were passing. Our gaze paused appalled on sweeping walls of granite even while our nailed boots sank into soft turf, from which peeped the gay-eyed potentillas and gentians.

Once or twice we passed little caves beneath the crags with entrances partially sheltered by primitive walls. We could only conjecture that hermits had dwelt, perhaps even now dwell, in these, who had cut themselves off from the world to rest and meditate near the source of their sacred river.

On the pastures were shepherds minding their flocks. We passed the last of them ; the hillsides became rockier ; the mountains closed in about us.

We entered a stony waste of water-worn boulders, washed down from the mouth of a side valley by spring floods. This valley contained a glacier, and, as we suspected, the glacier discharged a torrent of formidable size. We had been following a rude track to the edge of the stones, and hoped, therefore, to find a bridge across the torrent, but when we came to it, not only could we find no bridge, but we experienced grave misgivings as to the possibility of fording it. The mists had closed down upon us, and, as it was impossible to see far, Greene ascended the bank of the torrent in search of a bridge or a snowdrift, while I looked for a ford. The torrent was a steep one, and its waters tumultuous. In one place it was divided into two by a bank of boulders, and, as it was slightly less steep here, there seemed a chance of fording it. Presently, when Greene returned unsuccessful, we determined to try and effect a crossing. I went first, with a rope tied round my waist, held from the bank upstream, so that it would be of maximum assistance in preventing me from being washed off my feet. The depth of the torrent was not more than three feet, but what it lacked in depth it made up for in steepness and energy, and even with a rope it was all I could do to avoid being torn from my foothold. Green followed, likewise tied to a rope. Now that we had a hand-rail of rope stretched across, there seemed no need for each of the porters to be roped separately; the hand-rail should suffice to prevent them from being swept from their feet.

The Old Soldier came next, carrying my tent, sleeping-bag and other equipment. Although ungainly in appearance, his strength is prodigious, and he crossed with

WHERE THE GANGES FALLS

"LIKE THE SLENDER THREAD OF A LOTUS FLOWER"

scarcely a pause, a broad grin on his face. Our old friend the Egg-wallah followed, carrying our box of provisions on his back. For a few yards he went well. He crossed one branch of the torrent to the central bank of boulders, and then essayed the other. He would have been all right had he gone quickly, but he hesitated in the worst part of the torrent when he was about two yards from the bank. For a few moments he struggled to maintain his foothold, but the torrent was too strong for him and, though he clung tightly to the rope, he was swept from his feet. Even then, had he kept his wits about him, he could have reached the bank, by pulling himself a yard or two along the rope, but instead of doing this he clung helplessly to the rope without moving, petrified with fear. We yelled to him to advance, but he seemed incapable of doing anything. It was all over in a second or two. The torrent clutched and pulled at him remorselessly ; first one arm gave out ; he hung for a second or two by the other, then let go. In an instant he disappeared into the raging waters. He reappeared a few yards lower down on the edge of a vertical fall, quite ten feet in height, then vanished over it ; almost before we had time to think, he was dashed over a lower fall, and another and another. It was a terrible spectacle. For a moment we paused, horrified, then raced down the bank leaping from boulder to boulder. It seemed certain that he must perish, dashed into pulp on the rocks, and we had given up all hope, when to our amazement we saw him crawl slowly out of a pool.

Greene was the first to reach him. At the best we expected to find many broken bones, but an examination disclosed nothing worse than severe bruising and superficial cuts. His escape had been a miraculous one, for he had been carried about a hundred yards down a raging torrent through a total vertical height of at least forty to fifty feet, and over a series of falls up to fifteen feet each in height. The poor old man's clothes had been torn from him with the exception of his shirt, and he was groaning and shivering in an access of terror and cold.

Naturally, we had given no thought to the load that had been carried down with him. We had seen it bobbing about for a few moments, but it had then disappeared, doubtless smashed to matchwood. Our attention was now called to it by two or three of our porters on the opposite bank, who were declaiming its loss. They had chased not the poor old Egg-wallah, but the load ! To our Darjeeling men a few Egg-wallahs mattered but little, but the sahibs' food was of paramount importance. Such is their mental outlook, an inexplicable one to a European mind. It was a striking instance of the utter callousness of one Eastern race for another. The Egg-wallah was a Hindu, our Darjeeling men Buddhists. His life to them was worth no more than the snap of a finger. The sahibs' comfort and convenience was of greater importance. This incident by itself goes to show how deep is the gulf between East and West, and how abysmal is that other gulf between religion and religion in the East.

We rejoiced in the recovery of the Egg-wallah, but we bemoaned the loss of our food. It was best to return to the nearest pastures, where there was plenty of fuel. But how to get the Egg-wallah back across the torrent ? He was in a state of collapse, and incapable of doing anything for himself. Luckily, higher up, there were two large boulders, one on either side of the torrent ; between these we fixed a rope. From this the Egg-wallah was suspended by loops and hauled across the torrent without a further wetting. Greene, the Old Soldier and I followed, re-fording the torrent one by one, tied to ropes.

It was now late in the afternoon, and chill mists enveloped us. We were soaked to the skin and shivering from inaction. It was a relief to find a grassy hollow around which dwarf juniper was growing in abundance. We made a great fire, and under its cheering influence even the Egg-wallah forgot his troubles, and we ceased to remind each other of the delicacies now absorbed by Mother Ganges.

To our surprise and delight, not only was our hunger appeased but our palates were titivated by Nima Dorje, who on Kamet had proved himself to be a far better cook than Achung, and who now produced unsuspected delicacies from the porters' food. He was a modest little fellow, and his aptitude for cooking had been obscured by his cinematographic activities. We vowed that Achung must go. His day of reckoning had come. No longer must he be allowed to spiflicate the digestions of the expedition. Nima Dorje should reign in his stead.

As the sun was setting, we decided to go for a stroll. We did not intend to go far when we left the camp, but the beauty of the evening tempted us on and on up the slopes above. As we climbed, Nilkanta came into view. There are peaks in the Badrinath Range of greater height, but none to equal it in beauty of form and grace of outline. The sun had set, and its upper slopes were bathed in a cold pure afterglow. It is a peak built up of ice-ridges so fine and transparent that their edges merge imperceptibly into the sky, ice flutings, the continuous sweep of which emphasises height and steepness, and precipices crowned by ice-bastions that yield savagely to gravity in dreadful avalanches.

We scrambled on, mounting diagonally across the rough hillside. When next we paused we saw that the afterglow had ebbed from Nilkanta. The great peak was no longer queen of earth or sky, but ashen grey, nebulous—an afterthought, on the starry page of Heaven.

Before we turned campwards, we made a discovery. The torrent that had nearly caused the death of the Egg-wallah was securely bridged with snow avalanche débris ! Greene must have got within a few yards of this natural bridge, but owing to the mist had not seen it.

We hurried downwards. Tropic night rushed to meet us, dragging by its locks a white mist. Into this mist we plunged. Soon it was dark, and we could neither see nor hear our camp. The hillside was indefinite and complicated, and it was difficult to maintain the right direction.

We began to experience doubts as to whether we should find the camp. We shouted. There came no answer. Suddenly, we smelt the familiar odour of burning juniper. Like bloodhounds we followed the trail, and in a few minutes rejoiced to see the dull glow of burning juniper through the mist.

And so the day ended by the camp fire in companionship and happiness, warmth and comfort, while the light mists eddied and disappeared, and far away a dark ridge stood out from the night as a brilliant moon swung up into the stars. It was nearly midnight when we turned into our sleeping-bags. We were lulled to sleep by the deep voice of the Alaknanda speeding on its way towards the teeming plains of India.

The following morning we set out to visit the source of the Alaknanda, taking with us the Old Soldier and Passang.

Crossing the torrent by the snow bridge we had noticed the previous evening, we descended boulder-strewn slopes. Between these and an ancient moraine was set a little alp, a green oasis in the midst of the hungry rocks. There, to our surprise, we found a shepherd and his flock. How was he to descend the valley when the snow bridge melted or was washed away? Possibly, the villagers would make a bridge for him late in the summer, when the cold of autumn compelled him and his flock to retreat to lower levels. Why had he gone so far up the valley when he might have remained on one of the more fertile alps lower down? Was it because he wished to cut himself off from his fellows and while away the summer near the source of the sacred Alaknanda? He might have chosen a worse spot. How could such a man employ himself when he could neither read nor write? Some might envy him. Knowing nothing of the city, he was content. He had never heard the hammering of a typewriter, or breathed the stuffy air of an office. He recked nothing of financial crises; income-tax inspectors knew him not. His domain was the green pastures; his walls were the mountain peaks, his roof the ever-changing sky. A handful of grain a day was all that he needed. Time was not something to be cajoled or defied—it passed.

We climbed the moraine, and, descending on the far side, found ourselves in a wilderness of boulders. Before us we could see the Alaknanda winding tortuously between its rocky banks. Up and down we toiled, up over stony ridges and down into little dells pink with willow-herb. We breasted the last boulder-strewn ridge and gazed across at the muddy waters of the Alaknanda, surging from the combined snouts of the Bhagat Kharak and Satopanth Glaciers.

We had expected something beautiful ; we had promised ourselves a thrill ; neither expectation nor promise was fulfilled. As we gazed upon the rushing muddy waters beneath us, and the dirty ice of the Bhagat Kharak and Satopanth Glaciers, we felt that this was not a worthy setting for the birthplace of India's holy river. Here were no blue caverns of ice, but two torrents befouled with glacier mud, seeping unimpressively from beneath the snouts of two glaciers and uniting into one torrent a hundred yards lower. Yet, if beauty there was none, the scene was possessed of a certain wild impressiveness. Sheer desolation imparted a weirdness and magnificence into the landscape. Dimly seen through the swirling mists, dark precipices loomed forth. The air trembled with the thunder of the torrent. The huge boulders around, cast down by gravity and glaciation, were silent witnesses of forces ever at work fashioning the great peaks.

We returned by a different route, passing on our way a bank of strawberries, but their fruit was watery and tasteless.

We followed the Alaknanda until we came to the torrent in which we had lost our box of food. We ascended it in the hope of finding some of the food—possibly it might have been washed into back-waters. Soon our search was rewarded. We discovered tins of condensed milk, macaroni and tea, a large cabbage, a bag of very damp sugar, the

THE SOURCE OF THE ALAKNANDA

Egg-wallah's trousers and one shoe. But, alas, of the delicacies, which included a tin of preserved ginger and half a bottle of rum, there was no sign. We did not think it worth while bringing back the Egg-wallah's trousers. Before their immersion they were none too savoury. During the interim they had certainly had a wash, but that was all that could be said for them. The Egg-wallah, however, had a different idea as to their value, and subsequently put in a claim for ten rupees, a claim which, to his intense surprise, was recognised, for, even though his trousers were not worth an anna, the poor old man deserved something for the fright and knocking about he had received in the torrent.

We spent the remainder of the afternoon lounging about in camp. The weather was clearer than it had been heretofore, and we could see a col at the head of the Satopanth Glacier. This must have been the col crossed by Meade when he explored the head of the glacier, and which apparently led, without difficulty, into the Kedarnath Valley system.

We spent another happy evening round the camp fire, and next morning reluctantly packed up and started off back to Mana. Would that we had had a few weeks more left in which to explore the Badrinath Range and climb some of its magnificent peaks! We could only register a vow to return.

The weather was threatening as we descended the valley. On the way we met Beauman, who was coming up to visit the source of the Alaknanda, which he hoped to accomplish in one day from Mana, but, as the weather was deteriorating, he returned with us to Mana.

The same evening that we arrived back at Mana we were joined by Birnie, who had descended from the Arwa Valley. He told us that doubtful weather had rendered the original scheme of re-crossing the Badrinath Range by a pass into the head of the Bhagat Kharak Glacier inoperative, and he had been forced to keep within reasonable distance of the 19,000 ft. camp, in order to have a base to retreat to in the event of really bad weather. He had crossed the 20,000 ft. pass in a heavy snowstorm and descended some three or four miles down the glacier (11)[1] on the Gangotri side of the watershed, and made his Camp II some five miles from the junction of this glacier with the main Gangotri ice-stream. Next day he ascended a glacier (10) leading up to an apparent pass to the north-east of the 23,240 ft. peak and reconnoitred the pass, which was forced up steep snow-slopes. Descent on the far side was found to be possible but difficult. As the pass led back into the Arwa Valley, and not into the Alaknanda Valley, as he hoped, he returned. From the pass a view of several miles was obtained down the main Gangotri ice-stream.

He next ascended another glacier (9) leading back towards the watershed and partially reconnoitred an obvious pass at its head. Camp III was made at about 17,500 ft. On the following day, reconnoitring was continued with Gian Singh, a local porter. After some step-cutting this second pass was reached. Descent on the far side was found to be steep but practicable. Unfortunately, however, the pass did not lead to the Bhagat Kharak Glacier and the Alaknanda Valley as hoped, but into a subsidiary glacier flowing into the Arwa Valley. The route

[1] See map p. 280.

over this pass is liable to be overwhelmed by ice-avalanches, but a safe camping-site (Camp IV) was found.

Next day, Birnie, with the whole of his porters, returned to the pass. The porters were lowered one by one through a cornice, and 2,000 ft. of very steep snow-slopes were descended by the party. After a careful descent the easier glacier (2) was reached. Luckily, there was no ice to give trouble. This pass is only possible for laden men under good conditions, as ascent or descent on the Badrinath side of the watershed would involve too great a strain. Camp V was made at 16,700 ft. The local men showed up exceptionally well, and several of them became skilled in handling the rope and ice-axe.

After a long, tedious march, Birnie found himself once more in the Arwa Valley on July 29, and descended to Mana.

Shipton and his porters were the last to return. He had climbed a peak estimated at about 19,000 ft., which rises directly above Mana. No great difficulties had been encountered. From the summit he had had a beautiful view of the Mana Peak and its glaciers. Before leaving Mana, we conversed with an educated Hindu pilgrim who could speak good English. He seemed to have some doubts as to the source of the Ganges. The Sarsuti River was, he argued, with truth, considerably longer than the Alaknanda River, and therefore the true source of the Ganges must be in the glaciers near the Mana Pass. He told us something about a traditional pass said to exist between Badrinath and Kedarnath. By this pass it was, he affirmed, an easy day's walk of three miles between these two places. The surveyors, however, think differently ; the distance is over twenty miles on the map as the crow flies, and it would be necessary to cross several passes, the highest of which is the 20,000 ft. pass reconnoitred by Meade. It is not wise to try to cross these holy snows of Himachal. A pilgrim had once attempted a passage of the range, but he had not got far up the valley leading towards Nilkanta when he was seized by the devil, who sank with him into the ground. His basket was left, on the hillside, and may still be seen. Possibly as a result of this outrage, there was a terrific fight between the god Vishnu and the devil, and the footprints of the combatants are visible now in the hillside. Vishnu won.

CHAPTER XXIV

DOWN THE PILGRIM ROUTE

On July 31 we packed up our belongings and moved camp to Badrinath.

We pitched our tents near the dak bungalow opposite to the town, on pastures covered with edelweiss. The same afternoon we were received with much pomp and ceremony by the Rawal. An address was read to us by his interpreter from the foot of the temple steps. This address was couched so delightfully that I make no excuse for giving it here in full.

" *To Mr. F. S. Smythe and other members of the British Himalayan Expedition.*

" Dear Sirs,—Please allow us to extend our most hearty and loyal congratulations to all of you—members of the British Himalayan Expedition—on your glorious achievement in successfully completing the conquest of Mount Kamet. It is probably the ninth occasion on which you and your honoured party have alone been privileged to set foot on the highest summit yet attained. It is indeed a matter of glory to you, not less to the Empire, to have opened a new chapter in the pages of history in this heroic direction. It is therefore no surprise to us to learn that your manly enterprise and commendable achievement is being deeply appreciated far and wide and is being applauded as the most gallant and daring expedition of the present age. Let us thank Almighty God for having accorded us this noble opportunity to thank personally the brave sons of a brave Empire to whom all heads bow in reverence. And speaking about ourselves, we need hardly assure you that our joy knows no bounds for more reasons than one, for we can with some pride express that Mount Kamet stands in a district to which we have the honour to belong. We are therefore extremely gratified to feel that this holy peak has achieved an International fame and distinction to-day which have certainly elevated our heads and existence in the eyes of the civilised world.

"It is God's will that we have been honoured to welcome you here in this holiest place—the premier shrine of India—where every year during summer nearly 50,000 pilgrims yearly flock on pilgrimage with single-minded devotion and religious-vented mind. We need hardly mention that we are living in a district surrounded by a series of unsurmountable hills, devoid of almost all sorts of modern facilities, though it may be said to the credit of our benign Government that we are at least enjoying some of the facilities that were hitherto entirely unknown to us. But this unhappy district has frequently suffered from the severest type of famines in the past several years owing to the ridiculously poor condition of agriculture and lack of irrigation. It is only a few merciful showers of rain at times that save the inhabitants from regular starvation. Trade in the district is negligible, and whatever money we get from military and other Government services is barely sufficient for our living in view of the exorbitant rates of foodstuffs due to the lack of better communication in the district. The apathy of our miserable plight can better be illustrated from the fact that during the famine of 1918–19 grain could not be imported into the district from plains on any imaginable hire! Desperate efforts were then resorted to, and you will be agreeably surprised to know that we could get a little quantity of grain by post parcels only! Can anything be more deplorable and miserable? Some of the mule-carriers that volunteered to do the service could only reach up to Nandprayag—a place fifty-five miles below from here—on charging a hire of Rs. 24 a maund![1] Sirs, this is how we are living in this twentieth century! All over India we hear reports that the rates of grain have gone unprecedentedly low, but here in the hills we are getting it at the same old rates and that also of a bumper harvest, i.e., wheat 3 seers[2] and rice 2½ seers a rupee. We need hardly dwell upon the fact that this deplorable condition is all due to the absence of communication in the district for which we have long been striving hard.

"The Government, realising the apathy of this country, surveyed the line from Rikhikesh to Hardwar for a railway some ten years ago, at an expense of a few lacs of rupees, but the idea of a railway line was probably dropped as it was not found remunerative. But the Government did not leave the matter altogether, for it then surveyed a line from Lansdowne to Karanprayag, via Vyasghat, Musagali and Adbadri for a cart-road some five years back, but owing to the financial stringency in the Government budget, the proposal could not as yet be taken in hand

[1] 80 lbs. [2] One seer = 2 lbs.

and nobody can say when it may ultimately materialise.

"It is indeed a pity that the loyalty and services of Garhwalis was not adequately rewarded and respected. We may affirm here, without violating any canons of modesty, that the association of our community with the British Army has been long, and the meritorious services rendered by the Garhwali soldiers in every theatre of war both on the Indian frontiers and in the far-off climes in the service of His Majesty the King Emperor is now a matter of history. Our two gallant brothers obtained the coveted Victoria Cross for their heroic front; one of them died in duty and the other is fortunately living. This small district with its humble resources, out of loyalty and devotion to the Crown, wonderfully served the Empire during all periods of her crisis, but it is sheer misfortune to assert that our most legitimate and rightful demands in this respect have not yet been acceded to nor do we see chances of its adoption in the near future. In this way, obviously it appears to us that we are doomed to live in our present deplorable and helpless state for a number of years to come.

"We fully trust, sirs, you have with deep interest sympathetically listened to this story of our poverty and backwardness. We re-affirm that the culminating point of our moral, material and economic progress solely depends upon the question of CART-ROAD.

"Though we quite realise that the Government is at present running under great financial stringency, it cannot be concealed that the Government has unlimited resources at its disposal if it at all wills and cares for its poor and loyal subjects of Garhwal. The Government can conveniently earmark some money annually for the purpose, and we are sure, without any great embarrassment to the Government, the work can be finished within a very few years. We need hardly impress upon you the fact that with the opening of this new line the number of pilgrims, besides local traffic, will increase many more times ahead, and will far improve the economic and commercial status of the district.

"We therefore most earnestly and respectfully beg you to lend the weight of your influence to this demand to the Government when you come across with the higher authorities and thus considerably increase the chances of its fulfilment. We are convinced, sirs, that if you evince some real interest in the matter, the Government would in all likelihood pay more attention towards it. Let it be candidly said that our main purpose in bringing our standing grievance in this respect to your notice is fervently in the hope that you will leave no stone unturned to get it redressed, in order that peace and prosperity may as well reign in the district for the first time during the 130 years of the British rule in Garhwal.

"We are afraid we have rather far travelled beyond the range of your active interest, for which you will very kindly forgive us, but in fact we could not resist the temptation of putting forth our humble yet acute case to your benevolent notice since we are positively certain that you will not fail to pay sympathetic and lively attention and care in this matter.

"Lastly we beg to assure you, sirs, of our steadfast devotion to the Crown and our determination to continue to serve it as the sword arm of India.

"With very best prayers for your long life and prosperity,

"We have the honour to remain,

"Dear Sirs,

"Your Warm Admirers,

"His Holiness the Rawal of Temple Badrinath and the Public of Badrinath (Garhwal Dist.).

"Badrinath (U.P.),
"*August* 1, 1931."

I fear it may be a long time before the Rawal and the people of Badrinath get their cart-road, for the expense of constructing and maintaining such a line of communication would be enormous.

We were scarcely fit subjects for such a flattering address. Our beards were long, our clothes worn; our nailed and granite-like boots seemed awkward and clumsy amid the barefoot or sandalled pilgrims. The local photographer, who had been summoned for the occasion, can be excused if the picture he took was tilted to one side.

After the address had been read, Birnie delivered a lecture in Hindustani on the expedition. No lecturer can have lectured to a more unusual audience. Pilgrims thronged the temple steps. The aged and the infirm were brought on litters to listen. The stone-paved square without the temple was thronged by the populace of Badrinath. They listened with the greatest interest as Birnie explained in detail how Kamet was climbed. He illustrated his lecture by producing various items of

TEMPLE STEPS, BADRINATH

equipment. Our Darjeeling men swaggered nonchalantly through the throng, bearing with them tents, ice-axes, ropes, sleeping-bags and other expedition equipment. Great applause greeted the conclusion of this lecture. I made a speech in English, which was translated into Hindustani by the Rawal's secretary. From the impassioned harangue on the part of the interpreter, it was obvious that what I said was both ornamented and magnified—possibly just as well, for the flowery idioms of the East are outside my experience.

At the conclusion of these ceremonies we were entertained to lunch. The Rawal informed us that he himself was unable to attend, as he had to meditate and pray in the temple. After nearly three months of Achung, the lunch seemed a masterpiece of cookery. There were creamy rice, curiously flavoured and spiced, small pies, fruit, and many queer sweetmeats. These were washed down by "Himalayan tea," the flavour of which remains a unique and unhallowed memory. Replete to bursting-point, we tottered back to camp and spent the remainder of the day sleeping off our shameless gluttony.

Next day we were shown round the temple by the Rawal. Inside it is an inner shrine where reposes the sacred image of Vishnu. The idol is not more than three feet high, and it is made of a black stone and marble. It is clothed in a rich gold brocade. In order to see it, a large mirror was procured, and from this the sun was reflected into the temple. In front of the image are a number of lamps and a table also covered in brocade. In the forehead of the image there is a solitary diamond of moderate size. It is said that the properties, such as dresses, eating-vessels, etc., belonging to the image are not worth more than 5,000 rupees owing to the fact that the original gold ones were stolen by some robbers, who made their way across the snows in winter. The idol is provided with a meal every afternoon. Dishes are placed before it, and the doors of the shrine closed, so that the image is left to consume its meals in quietness. Not until after sunset are the doors again opened. Attendants prepare the idol for bed, and the doors of the shrine are again closed until morning. There are many attendants, both male and female, and the usual dancing-girls. No one is allowed inside the inner apartments of the temple except the servants, and only the Rawal may touch the idol.

Many come hundreds and even thousands of miles to visit Badrinath and Kedarnath. What is the reason behind this long and toilsome pilgrimage from the plains of India? Some, who have lost their husbands, wives or children, believe themselves to be under a curse for some offence committed during a former existence, and undertake the pilgrimage to expiate their crime against the gods. There are many Yogis among the pilgrims who believe that only by pain and toil may they acquire merit or rid themselves of their sins. Many of these even renounce their names and identity. Included among them are those of noble family and the lowest of the low. These Yogis practise detachment and abandon everything in order to meditate, and it is their aim to rise superior to bodily needs or ailments. Some fast for weeks on end without clothing or shelter save rude caves in the mountain-side. These ascetics cover themselves with ashes, whilst the Sanyasis and Gosains (devotees of Siva) wear a red wig of coiled and matted hair over their shaven heads, which gives them a wild and ghastly appearance. A leopard- or deer-skin is their dress. They carry a rind or a gourd, in which the charitable place gifts of food, a pair of tongs for making their fire and an earthen water-jug. Another sect is the Kanphata Yogis.[1] These wear ochre-coloured garments. They dedicate themselves to Bhairava, a terrible mountain deity. The religion of some of these Yogi sects is associated with indescribable rites. It is not long since human sacrifices were offered on the altars of the temples in Kumaun and Garhwal. Even nowadays the initiation ceremony into the Kanphata caste consists in drawing blood as an offering to their god. It is for this reason that they slit their ears. Unlike the Hindus, they do not burn their dead, but enclose them in a coffin in an upright position, or else throw the corpse into a river.

After visiting the temple we were conducted by the Rawal to an enclosed bathing-pool which is fed by a hot sulphurous spring. This, like the waters of Lourdes, is reputed to be capable of cleansing and invigorating body and soul. In Europe its waters would probably be drunk for their medicinal properties, but at Badrinath they are used merely to bathe in.

Below the bathing-pool there is a flight of steps, worn by the tread of countless feet, that leads down to the Alaknanda. Where these steps disappear into the torrent there is an iron bolt, to which pilgrims cling while immersing their bodies in the grey glacier waters of their sacred river. Close by is another hot spring which issues steaming

[1] Kanphata means "ear split," because the lobe of the ear is pierced and a pendant of rhinoceros horn, agate or gold passed through.

from a rock, whilst a few yards away, and projecting from the river water, is a large boulder pierced by a hole, through which the god Vishnu is reputed to have poked his finger.

In camp that evening we realised sorrowfully that it was our last night in the High Himalaya. The morrow would see us marching downhill into tropical heat. Had the weather been bad we could have turned plainwards without regret. But it was not bad ; it was perfect. The sunset was a peaceful one. Our one regret was that a few clouds obstinately concealed Nilkanta. We knew that from our camping-ground there is a view of that marvellous peak, and it would be disappointing to leave Badrinath without seeing it.

The evening was cool, and we dined in the mess-tent. After dinner we came out for a final pipe and a stroll. The camp and the Alaknanda Valley were in deep shadow. The night was very still. We could hear the low thunder of the Alaknanda and the murmur of Badrinath. We could smell the sweet scent of pastures still warm from the sun. The moon was rising. Suddenly our attention was arrested. We saw Nilkanta. It was bathed in brilliant moonlight and was framed by the dark walls of nearer mountains. It was difficult to believe that it was a mountain and not some product of the infinite manufactured by the stars.

Later, when the camp was sleeping, I lay awake gazing through the doorway of my tent at Nilkanta : later still, in dreamland, I sought refuge on that serene summit from the uneasy phantasms that beset the wanderer through the valleys of sleep.

The dawn was sparkling and fresh, and we saw Nilkanta

NILKANTA – MOONLIGHT

lit gloriously by the rising sun. Its snows were the last we were to see on our march back to Ranikhet. Just as we were about to leave, a local resident, Pandit Nerian Dutt, who informed us that he was a retired banker, begged us to come and see his garden. We did so, and we were surprised at the number of flowers he had managed to cultivate in the rocky soil. He was a charming old gentleman of a type not often seen nowadays in India. He loaded us with fruit and other delicacies, and informed us that he had sent word down to Joshimath to inform the steward of his orchards there that we were coming.

That the path below Badrinath is dangerous and impassable in winter was evidenced by the avalanche snow lying in the Alaknanda Valley. The sun had been melting it for months, but in such quantities had it accumulated that in several places it still bridged the Alaknanda River. One bridge was an extraordinary freak of nature, and resembled a brickwork bridge, owing to the snow being curiously veined with streaks of dirt.

Down and down we tramped. Gusts of heat met us. The valley walls closed in upon us. Dust whitened our boots. Runnels of sweat coursed down our foreheads as we approached the dak bungalow at Pandukeswar.

During the past two months we had forgotten that flies existed. Now, as swarms of them settled on our food, we were disagreeably reminded of this curse of Himalayan travel in the lower valleys.

Night fell dark and ominous, with a flicker of lightning to remind us that we were approaching the foothills. Insects whirred and fluttered about us as we ate our dinner ; a hundred moths committed suicide in the candles.

We awoke next morning to hear a series of crashes. A huge boulder was falling down the opposite side of the valley. It bounded down in a series of leaps, plunging at last, with a splintering crash, into the forest beneath.

The path, in the way that Himalayan paths have, played a bad joke upon us that day. We were congratulating ourselves on having all but reached Joshimath when it turned uphill and we found ourselves confronted with an ascent of some 1,500 ft.

At Joshimath there is a hospital at which Lewa had been detained as his feet were considered too bad to allow of him being carried to Ranikhet. The hospital is under the charge of a native doctor whose cleanly methods and efficiency impressed us not a little. Poor Lewa's feet were not a pleasant sight. Mortification had set in : his toes resembled burnt cinders ; on the edges of the affected areas cracks had opened up down to the bone, oozing blood and pus. But, despite the terrible appearance of his feet, Greene was satisfied that not only would they be saved, but that at the worst he was not likely to lose more than the top joints of his toes. A welcome surprise awaited us at Joshimath. Pandit Nerian Dutt had been as good as his word, and we feasted on mangoes from his orchard. How good those mangoes were ! We vowed that we had never tasted anything like them. Even to a sophisticated palate, a mango is a gift from the gods, but it must be perfectly ripe—not under-ripe, when it is disappointing, or over-ripe, when it tastes of paraffin, but ripe to the hour ; it is then a peerless fruit.

As we descended the Lower Alaknanda Valley the heat became more intense. Pilgrims were toiling up the path.

SNOW BRIDGE OVER ALAKNANDA

Those who were too old or crippled to walk were carried on litters, whilst others rode ponies. They eyed us incuriously and apathetically. Many looked starved and worn-out by their journey. We encountered also the postman. In order to ward off wild animals and evildoers, he carried a spear with a ring of bells round the shaft.

The farther we proceeded southwards, the heavier became the rainstorms, but by starting at dawn every morning we were able to avoid both the heat of the day and the torrential downpours which occurred almost every afternoon. The march was dull and uneventful. We managed to keep in good health save that for two days I suffered from an attack of fever.

On August 13 ponies carried us up the sun-baked hill-side to Ranikhet. In the hospitable club there we soon forgot the toil, the heat, the flies and the smells of the past ten days. Our beards came off; we wallowed in hot baths; we ate well-cooked food; we slept between sheets. Civilisation claimed us, and at the time we would not have had it otherwise. A real appreciation of life is made up of contrasts. Civilisation cannot be properly appreciated unless you have lived in the wild. Comfort can only be judged by discomfort. No man can claim to be a gourmet until he has sampled native cooked food. For the past three months we had lived as men can only live in the wilds. Our eyes had searched wide horizons; we had sweated and we had shivered; we had experienced comfort and discomfort; we had gazed upon ugliness and beauty; we had known comradeship; we had found peace.

A few mornings later I saw the Himalaya for the last time. The forest was whispering the secrets of the slow dawn wind ; the call of a cuckoo came joyously from a distant ridge. Day was already fashioning her twisted pillars of cloud. Into the stainless air, and at an immeasurable distance from the common things of earth rose the everlasting hills.

CHAPTER XXV

THE MEDICAL ASPECTS OF HIGH CLIMBING

by Raymond Greene

PHYSIOLOGICAL CONSIDERATIONS

THIS is not the place to discuss in detail the physiology of great altitudes. The questions which arise are highly technical and often highly controversial. Any attempt to convey untechnically the salient features of these questions is bound to be incomplete, and, if at times dogma is found in place of hypothesis, I shall, I know, be pardoned by those who have themselves attempted the popular exposition of an abstruse subject.

We may divide the evil effects of great altitude into three parts : mountain sickness, acute and chronic, and altitude deterioration. Mountain sickness in either form is due to oxygen lack. The acute form does not concern us here. It is met with where civilisation has made it possible for men to ascend to great altitudes before their bodies have accustomed themselves to the changed conditions. From this disease are suffering the faint and vomiting railway travellers of the Andes, Jungfraujoch or Pike's Peak, who, raised suddenly untrained to these great heights, gaze with envy upon the happy climbers whose physical fitness and slower rate of progress have made them immune to gastric disturbance. It has been said

They climbed the steep ascent to Heaven through sorrow, toil and pain.
O Lord, to us may grace be given to follow in the train.

It is a prayer which will never pass the lips of those who have experienced the disadvantages of speed.

The chronic form of mountain sickness is met with in all those who attempt to climb the greater peaks of the world. Its manifestations vary according to the physical fitness of the individual, the rate at which the ascent is made, the conditions under which the climber is living, and his power of "acclimatisation." There may be breathlessness on the slightest exertion, lassitude, headache, sleeplessness, blueness of the lips, frostbite, and an insidious impairment of the mental processes.

Breathlessness in the thin air of high mountains is the symptom of oxygen lack which impresses itself most forcefully upon the climber. We experienced it first during the last few hundred feet before our arrival at the Base Camp (15,800 ft.). Here it was too slight to be a serious inconvenience. But even at this altitude one of us suffered during his first night from "Cheyne Stokes Respiration," a form of breathing, associated with lack of oxygen, in which periods of breath-holding alternate automatically with periods of deep breathing. Two members were comfortable till they fell asleep, when they awoke panting. These symptoms passed after one night, but from Base Camp onwards a steady increase in respiratory symptoms occurred. Though as much time as we could afford was given to acclimatisation, it was not until Kamet had been climbed and our activities had been transferred to the

Badrinath Range that we found ourselves able to move quickly without laboured breath. At Camp Three (20,600 ft.) I noted in my diary : " Small sudden movements, such as turning over in bed, made me pant a little, and I panted for three minutes after a short glissade. But I can keep moving slowly and rhythmically for prolonged periods without undue fatigue." Above Camp Three we all found our rate and depth of breathing much increased. I found one breath necessary to each step. From Camp Five onwards, two breaths were taken to each step and frequent pauses were necessary.

Lassitude affected very differently the several members of the expedition. It is a symptom a little difficult to evaluate, for the spirit of competition is ineradicable among even the most intimate friends. Two of the Europeans, however, confessed to it at Camp Three. " X and Y," I noted, " stayed in camp. They feel well when they are doing nothing, but become very tired on the slightest movement. X complained also of a sense of suffocation on movement." I treated him with large doses of ammonium chloride, with apparently good results. This is a point to which I shall return. Y recovered without treatment, but it is worth noting that he lost two stone in weight on the expedition. If Argyll Campbell[1] is right in supposing that loss of weight may be taken as a criterion of lack of acclimatisation, the more honour is due to Y that he reached the top. He was one of the two who suffered from heart strain as a result of his climb. No such sense of shame deterred the porters from confessing their weakness, and several were sent down from Camp Three to the Base.

[1] J. A. Campbell, *Journal of Physiology*, lxiii. 4. 325.

Headaches were never sufficiently severe to interfere seriously with our enjoyment, but the complaints of the porters produced a steady drain on the supplies of aspirin and phenacetin. One tablet of Veramon cured the worst cases. Restlessness at night was experienced by all of us, but a tablet or two of allonal usually produced sound sleep.

Despite careful observation, no cyanosis (blueness) was observed in any member of the expedition, whether at work or at rest, at any point below 24,000 ft. Between 24,000 ft. and the summit I was alone and unable to observe. On the summit we encountered a very cold wind, and it was impossible to determine whether the blueness of my companions was due to lack of oxygen or to cold. My opinion is that they were no bluer than they would have been at sea-level in such a wind.

The mental effects of great altitude have wrecked the pleasure of many expeditions. The impairment of judgment and control produced by insufficient oxygen often makes men irritable and quarrelsome. That no quarrels occurred on the Kamet expedition is, in my opinion, due partly to our conscious effort never to ascend far above our acclimatised level, but chiefly to the fact that we belonged to the same generation. At sea-level youth and age cannot live together. It is far truer above 20,000 ft., where men find it more difficult to control their natural spleen and to adopt a cheerful attitude towards their own discomfort and the faults of their fellows.

The special senses at great altitudes are frequently blunted, though this was a change not noticed by the majority of the expedition. I noticed no change in our upward progress, but the improvement on the quicker return journey was to me dramatic. Early on June 26, in fast-falling snow and a bitter wind, we began the double march to Base Camp. My frostbitten toes made walking painful. The wind seemed to find its way into every chink and buttonhole of one's clothing, and the snow fell so fast that no sight of distant mountains diverted one's attention from present misery. In the neighbourhood of our old Camp One the snow began to fall less thickly, and far ahead we could see the end of the East Kamet Valley, and the dark and snow-streaked rock peaks lying above Base Camp. It was at this point—at about, I suppose, 16,500 ft.—that a change came over my feelings. Haldane[1] has written how, in his experiments on the effects of low air-pressure, he sat in his steel chamber with the pressure gradually rising towards the normal: and how, at a certain level, the electric light glowed suddenly more brightly. At first he thought that the current had been increased, but later he came to realise that the change was in himself and not in the current. For me, shut in no steel chamber, but walking slowly down the East Kamet Glacier, depressed by wind and weather and painful feet, the whole aspect of life as suddenly changed. I began once more to appreciate the pleasures of the senses. The peaks beyond the Raikana Glacier drew nearer. The snow was whiter and more scintillating. When, little by little, patches of sky began to show between the banks of cloud, they seemed a brighter blue than the skies of Kamet. One began to hear and to smell more acutely. It is clear that not only are one's senses dulled by lack of oxygen, so that

[1] Haldane, Kellas and Kennaway, *Journal of Physiology*, liii. 3. 183.

the light in the steel chamber becomes dull and the Himalayan sky less blue, but that all one's mental processes suffer a like fate. Especially, at great heights one does not gloat over one's pleasures. One loses, as Goethe has put it, " the capacity to submit to impressions; to be delighted, touched and exalted." But now this capacity was suddenly restored. Eye and ear and nose were restored to sensuality.

Frostbite is a constant danger at great altitudes. It may occur as a dry gangrene or a moist form with large blisters full of fluid. Lewa, the sirdar, suffered so severely that he had to be carried down the mountain and back to hospital in Joshimath. He lost the end joints of all his toes. Of the six European members of the expedition, three were slightly bitten. The danger is greater on high mountains, not merely because of the extreme cold, but because the heart, deprived of its proper supply of oxygen, works with diminished efficiency. The circulation is slowed and the output of the heart per minute is greatly diminished. The brunt of this disease[1] is borne by the skin, where the blood becomes almost stagnant where the skin is subjected to pressure.

Before describing the third effect of great altitudes, the so-called high-altitude deterioration, it is necessary to explain what is meant by " acclimatisation." A man ascending rapidly in a balloon to 20,000 ft. would die. Yet six men spent a fortnight above this height and suffered no harm. The changes which occur in the body which make this possible may be grouped, according to our present knowledge, under three heads. In the first place, in the well-trained person, it is claimed that oxygen

[1] Barcroft, *Respiratory Function of the Blood*, i. 129.

"secretion" by the lung-lining increases the oxygen supply to the blood at a very early stage of the ascent. The cells of the lining of the lung actively remove oxygen from the air and transfer it to the blood.[1] The existence of oxygen secretion is denied by many physiologists. In this battle of the giants I do not propose to take a part.

In the second place an increase in the hæmoglobin of the blood undoubtedly occurs. At an early stage oxygen-want causes a contraction of the spleen, which forces out into the blood stream a part of its store of red corpuscles. Thereafter, by a more gradual process, the bone marrow, the factory of red corpuscles, enlarges and steadily increases its output. But this increase will not make possible the continuance of life at great altitudes. The red corpuscles are the means by which oxygen is carried from the air to the tissues. The new corpuscles cannot do their work unless at the same time more oxygen is supplied for them to carry. This is brought about by the third and most important aspect of acclimatisation, deep breathing.

The first deep breathing of the ascending climber is believed to be brought about by oxygen-want, which increases the susceptibility of the respiratory centre in the brain to changes in the acidity of the blood. The climber responds to oxygen-want by breathing more deeply. In so doing he washes carbon dioxide out of his blood and so lowers the acidity of the latter. An "alkalosis" is thus produced. The most important element in acclimatisation is the overcoming of this "alkalosis" by an increased excretion of alkalis by the kidneys. Thus a compensation towards "acidosis" is produced, and permanent deep

[1] Haldane, *Respiration*, ix.

breathing, with an increased oxygen supply, follows. It had been suggested by Haldane that the process of overcoming the " alkalosis " of high altitudes might be accelerated by the administration of ammonium chloride, a salt which is split up in the body into ammonia and hydrochloric acid. Acting on this suggestion, I took a dose of seven grains of ammonium chloride three times a day for the whole period which I spent above 15,000 ft. A single experiment of this sort cannot be regarded as of any scientific importance. Nor was it obvious that I acclimatised any better than any other member of the expedition. I was, however, the only member of the expedition who did not lose weight.

I have left to the last the discussion of the problem of altitude-deterioration, a subject which has recently received publicity both in scientific and lay journals. By some its very existence is doubted. To others its importance ranks equally with that of acclimatisation. To my mind it is an established fact. It is of no significance for a climber to say, "I have lived for many days above 20,000 ft. and I have never seen it." As well might a doctor deny the existence of malaria because in his passage through a mosquito-ridden valley he had never seen a case. Its occurrence depends upon many factors, and the experience of Odell[1] on Everest and some members of the Bauer expedition on Kangchenjunga show that it is sometimes avoided.

We first hear of altitude deterioration in the sixteenth-century writings of Mirza Haidar, who, describing the condition as " dam giri," ascribed it to the poisonous

[1] Norton, *The Fight for Everest*, iii. 5 (by N. E. Odell).

exhalations of rocks, and counselled sufferers to seek a cure by a return to the neighbourhood of forts and villages. Most Himalayan expeditions have observed some form or other of deterioration. After prolonged residence at great altitudes their members have lost appetite and weight. Some have shown signs of heart trouble. There has been a failure of energy, and often they have returned to the valleys "sick men." Barcroft's expedition to Cerro de Pasco, living in conditions of luxury, noticed signs of mental deterioration. After describing his own impressions, he adds[1]: "The experience of residents at Cerro de Pasco is definitely that concentrated thought is more fatiguing to the mind there than at sea-level. It was put to me in this way. Accountancy (which I suppose is largely mechanical) is done up to the same standard at Cerro as in New York, but the drafting of a complicated report at Cerro, on which important financial decisions hinge, involves a degree of mental wear sufficient to demand a holiday 'trip to the coast.'"

On the Kamet expedition the deterioration was slight, but in my view none the less present. We were conscious on the second part of the expedition, at the 19,000 ft. camp in the Badrinath Range, of a very fine degree of acclimatisation. We could climb at 20,000 ft. at almost Alpine speed. But we were also conscious of symptoms, slight but definite, of degeneration. When I read to the other members of the expedition what I wrote at this high camp, which is in substance, and to a large extent in word, what I repeat here, it was agreed to by all present as a fair account of our condition. Our appetites had begun to suffer. We ate less

[1] Barcroft, *Respiratory Function of the Blood*, i. 165.

heartily than on Kamet, though our camp was 4,000 ft. lower. A lack of energy began to show itself. Off days were more welcome. A fear, amounting in one or two of us to horror, of exchanging our tents for the more conventional comforts of houses, died in us. The delights of beer were more frequently mentioned. In general, a tendency to go home began to be manifest.

In the face of this body of evidence it is idle to deny that deterioration occurs. We cannot with such certainty ascribe it to a definite cause. Of the possible causes, prolonged oxygen-want must take the first place. Experience and experiment point this way. Barcroft in luxury at 14,200 ft. experienced deterioration. The Shackleton expedition of 1914, at sea-level, but in other respects living under conditions similar to those on a great Himalayan peak, did not experience it.[1] The experiments of Argyll Campbell[2] showed that rabbits, rats and mice, well fed and acclimatised, can exist in a decompression chamber for at least seven days under continuous exposure to low oxygen pressure equivalent to that at the top of Everest. The animals exhibited some activity but deteriorated rapidly. Cats, a monkey and cavies could not tolerate the condition for so long a time. The animals lost appetite, weight and energy, as do human beings. On post-mortem examination, degenerative changes were found in the heart, liver and kidneys.

It is argued, with truth, that the experiments of Campbell are not strictly applicable to the question : that we do not know that what happens to another animal happens to a

[1] J. M. Wordie, personal communication.

[2] J. A. Campbell, *Journal of Physiology*, lxiii. 4. 325.

man. But animal experiment was ever found to be a useful indicator of changes occurring in man, and until human evidence in either direction can be obtained we must bear in mind the probability that the degenerative changes occurring in Campbell's animals occur to a certain extent in man. It has been argued that all the Everest climbers became fit on their return to lower altitudes. So did the animals. No mountaineer has yet been found who will on his return submit to an autopsy in the cause of science.

But other factors may play an important part in the production of deterioration. Of these the psychic is, in my opinion, the most important. Men become stale, in the sense that a boat's crew may, in training, become stale. They become " sick of the job," and their changed mental attitude is reflected in a diminution of " energy." This mental change is probably itself partly due to prolonged oxygen-want, but it may be increased by uninteresting food or by a badly chosen " crew." I am convinced that the success of the Kamet expedition was largely due to the skill with which the personnel was chosen.

Dr. John Cowan of Glasgow, in a series of personal communications, has impressed upon me the possibility that C-vitamin shortage may have a bearing on the problem. Our care that as far as possible the Kamet expedition was never short of this vitamin, which is contained in fresh food, especially fruit and vegetables, may in his view have prevented serious deterioration.

Apart altogether, however, from the possibility of vitamin-shortage, it is essential that any expedition living under conditions of meteorological discomfort must be provided not merely with a full diet, but with an interesting, varied and palatable one. The appetite must be stimulated. At great altitudes a man will rather underfeed than feed on what is lacking in appeal. Of Antony, Octavius Cæsar said : " In the Alps, it is reported he did eat strange flesh which some did die to look on."[1] What was possible to Antony in the Alps is not necessarily possible to others in the Himalayas.

It is probable that many other factors may enter into the problem. I hope that by stimulating controversy I may be instrumental in bringing some to light. The importance of the subject to climbers is great. I have pointed out elsewhere that the question of the climbing of Everest depends upon the opposing factors of acclimatisation and deterioration.[2] But the knowledge that, from whatever cause, deterioration undoubtedly occurs, has in the past bulked too largely in the strategy of climbing. It gave rise, until recent years, to the habit of rushing peaks, a habit unsound in theory and disastrous in practice. The Kamet expedition, which attacked its objective by slow siege tactics, never climbing far above its level of acclimatisation, left Kamet a group of six fit men, who instead of creeping back to Ranikhet, triumphant but broken in health, proceeded over several high passes to another district where they explored many unknown glaciers and climbed ten high peaks.

EQUIPMENT

The choice of medical equipment for an expedition to the Himalayas or to any mountain range at a great

[1] W. Shakespeare, *Antony and Cleopatra*, i. 4.
[2] Greene, *Nature*, November 23, 1931.

distance from ordinary sources of supply is made difficult by opposing factors. On the one hand is the impossibility of replenishing the supplies or of rectifying an omission : on the other the necessity of confining the weight of luggage to the minimum consistent with safety. The advice of experts is often difficult to elicit, and apt to amount to no more than an admonition to take " bags of castor oil," but in planning the equipment of the Kamet expedition I was greatly helped by the verbal advice of Doctor Longstaff and by Major Hingston's chapter in *The Fight for Everest.*

The medical equipment was packed in two " Venesta " three-ply wood cases. One of these, the stock box, measured 25 × 17 × 13 inches, and weighed at the beginning 60 lbs. : the other, for daily use, measured 12 × 12 × 21 inches, and weighed 35 lbs. In addition, I carried in my own rucksack a few dressings and instruments which might at any moment be urgently required. The quantities of drugs and dressings were estimated for a party of six Europeans and about seventy porters. In addition to the care of these, the medical officer is expected to undertake the immediate cure of all the ailments prevalent in the villages through which he passes. News spreads rapidly, and more than once I entered a small village to find a clinic of some thirty patients awaiting my arrival. It is impossible for a small expedition unsupported by public funds to carry sufficient supplies adequately to deal with such a situation. I was forced to content myself with the administration of effervescent tablets of Epsom salt, given with a feeling of thankfulness that I should not pass that way again. I can imagine no more satisfying holiday for a medical man than a tour through the valleys of the Himalayas adequately equipped to treat these charming people with the skill and care they deserve.

In the list which follows, the first column of figures shows the quantities taken ; the second the quantities used. Often it will be seen that little of the amount taken actually came into use. But I do not think it would be safe for this reason to reduce the quantities. It must be remembered that the health of the expedition was, throughout, extremely good, and that no serious accident occurred. All expeditions cannot expect to be so lucky.

Dressings :

Boric lint	24 ozs.	22 ozs.
Cotton wool	60 „	30 „
Bandages, 3 in.	24	4
„ 2½ in.	24	18
Lister's gauze	6 yds.	0
Crêpe bandages	6	2
Gamgee tissue	½ lb.	¼ lb.
Zinc oxide plaster, 3 in.	30 yds.	10 yds.
„ „ „ 2 in.	20 „	10 „
Oiled silk (18 in. width)	2 „	½ yd.
Plaster of Paris bandages	6	0

"*Elastoplast*" *Dressings* :

(These were presented to the expedition by the manufacturers. They proved invaluable. They were subjected to a temperature variation of about 120° F. and were completely unimpaired.)

Gauze plaster strips 1½ in. width	18 yds.	4 yds.
Elastic bandage, style A, 2½ in. width	36 „	3 „
Finger dressings	24	18
Boil dressings	9	6
Emergency wound dressings, 4 in. sq.	36	14
„ „ „ 3 in. sq.	36	14
Vaccination dressings (small)	12	7
„ „ (large)	12	3

Jaconet, rubber tubing, safety-pins, silk worm gut (50 twelve-inch lengths in spirit), sterile catgut, Gooch's splinting, poroplast splinting, Thomas's splint (the author's modification) with extension appliance, Carr's splints, tourniquet, selected suture needles, Higginson syringe, stethoscope, clasp knife, dissecting forceps, dental forceps, six pairs of artery forceps, bullet probe, three pairs of scissors, hypodermic syringe with needles, throat spray, a dozen throat brushes, twelve clinical thermometers, sphygmomanometer.

Omnopon in "Tubanic" syringes	12	2
Morphine sulphate (tablets of ½ grain)	20	0
Cocaine hydrochloride (lamellæ gr. 1/20)	24	14
Allonal tablets	300	200
Medinal tablets	10	5
Veramon	10 (insufficient)	10
Magnesium sulphate, effervescent tablets, each of 60 grains (B. W. & Co.)	150	100
Eucalyptus tablets	6 boxes	Distributed
Castor oil	1 pint	16 ozs.
Ammonium bromide, 5-grain tablets	4 ozs.	0
Aromatic chalk and opium, 5-grain tablets	200	0
Santonin, 2-grain tablets	½ oz.	0
Chloral, 5-grain tablets	4 ozs.	0
Tr. camph. co. 5-grain tablets	4 "	2 ozs.
Ipecac, 5-grain tablets	4 "	2 "
Quinine bihydrochloride, 5-grain tablets	12 "	6 "
*Sodium bicarbonate, 5-grain tablets	4 "	3 "
Phenacetin and caffeine, 5-grain tablets	8 "	2 "
*Aspirin, 5-grain tablets	4 "	3 "
*Sodamint, 4-grain tablets	4 "	3 "
*Tr. Iodi (in three bottles)	4 "	2 "
Pigm. mandl.	4 "	3 "
Adrephine	2 "	½ oz.
Vaseline	3 tubes	1 tube
Collodion	2 ozs.	1 oz.
Ung. hydrarg. nit. dil.	2 "	0
Ung. sulphuris	2 "	0
Paroleine spray solution	2 "	1 oz.
Chloroform	2 "	0
"Neko" soap	6 tablets	Distributed
Hemoplastin	12 c.c.	0
Antidysenteric serum	200 c.c.	20 c.c.
Sodium sulphate	1 lb.	0
Potassium permanganate	2 ozs.	0

* Individual members brought their own supplies in addition.

CHAPTER XXVI

THE FLOWERS OF THE KAMET AND BADRINATH RANGES

By R. L. Holdsworth

LET ME confess at the outset that as the botanist of the Kamet expedition of 1931 I am an impostor. My qualifications for the post are wholly inadequate, and my opportunities for doing the job thoroughly were naturally rather meagre. Knowing this well enough before I set out, I determined that my collections and botanical notes should be strictly selective, and limited to those species which I thought would be of value to English gardens, and particularly to the growing number of people whose particular interest lies in the cultivation of hardy mountain plants. I did not attempt to record in detail the forest trees, nor any but the more outstanding of the shrubs we met with in our wanderings ; and, in the case of plants, I refused to notice the many hundreds which had no definite beauty or daintiness to recommend them. In the case of such a well-represented genus as potentilla this duty was urgent ; otherwise my collection would have been impossibly unwieldy. For the same reason I did not collect plants at all from regions so relatively low down that their hardiness would be doubtful ; and I must confess that in observing this plan I sometimes erred. I fell, for instance, a victim to the charms of that gorgeous climber *Gloriosa superba*, which is nowhere hardy in Great Britain, while rejecting the two roscæas (*R. alpina* and *purpurea*), which I thought looked tender, but which I find are not.

The alpine districts of Garhwal are not reached until you are in the neighbourhood of the Kuari Pass. In the foothills round about Naini-Thal and Ranikhet, snow falls, but never lies for long on end. The foothills are covered with a mixed hill jungle, conifers and rhododendrons only making their appearance on the highest tops at about six thousand feet above the sea. There is here no noticeable rush of vegetation in spring, caused by the melting of the snows, as in the Alps. The cold weather comes to an end and the hot weather begins about March or April. In the middle of May, when we arrived, the ground was already parched and brown, as in midsummer, and it remains so until the rains come towards the end of June.

The climate of the whole area covered by our march up to, and return from, Kamet, and consequently the flora, approximates to that of Kashmir. The summer monsoon is, I believe, greater than in Kashmir, though not a quarter of what is commonly experienced in Sikkim. On the other hand, as soon as you have reached the genuinely alpine districts, judging from the level of the snow in June and the size of the débris of winter avalanches, you are in a region subject to a considerable winter snowfall. From this one concludes that the flora is at least as rich as, probably richer than, that of Kashmir; though of course not so varied in the number of species as in the Eastern Himalaya. On the other hand, since climatic conditions more resemble those of our own European ranges, the species will probably take more kindly to cultivation in British rock-gardens, as indeed many already do.

The earlier stages of the march up to our Base Camp from Ranikhet took us over five intermediate and subsidiary ridges of 6,000, 8,000, 9,000, 10,500 and 12,500 ft. above sea-level. Thence we dropped down to the Dhaoli River at 5,000 ft. and, continuing up its valley in a series of impressive gorges, reached the last group of Bhotia villages at over 10,000 ft. The Base Camp on the Raikana Glacier was pitched two marches from here at 15,500 ft. I mention these rather tiresome figures because I wish to try and make it clear that, at any rate in this part of the Himalaya, few genuinely alpine plants are to be found until you are over 10,000 ft. above the sea. Since the tree level extends in many places to over 12,000 ft., we were marching most of the way through forest, though often the southern slopes of the hills were grassy and bare of trees. At Ranikhet I noticed no herbaceous flowers worth mentioning until our return in the rains, and then only two species of begonia, and *Roscœa purpurea*. The forest was mostly light, and consisted of a tall fir-tree, not unlike a Scotch fir, one of the Himalayan oaks (we met a second species later), and *Rhododendron arboreum*. Lower down in the valleys, cactus species and wild figs grew, while bananas and mangoes were cultivated. At the first ridge we crossed, at 6,000 ft., we were in a forest of more varied conifers, including, I think, deodars. Here, on a grassy hillside, I found no real alpines except a pretty polygala (*P. crotalarioides*), a rather dingy harebell, and a single plant of that well-known friend of man, *Androsace lanuginosa*. Our camp at Lohajang at 8,000 ft. looked distinctly more alpine in character.

As we neared the pass we passed through a thick undergrowth of three kinds of cotoneaster, a white-flowered rose, and, in prodigal abundance, the gay, rose-coloured *Indigofera Gerardiana.* Lurking coyly among the shrubs and, on the actual pass, in long grass I found a dainty delphinium (*D. denudatum*). But still, I murmured to myself, no primulas ! I had, as a matter of fact, come across a few plants, low down—no higher than 4,000 ft.—of the common *Primula denticulata.* A plant's good nature in cultivation is always betrayed if it consents to such an extreme range of climatic conditions as this amiable species. Later on I found it equally happy and far more profuse at over 14,000 ft. Yet surely I had read of Farrer and Kingdon Ward finding a wealth of primulas below 8,000 ft. And so far only one rhododendron ! I began to say unkind things about the botanical barrenness of the land.

The northern slopes of this pass led us down through a forest of oak and tree rhododendron—great gnarled trunks, sometimes three feet thick, though the scarlet or pink flowers were almost over. The scene at times recalled the North Devonshire combes. There was no impenetrable dankness, no dense tangle of leech-haunted undergrowth, such as one reads of in Sikkim or Upper Burma. It was a pleasant stroll down rough but recognisable footpaths. Round the forest streams grew thickets of bamboo, and among these I saw for the first and last time a fine group of the great *Lilium giganteum,* not yet in flower. Shrubs were too many to name, but I noticed a viburnum and a big Pieris (*P. ovalifolium*).

Our third ridge took us up to above 9,000 ft. It was, in fact, a ridge that merged itself in the snow and ice of

Trisul. In open glades of the forest the grass was starred with flowers : large-flowered wild strawberries ; a common-looking erigeron ; a gentian, microscopic, pale blue, horticulturally worthless, and probably annual as well (*G. aprica*) ; and last, and a long way best, a species of anemone which certainly ought to be in cultivation, if it isn't, since it grows in Kashmir—*Anemone obtusiloba.* This desirable thing from silky, almost prostrate leaves opens wide its big flowers of white, with a dark-blue reverse to its petals. Or sometimes it is pure hepatica-blue all over. Unfortunately, I never found it in seed, since it never occurred, so far as I could discover, north of the Kuari Pass, except in its yellow form, which is so distinct that I am surprised that it is not given specific rank, as it is a genuine high-alpine, growing on inhospitable rocks and screes at over 16,000 ft., while its prettier sister never rose above 11,000 ft. In amongst these rambled the prostrate *Gaultheria trichophylla*, whose pink flowers and even more handsome big blue berries would "justify its inclusion in the choicest garden," as catalogues say.

Things gradually improved. We were now among ranges where the increased luxuriance of forest and meadow bore witness to the snowy source from which they drew their sustenance. Round about the 10,000 ft. contour two more rhododendrons appeared : *Rhododendron barbatum*, which I did not see in flower, but which appears to be rather more of a tree than a bush ; and *Rhododendron campanulatum*, with its great bells of pale pink or purest white, which is certainly more of a bush than a tree, and which guards the frontier line between the forest and the alp. At about the same level, too, I got my first real thrill : as I passed by shady forest rocks I noticed a few gleaming eyes of rich rose, and for a few hectic minutes I left the path and laboured arduously. I remember the indulgent and slightly cynical smiles of my companions when I solemnly announced to them that the most important event of the expedition had taken place, as I had discovered a primula that really mattered. I knew sufficient botany to realise that it belonged to the most desirable *petiolaris* section, and, since it wasn't *Winteri*, and it wasn't *sonchifolia* I vainly hoped it might be new. But Professor Wright-Smith of Edinburgh—to whom I must here acknowledge my indebtedness for identifying and naming practically all of my extremely amateurish collection of specimens—has since shattered my illusions and named it *Primula sessilis*. And, now that we know it is not new, I don't mind admitting that it is not *quite* so beautiful as *Winteri*, lacking that plant's mealy foliage and purity of pale mauve. Yet an attractive plant it is, especially as I saw it later on, growing in the rocks of the open alp up to 12,500 ft. in great abundance, but never, so far as I could see, crossing north of the Kuari Pass.

I think that it was on the northern slopes of this fourth ridge that I met *Pæonia emodi*. This also is a Kashmir plant, and, I believe, is in cultivation, though I have never seen it in catalogues. Here in deep forest and in more open glades it grew literally in groves, the huge, single, cream-coloured flowers rising three feet from the ground—a magnificent plant for the select border, or, still better, for the very select wild garden.

Looking through my book of specimens, I find that my next good day for plant-hunting was on the south side of the Kuari Pass—a day which had been originally set aside for hunting in the literal sense of the word. A local shikari had volunteered to show us game—gurrhal and possibly thar, with just the chance of a black bear. Birnie and I went out in the early morning. Jungle fowl and monaul pheasants were everywhere, and once something big crashed away invisible in the dew-drenched undergrowth. At the top of the ridge we at last caught sight of two gurrhal a good distance away, but my attention was now distracted from the hunt proper to the hunt incidental, when I found myself taking cover behind a delightful dwarf rhododendron with wide-open crimson flowers (*Rhododendron lepidotum*). The gurrhal escaped unscathed from my rifle—I could only get a snap shot as she walked through bigger rhododendron scrub—but the dwarf rhododendron could not run away any more than could many another treasure. Here I found *Primula denticulata* again, and on sunny, drier spots the first few plants of a species I was to see later in prodigal abundance—*Iris kumaonensis*. *Anemone narcissiflora*, probably the variety known as *tetrasepala*, was just beginning to unfurl its silken chalices. There was a handsome thing like a silky-leaved broad bean with deep maroon flowers, called *Thermopsis barbata*. There first I saw the lovely silver and golden *Potentilla argyrophylla*, with its deep crimson variety, and a form of the shrubby *Potentilla fruticosa* ; there also I found the lovely gentian-blue *Corydalis Kashmeriana*, which I didn't know was a bulb, or I should certainly have collected it ; there I first found my one Kabscia saxifrage (*Saxifraga imbricata*) with its stemless white flowers ; and *Lloydia serotina* that grows wild on some of our Welsh hills ;

and, last and best of all, and so enchanting as to make the heart leap as one saw its pendent cups of pale blue silk hanging from some vertical cliff, *Isopyrum* (its older name) or, more correctly, *Paraquilegia microphylla*. Of this, alas ! not a seed did I succeed in getting ; nor of its still more lovely cousin, which I found later, of pure white just touched with blue—*Paraquilegia grandiflora*.

On the northern slopes of the Kuari Pass the winter's snow still lingered, and spring was just awakening at 12,500 ft. I found nothing fresh here worth mentioning save my second dwarf rhododendron (*R. anthopogon*), with its aromatic dark green leaves and dainty flowers exactly the colour of Devonshire cream ; a second and still more insignificant gentian ; a yellow geum like *montanum* of our own Alps and growing in the same alpine situations—*Geum elatum* ; and an insolent profusion of *Primula denticulata*. Those who have witnessed with pardonable pride the cabbage-like masses this plant makes in our own gardens will possibly be surprised to learn that at this height it was growing smaller in stature than our native *farinosa*, though with larger flowers. Yet at one spot the ground was a solid purple for hundreds of yards with its millions.

Down for the last time we dropped to 5,000 ft. in the gorge of the Dhaoli River, to the level of flies and dust and cattle and comparative aridity. These big river valleys are definitely drier than the ridges on either side—an observation which was confirmed on our return journey down the valley of the Alaknanda Ganges, where we often walked completely dry, while monsoon storms raged in the hills on either side. Consequently of alpines proper I found but few. I can only record from these levels the two androsaces—*lanuginosa* and *primuloides*—and a sub-shrubby cliff-dweller, something like a rich rose penstemon, called *Amphicome arguta*, of which I got good seed.

Our way led us through precipitous gorges, sometimes naked of vegetation, sometimes sparsely clothed with gnarled and picturesque deodars, to the last group of villages, where, at 10,000 to 11,000 ft., the valley opens out again. Here we were clearly under the influence of the droughty winds of Tibet, blowing down unchecked from the Niti Pass and the Raikana Glacier. The forest ended, and the bare moor was clothed with a painfully prickly undergrowth of wild roses, and two gorse-like bushes which rejoice in the name of *Caragana Gerardiana* and *crassicaulis*, and which grow just high enough to torture your bare knees. Here on the evanescent snowfields, alone, I enjoyed my first ski-tour. I climbed to a peak of between 15,000 and 16,000 ft., and, prolonging my run some distance by using the compacted snow of an old avalanche, I ran down 4,000 ft. on perfect spring snow. Where the snow gave out, I took off my ski and basked amid masses of the azure blue *Iris kumaonensis*. This plant begins at about 10,000 ft., choosing always the stonier, bleaker, sun-scorched spots to grow on, and followed us up almost to the Raikana Glacier Base Camp. It blooms as soon as the snow has left it. I brought back its rhizomes, some of which I hear are making a good recovery.

By June 1, winter had barely left the Niti Valley and the Raikana Valley beyond. The hillside was bare and brown, and scarred with avalanche snow. I may as well leave the description of its floral beauty for some weeks, until

Kamet has been climbed, and we could rest our eyes, seared and dazzled by three weeks of ice and snow and rocks, on green meadows and brilliant flowers. The great difference between these and alpine summits is that whereas, when one stands at the top of a great peak in Switzerland, one can always rest the eyes on some green valley at one's feet, here, so vast is the scale, and from the midst of so vast a glacial system does Kamet rise, that for days on end one sees nothing but stark black and red rocks, white snow, and green ice. Plants, of course, grew—dingy and uninteresting things—even on the chaos of boulders and moraine with which the lower lengths of every Himalayan glacier are strewn. The highest plants I collected were from an unnamed peak of 20,500 ft. in the second part of the expedition. Smythe actually found one on the rock wall of Kamet, at over 21,000 ft., as he was hammering in a piton. He threw it down to me, who was at the other end of his rope ; but I failed to make the catch, and the adventurous crucifer, as it probably was, was lost to science.

On our way down from the Base Camp, we found that three weeks had worked wonders. First of all a tiny and exquisite androsace, of the *Chamæjasme* section—*Androsace globifera*—was in bloom, with its tiny balls of silver wool and comparatively huge flowers of rich cerise. Drabas and another choice crucifer with flowers of mauve and white and yellow and *Geranium pratense* decorated the bare river gravel. On grassy patches, potentillas, red and yellow, ran riot ; while, true to its name, the almost top-heavy blooms of *Anemone rupicola* haunted the rocks. On peat-beds where the creamy dwarf rhododendron grew, *Cassiope fastigiata* recalled our own marsh heather. *Viola biflora*, denizen of woodland paths in the Alps, appeared here on the bleak mountain-side. At one point, to my great joy, I found *Meconopsis aculeata* in bud ; but more of that later. At another, where water oozed through and over a slaty scree, I found a third primula, the well-beloved *involucrata*, and on dry rocks by the path-side a dainty cousin of " the King of the Alps," *Eritrichium strictum*. Everywhere—on rocks, on grass, and in scree—*Androsace primuloides* was in prodigal splendour, but never so dainty as where its nodding umbels danced in the breeze from the top of a rocky bluff. Back in the highest villages at " cow-level," *Anemone rivularis* was coming into bloom—a domestic, home-loving creature this, unhappy on the open moor, but revelling in the well-manured grass by the path-side.

In order to accomplish the second objective of our expedition, the exploration of the Alaknanda–Gangotri watershed, it was necessary to cross the Kamet Range at some point which brought us down into the Badrinath Valley not too far from Badrinath. Smythe decided to make use of the Bhyundar Kanta Pass leading to the Khanta Khal Pass, the first a glacier pass of nearly 17,000 ft., the second consisting of grass and scree at about 15,000 ft. The Bhyundar Valley, which lies between these two, is a valley of astonishing beauty, containing the richest flora, both in respect of variety and luxuriance, that we had ever seen. The big glacial valleys themselves such as the Mana and Raikana Valleys, are too exposed to Tibet to provide a really rich flora. Moreover, their floors consist of recently accumulated glacial débris, and the combination of poor soil and comparative aridity militates against luxuriance of plant life. In the Bhyundar Valley conditions are very different : here the dry winds of Tibet are shut off by steep mountain walls, and the valley runs down steeply in a south-westerly direction, to join the Alaknanda Valley near Joshimath, providing a funnel up which, as we passed, one could see warm, steamy monsoon clouds surging as from a kettle's mouth. Probably the valley receives a very much bigger rainfall than the Raikana or Mana Valleys. It would be interesting to know. If such is the case, the great depth of rich soil on the valley floor might be explained by the more rapid denudation of the mountain walls on either side. For the benefit of any future plant-collectors who may explore these parts, it is worth noting that the best results are to be expected from these smaller side-valleys running east and west, where similar climatic differences may be expected. Again I noticed that, where the alpine forests consist of birch-trees, one may also expect good things in the way of plants.

It was a miserable day when we crossed the Bhyundar Kanta Pass. The wind blew, and a cold rain fell on the snow-covered glacier. My frostbitten toe cried out in anguish. The pass itself was swathed in flying mist, and was only discovered with difficulty. We were all soon soaked to the skin. At the top we had to wait for the porters, who were making very heavy weather of the march. Eventually the cold and wet made us so miserable that we dropped down some 400 ft. on the other side to get out of the wind. The snow soon gave out on to steep, shelving rocks intersected with runnels of water. We halted here to continue our vigil. All of a sudden I realised that I was simply surrounded by primulas. At once the day seemed to brighten perceptibly. Forgotten were all pains and cold and lost porters. And what a primula it was! Its leek-like habit proclaimed it a member of the *nivalis* section. All over the little shelves and terraces it grew, often with its roots in running water. At the most it stood six inches high; but its flowers were enormous for its stature, and ample in number—sometimes as many as thirty to the beautifully proportioned umbel, and in colour of the most heavenly French blue, sweetly scented. Only occasionally did they deepen to lilac, and in one case I picked an almost perfectly pure white flower. I am not understating the case when I say that it puts *Primula* "*Linda Pope*" completely in the shade. I am disappointed, however, to have to say that the "powers that be" do not allow it specific rank, but relegate it firmly to the humble status of "a form of *Primula nivalis macrophylla*," which I happened to find myself later. Yet I *will* state my case on behalf of the plant. The two forms are absolutely different in size and stature, the type plant being twice the size and having quite broad leaves. This pale blue form, in addition, has very narrow leaves, grows always within a belt of 1,000 ft. round about the 16,000 ft. level, and insists on the wettest situation, close to the melting snow, while the deep purple type-plant is content with a normal peaty bank 2,000 ft. lower down. This blue primula will be a devil to cultivate, so extreme are the conditions which it seems to demand. But anyone who can manage it will have a real treasure.

On harder, drier banks of peat I came across the first of two tiny dwarf primulas (*P. minutissima*) tiny in size, tinier even than the European *Primula minima*, with narrow, serrated leaves and a bright pink, starry flower. In the same sort of place there were dense hummocks of silvery wool, covered with the charming white flowers characteristic of the haughty *aretian* section of androsace. This turns out to be the extremely rare *Androsace poissonii*. It resembles very much *Androsace helvetica* of our own Alps, though, unlike *helvetica*, which insists on growing in rock-walls, it spreads into big masses in open peaty places and seems to need no stone. As a testimony to its minute charm I need only say that, though barely half an inch high, it impressed its personality on all the members of the expedition without my aid. Lower down, first *Androsace globifera* and next *primuloides* resumed the family history, and *Primulas denticulata* and *involucrata* took up the tale of primula. Still in mist and rain we stumbled over a glacier and crossed the moraine on to its right bank, where slopes of rich red loam provided a home for a thousand lovely flowers. The two dwarf rhododendrons ran riot, and in amongst them the *Anemone narcissiflora* grew in drifts of huge plants. Lower down we were to see it turn the hill-side white four miles away ! Soon in stately groups, among giant boulders, shone the first flowers of the Kashmir blue poppy—*Meconopsis aculeata*—blue as the sky at dawn, and even on that gloomy day shining from afar, as though it contained in its silky petals enough radiance to be independent of the sun. It seems a pity that we see so little of this poppy in cultivation. It is of course a biennial, but seems in nature to have few fads, provided that it can enjoy the shady side of a great boulder. In fact, I learnt to seek out from afar such wildernesses of tumbled stones, sure of finding there my poppy. It was interesting to notice its seed germinating by the million in little rock caverns in dense shade, where none could live for long. Nature's way with blue poppies at any rate is the "survival of the fittest." Only once did I see a dingy colour form of this, the only species I found.

Rough alp gave way to lusher meadows, where among primulas, geranium and forget-me-not grew four choice bulbs. First I was puzzled for a long time by a graceful indigo-coloured flower. Not till I had dug a bulb up did I come to the conclusion that it was a nomocharis (*N. nana*). Another, daffodil-yellow, and lily-like, I easily recognised as such. This turns out to be *Nomocharis oxypetala.* The third was a fine green and chequered fritillary (*F. Roylei*). The fourth was a lloydia, with a rich chestnut centre to its pearly star (*L. Tibetica*). Still lower down the valley, at 11,000 or 12,000 ft., we were over knee-deep in grass and flowers. Here in the light shade of shrubs I found two plants of a rosy cypripedium (*C. Himalaicum*), and the purple cart-wheels of a great aster (possibly *A. diplostephioides*) peered up at us from the rank herbage.

Two nights we camped in the lovely Bhyundar Valley, and where we pitched out tents it was impossible to cut a sod of turf from the ground without destroying a primula or a fritillary. For us it will always remain "the Valley of Flowers."

On the way to our next, the Khanta Khal Pass, by the streamside, growing with our own marsh marigold, and looking not unlike a semi-double form of it, with divided leaves, I gathered *Trollius acaulis*, which would be a welcome inmate of the small bog-garden. Higher up, at 14,000 ft. I had chosen a route diverging from that followed by our main body, when, by the side of a big boulder, a flare of the most imperial purple caught my eye. I hastened up, mystified, and found a huge and handsome primula, which turns out to be the typical form of *Primula nivalis macrophylla*. This is a stout-growing splendour, massive as the well-known *Primula chionantha*, which is the most amenable of the difficult group of *nivalis*, with huge flowers of deepest purple and a rich, almost meretricious scent, quite different from the dainty and distinctive odour of the pale blue form.

At the summit of the pass we admired again the dainty loveliness of *Androsace poissonii*, but our porters were far more interested in a curious white lichen, which is much prized by them as incense. Soon we were pushing our way through dense masses of dwarf rhododendron, *Geum elatum*, anemone, and a vast thistle-like plant, called *Morina persica*, with pretty pink flowers in the axils of its leaves. And so through still denser thickets of bamboo, berberis and wild roses till we reached the "Pilgrim Way," and thence up by the path polished by the feet of a million pilgrims to holy Badrinath.

In the last stages of our expedition we came across a few more noteworthy plants, though my own appetite was now rather jaded by the luxurious fare provided by the Bhyundar Valley. The big glacial valley leading up to the Mana Pass was too dry for much beyond the usual feast of androsace and potentilla, with here and there, among the big boulders which they love, a group of blue poppies. Higher up, as we entered the Arwa Valley, and I was traversing a peaty slope, my eye once more caught the unmistakably live glow of a primula. There were, as a matter of fact, two species growing side by side in the shade of a big boulder in dark moss-covered soil : the first another genuine dwarf—*Primula reptans*—only distinguishable from *Primula minutissima* by its rounded or spoon-shaped (not lanceolate) leaves, and by the amethyst (not pink) flowers ; the second—*Primula ellyptica*—is a species in the group of *farinosa*, and nearest in appearance to the well-known *Primula rosea*. It is, I believe, in cultivation, though only too rarely seen. It is less robust in habit than *rosea*, and its flowers, two or three to the head, are pure violet. In the almost completely stony floor of the Arwa Valley a handsome willow-herb revelled on a Spartan diet—*Epilobium latifolium*—whose gay magenta flowers our Darjeeling porters recognised and admired. More valuable and more subtly fascinating was a pale pink dwarf pyrethrum known as *Allardia tomentosa*, whose finely cut foliage is densely clothed in white wool. This also, I believe, is in cultivation. It should make a splendid moraine plant, though against a background of pale limestone, it should be remembered, both foliage and flowers would be almost invisible. Potentillas, of course, were happy in the dry stony ground. The daintiest of the *fruticosa* group was a variety called *inglesii*. It grows at a great height, from 16,000 to 19,000 ft., and hugs the rock-walls, forming a tight hummock, three inches high, of silky, emerald leaves, starred with moderate-sized but perfectly formed flowers of the usual metallic gold. Delphiniums are usually regarded as hearty, if not gross, feeders ; but here, in the most pitiless of shingles, with apparently no particle of soil, was one growing into lush clumps of ample leaves, over which nodded comfortable fat flowers of rich steely blue, frosted over with hairs—*Delphinium brunonianum*. No one who, not knowing its haunts, acquired a plant of it, would dream of treating it as a scree plant. The attractive genus of *cremanthodium* is represented on the Arwa Valley screes by one species only. I can best describe it, in the words of my diary, as " a dwarf high-alpine yellow sunflower, six inches high." I only found one specimen at 16,000 ft.—identified as *Cremanthodium plantagineum*. *Chorispora sabulosa* is one of the high-climbing crucifers, a compact tuft, smothered in dainty mauve flowers, which, if it were grown at home, would surely challenge the supremacy of the thlaspi genus. This also followed us up to 19,000 ft.

Having turned our backs regretfully at last on the regions of ice and snow, we returned to Badrinath, where the level pasture opposite the town was a sea of *Anemone rivularis* ; and on shorter turf grew an edelweiss, smaller and more tidy than the usual Alpine form. Curiously enough, the usual Alpine form was gathered in flower on a 19,000 ft. peak above the Arwa Valley by Smythe, Shipton and Greene. One would have expected the opposite, and that this very distinct small form would have been the higher climber. On these same fine lawns, but very rarely, grew the one species we found of a distinguished and increasingly popular Asiatic genus, *Cyananthus microphyllus*. It reminded me rather of the lovely autumn-blooming gentian of our own Alps, *Gentiana ciliata*, by reason of its steel-blue petals and fringe of hairs round the mouth of the corolla. The great race of campanula was scarcely represented at all in my collection. Two dingy weeds from the earlier marches have been identified as *Campanula colorata* and *sylvatica*, but *Campanula argyrotricha*, from rock-walls round Mana and Niti at about 11,000 ft., is a valuable plant of a different kidney, intensely saxatile in habit, and with dainty harebells of white, veined with chocolate. Last of all, on our way back in the Alaknanda Valley, by the roadside, in regions of sweltering heat and far below the level of any sensible alpine plant, I had almost put away my flower-press, when I suddenly saw on dripping dank cliffs a yellow-flowered primula. At first I was quite bewildered, wondering where I'd seen anything like it before, since I felt sure that I had. Eventually I realised that my ninth and last primula was one of the relatives (*Primula floribunda*) of the well-known greenhouse hybrid, *Kewensis*.

This account brings to an end my list of plants we found that are worth possessing ; but a few words may be added by way of summary. Botanically, our journey was more of a reconnaissance than a plant-collecting expedition proper. I have in every case indicated the height at which plants were found, in the hopes that this information will be helpful to any gardeners who come to possess the species we found. We were a small party of Europeans, and we were primarily engaged, all of us, in climbing. Botany and seed-collecting had to be incidental to the main object. I could not demand a day here or a day there in which to dry my seeds and specimens. My flower-press and seed-bags accompanied me up to the limit of vegetation in the back of my rucksack, and seeds and specimens had to take their chance. In the monsoon season, when we found many of our best plants, this chance was never very big, since it was difficult to get things dry. Moreover, in order to collect seeds properly it is necessary to revisit later in the season the spot where you have marked your plant in flower, so as to be sure of finding the seed ripe. We returned by a different way from our route up to the mountains, and so I missed the chance of finding ripe seed of many of the most precious plants. I did succeed in getting a few seeds and bulbs back in respectable condition, and these are in the hands of experts, though up to the time of going to press I have little news to give of their progress. I experimented with a few plants, extra specially rare or minute primulas and androsaces, packing them and, as I thought, sealing them hermetically in tins. But these, I regret to say, arrived either hopelessly withered or a stinking mass of corruption. To possess most of these plants we must rely on some professional collector thinking it worth while to visit the district and collect systematically. That his efforts would be worth while I hope I have proved. Of the plants I have mentioned, almost all are either not in cultivation, or else extremely rare. It is true, of course, that I discovered no new species, but it is by no means impossible that new species exist there and await discovery.

I have, I think, read, in one of Captain Kingdon Ward's books about plant-hunting in the Eastern Himalaya, that all the plants that grow above 12,000 ft. are almost impossible to grow in British gardens. This remark is especially applied to the smaller high-alpine primulas. Now, one cannot expect a high-alpine Himalayan primula to grow as easily and with the same treatment as Captain Kingdon Ward's triumphant introduction, *Primula florindæ*. But there are an increasing number of gardeners who can, and who find it worth while to compete with these beautiful difficulties, and who grow with triumphant success European high-alpines which come from heights where you get almost the same climatic extremities as in the high-alpine districts of the Himalaya. The few lucky and skilful gardeners who can grow *Eritrichium nanum* or *Jankæa heldreichi* need not be terrified by a primula from 16,000 ft. in the Himalaya. Of course, it is true that in the Himalaya the sun is nearly vertically overhead. But there are many easily grown Himalayans which submit meekly to our own less torrid sun. Again, conditions are admittedly more extreme in the Eastern Himalaya than in the more central ranges owing to the very heavy rain- or snowfall that the East receives. But I do not believe that actual height makes so much difference to ease of cultivation. Certainly in the Badrinath Ranges the edelweiss followed us up to 19,000 ft.; and what easier plant can man have to grow than the edelweiss? My experience on the Kamet expedition led me to conclude that in the alpine valleys of the Central Himalaya, from 10,000 to 14,000 ft. above the sea, conditions were much the same as in alpine valleys at from 5,000 to 7,000 ft. And we know from experience that most of the plants from this altitude in the Alps are easily cultivated in British rock-gardens. The high-alpine region of the Alps, from the botanical point of view, extends from 7,000 ft. to 10,000 or 11,000 ft., a height which is represented in the Central Himalaya by 14,000 to 18,000 ft. Most of the plants from this region in the Alps are successfully grown by careful rock-gardeners; so why should they not be able to compete with the high-alpines from similar regions of the Himalaya? To take an example: I noticed that the pale blue form of *Primula nivalis macrophylla* grows in almost precisely the same climatic situation as *Primula glutinosa* of the Tirol. The latter is cultivated successfully, so why should we fight shy of the former?

I have embarked on this argument because most of my own treasures came from great altitudes, and, if any expert collector goes out to Garhwal he must climb high for many of his plants. There are many enthusiastic gardeners who, I feel sure, would welcome these Himalayan high-alpines, and I write this in the hopes that some enterprising philanthropist will go and get us seed or plants, not merely of the easier, bigger species from comparatively low down, but of many a shy primula and gentian which haunts the more austere heights of that wonderful world.

INDEX OF PLANTS COLLECTED ON THE KAMET EXPEDITION, SHOWING HEIGHT AT WHICH FOUND

Abelia triflora	6,000– 9,000
Allardia tomentosa	13,000–15,000
Amphicome arguta	5,000– 8,000
Anaphallis nubigena	10,000–13,000
Androsace globifera	12,000–15,000
„ *lanuginosa*	6,000– 9,000
„ *poissonii*	15,000
„ *primuloides*	6,000–14,000
„ *rotundifolia*	5,000–13,000
Anemone narcissiflora	12,000–14,500
„ *obtusiloba* (blue and white forms)	8,000–11,000
„ „ (yellow form)	15,000–18,000
„ *rivularis*	7,000–12,000
„ *rupicola*	13,000–15,000
Arenarea glanduligera	16,000
Arisæma flavum	10,000–11,000
Aster diplostephioides (?)	11,000–12,000
Caltha palustris	11,000–13,000
Campanula argyrotricha	10,000–11,000
„ *colorata*	7,000– 9,000
„ *sylvatica*	6,000
Cassiope fastigiata	12,000–15,000
Caragana Gerardiana	8,000–12,000
„ *crassicaulis*	10,000–13,000
Chorispora sabulosa	16,000–19,000
Corydalis Cashmeriana	11,000–13,000
„ *govaniana*	10,000–11,000
„ *meifolia*	14,000
Crucifer (unknown)	13,000

Cremanthodium plantagineum	16,000
Cyananthus microphyllus	10,500
Cynoglossum Sp.	11,000–13,000
Cypripedium himalaicum	11,000–13,000
Daphne olæides	8,000– 9,000
Delphinium denudatum	7,000– 8,500
„ *brunonianum*	14,000
Draba lasiophylla	13,000–15,000
„ *incompta*	16,000–20,400
Epilobium latifolium	9,000–14,000
Erigeron Sp.	5,000– 9,000
Eritrichium strictum	13,000
Erysimum hieracifolium	6,000– 9,000
Fritillaria roylei	12,000–14,000
Gaultheria trichophylla	8,000–12,000
Gentiana aprica	4,000–12,000
„ *capitata*	12,500
Geranium pratense	10,000–14,000
„ *donianum*	12,000–14,000
„ *wallichianum*	9,000–11,000
Gerbera lanuginosa	7,000– 9,000
Geum elatum	12,000–13,500
Gloriosa superba	5,000– 7,000
Indigofera Gerardiana	6,000– 9,500
Iris kumaonensis	10,000–14,000
Leontopodium alpinum (type)	16,000–19,000
„ „ (small form)	10,000–12,000
Lloydia serotina	11,000–13,000
„ *tibetica*	13,000–14,000
Lonicera Sp.	15,500
Meconopsis aculeata	11,500–14,000
Morina persica	11,000–13,000
Nomocharis nana	13,000–14,000
„ *oxypetala*	11,000–13,500
Onosma Sp.	14,000
Oxalis corniculata	5,000– 9,000
Oxygraphis polypetala	12,500–13,500
Pæonia emodi	8,000–10,000
Paraquilegia microphylla	10,500–12,500
„ *grandiflora*	14,500
Parochetus communis	5,000– 8,500
Pedicularis siphonantha	14,000–15,000
„ *versicolor*	13,000–14,000
Pieris ovalifolia	7,000–10,000
Pleurospermum candolli	16,000–18,000
Polemonium cæruleum	11,000–13,000
Polygonum affine	11,500–13,000
„ *sphærostachyum*	9,500
Polygala crotalarioides	6,500
Potentilla ambigua	10,000–12,000
„ *argyrophylla* (yellow form)	11,500–13,500
„ „ (crimson form)	11,500–13,500
„ *fruticosa*, var. *inglesi*	16,000–19,000
„ „ „ *ochreata*	14,000–15,000

Primula denticulata	4,000–14,500
„ *ellyptica*	13,000–14,500
„ *floribunda*	3,500– 5,000
„ *involucrata*	12,500–14,000
„ *minutissima*	14,000–18,000
„ *nivalis macrophylla* (pale blue form)	15,000–16,500
„ *nivalis macrophylla* (type)	13,500–14,500
„ *reptans*	13,500
„ *sessilis*	10,500–12,500
Rhododendron anthopogon	11,000–14,500
„ *arboreum*	5,000–10,000
„ *barbatum*	9,500
„ *campanulatum*	10,500–13,500
„ *lepidotum*	9,000–14,000
Roscæa alpina	8,000–10,000
„ *purpurea*	4,500– 7,000
Saxifraga flagellaris	14,000–15,000
„ *imbricata*	10,500–19,000
Sedum crenulatum	14,000–16,000
„ *scabridum*	14,000–16,000
Senecio arnicoides	11,000
Strobilanthes alatus	6,000– 8,000
Thermopsis barbata	10,500–12,500
Trigonotis Sp.	12,500–14,000
„ *rotundifolia*	14,500
Trollius acaulis	13,000–14,000
Veronica capitata	14,000–16,000
Viburnum cotinifolium	8,000–10,000
Viola serpens	7,000–10,000
„ *biflora*	12,000–14,000
Wulfenia amherstiana	6,000– 9,000

APPENDIX I

SHORT SUMMARY OF EXPEDITION

1931.

April 22. Shipton and Smythe arrived at Ranikhet.

May 10. Birnie arrived at Ranikhet.

May 13. Fifty-five Dotial porters left Ranikhet with main stores under Sirdar Lewa. (Note : Five Garhwali porters were recruited *en route.*)

May 14. Beauman, Greene and Holdsworth arrived at Ranikhet.

May 18. Beauman, Birnie, Greene, Holdsworth, Shipton and Smythe left Ranikhet with eight Darjeeling porters and cook, two Gurkha N.C.O.s being picked up *en route*, and arrived Gwaldam.

May 19. Arrived Debal.

May 20. Arrived Lohajang.

May 21. Arrived Wan.

May 22. Arrived Kanaul.

May 23. Arrived Ramni.

May 24. Rest at Ramni.

May 25. Arrived Semkharak.

May 26. Arrived Khaliaghat.

May 27. Arrived Dakwani.

May 28. Crossed Kuari Pass. Arrived Tapoban.

May 29. Rest Tapoban.

May 30. Arrived Surai Thota.

May 31. Arrived Juma.

June 1. Arrived Malari.

June 2. Arrived Niti.

June 3. Reorganisation at Niti.

June 4. Reorganisation at Niti.

June 5. Arrived Goting.

June 6. Arrived Base Camp (15,500 ft.)

June 7. Preparing for high camps. Shipton and Holdsworth climbed 17,230 ft. peak near Base Camp.

June 8. Greene, Holdsworth, Shipton and Smythe establish Camp One on East Kamet Glacier at 16,600 ft.

June 9. First party establish Camp Two at 18,600 ft. Beauman and Birnie to Camp One.

June 10. Beauman and Birnie to Camp Two.

June 11. Rest day.

June 12. Greene, Holdsworth, Shipton and Smythe prospected site for Camp Three at 20,600 ft.

June 13. To Camp Three.

June 14–17. Prospecting route to Camp Four at 22,000 ft. and fixing ropes, etc., etc.

June 18. Shipton and Smythe to Camp Four assisted by Birnie and Holdsworth.

June 19. Remainder of party to Camp Four.

June 20. Holdsworth, Shipton and Smythe to Camp Five at 23,300 ft.

June 21. Holdsworth, Shipton and Smythe with Sirdar Lewa climbed Kamet, 25,447 ft. Nima Dorje, porter, reached 25,000 ft. Party frostbitten, Lewa's feet very badly frostbitten.

June 22. Lewa evacuated to Camp Three.

June 23. Birnie and Greene, with porter Kesar Singh,

climbed Kamet. Party frostbitten. Holdsworth reached Meade's Col, 23,500 ft., on ski.

June 24. Descended to Camp Three.

June 25. Main party to Camp Two. Beauman and Shipton with Lewa to Camp One. Holdsworth to Base Camp on ski.

June 26. Remainder of expedition to Base Camp.

June 27–29. At Base Camp.

June 30. Left Base Camp. Camped by Dhaoli River.

July 1. Arrived Goting.

July 2. Arrived Gamsali.

July 3–4. At Gamsali.

July 5. To Thur Udiar.

July 6. To Eri Udiar.

July 7. Holdsworth and Shipton reached point 300 ft. below summit of 19,815 ft. peak.

July 8. Shipton with porter Nima climbed 19,815 ft. peak. Beauman and Greene explored head of Banke Glacier.

July 9. Crossed Bhyundar Kanta Pass, 16,700 ft., descending to Bhyundar Valley.

July 10. Moved camp down Bhyundar Valley.

July 11. Crossed Khanta Khal Pass, 14,750 ft., and camped 1,000 ft. above Hanuman Chatti.

July 12. Arrived Mana.

July 13–14. Reorganisation at Mana.

July 15. To Ghastoli.

July 16. To 15,000 ft. camp Arwa Valley.

July 17. To 16,000 ft. camp Arwa Valley.

July 18. Greene, Shipton and Smythe climbed 19,500 ft. peak. Beauman, Birnie and Holdsworth explored glacier west of camp to 19,000 ft.

July 19. To camp at 19,000 ft., traversing *en route* 19,000 ft. peak.

July 20. Birnie, Holdsworth, Shipton and Smythe climbed to 20,000 ft. pass on watershed of Badrinath Range. Shipton and Smythe climbed 20,800 ft. peak above pass. Birnie and porter Dorje crossed pass and re-traversed watershed by another pass.

July 21. Shipton and Smythe with porter Nima attempted 21,800 ft. peak (Avalanche Peak), but returned in snowstorm.

July 22. Shipton, Smythe and porter Nima, and Birnie and porter Dorje, climbed Avalanche Peak. Smythe injured by avalanche in descent.

July 23. Beauman, Greene and Holdsworth climbed 20,500 ft. rock peak.

July 24. Decided to split expedition into three parties.

July 25–27. Beauman, Greene and Smythe returned to Mana.

July 25–29. Birnie with porters crossed 20,000 ft. pass and explored Gangotri side of watershed and returned to Arwa Valley by another pass. Holdsworth and Shipton ascended three peaks of 21,500 ft., 21,000 ft., and 20,400 ft. in neighbourhood of 19,000 ft. camp.

July 28–29. Greene and Smythe ascended Alaknanda Valley to source of Alaknanda River.

July 30–31. Shipton and porter Nima climbed 19,000 ft. peak near Mana.

August 1. Expedition at Badrinath.

August 3. Arrived Joshimath.

August 4. To Gulabkota.

August 5. To Pepolkota.

PEAKS CLIMBED BY HOLDSWORTH AND SHIPTON, NORTH OF 19,000 FT. CAMP

August 6. To Chamoli.
August 7. To Sonala.
August 8. To Karnaprayag.
August 10. To Lohba.
August 12. To Dwarahat.
August 13. To Ranikhet.

APPENDIX II

PEAKS CLIMBED BY THE EXPEDITION

Peak	*Height*	*Party*
Kamet*	25,447 ft.	First Party: Holdsworth, Shipton, Smythe; Porter Lewa. Second Party: Birnie and Greene; Porter Kesar Singh.
Avalanche Peak	21,800 ft.	Shipton, Smythe and Porter Nima; Birnie and Porter Dorje
Un-named	21,500 ft.	Holdsworth and Shipton; Porter Ang Nerbu
Un-named	21,000 ft.	Holdsworth and Shipton
Un-named	20,800 ft.	Shipton and Smythe
Un-named	20,500 ft.	Beauman and Greene
Un-named	20,400 ft.	Holdsworth and Shipton
Un-named*	19,810 ft.	Shipton and Porter Nima
Un-named	19,500 ft.	Greene, Shipton, Smythe; Porter Nima
Un-named	19,000 ft.	Beauman, Birnie, Shipton, Greene, Smythe; Porter Nima Dorje
Un-named	19,000 ft.	Shipton and Porter Nima
Un-named*	17,230 ft.	Holdsworth and Shipton

NOTE: In addition to the above five passes were traversed, three for the first time.

* Triangulated peaks. Other heights by aneroid only.

APPENDIX III

THE ASCENT OF KAMET

Showing distribution of personnel and tents on June 21, 1931
(*from information supplied by Captain Birnie*)

SUMMIT (25,447 ft.)

First Summit Party

Holdsworth
Shipton
Smythe
Lewa (Darjeeling porter)
Nima Dorje (Darjeeling porter)

CAMP V (23,300 ft.)

	Support Party
3 Meade tents	Beauman
1 Norwegian tent	Birnie
1 Porter tent	Greene
	Lance Naik Randhoj Kan
	Lance Naik Budhibal Gurung
	Passang (Darjeeling)
	Dorje "
	Nima "
	Ondi "
	Nerbu "

CAMP IV (22,000 ft.)

1 Meade tent

CAMP III (20,600 ft.)

2 Meade tents	Kesar Singh and 5
1 porter tent	equipped men (local)

CAMP II (18,600 ft.)

1 porter tent	Nima Tendrup (Darjeeling)
Shelters	Ang Nerbu ,,

CAMP I (16,600 ft.)

1 porter tent	Naitar Singh and 5 unequipped men (local)

BASE CAMP (15,600 ft.)

1 mess tent	Alam Singh, Achung, 2 post-
1 porter tent	men and 5 unequipped men (local)

Note.—The second ascent was made on June 23 by Birnie, Greene and Kesar Singh. It will be seen that Kesar Singh climbed from Camp III (20,600 ft.) to the summit in two days without having acclimatised higher than Camp III.

APPENDIX IV

WEATHER

HIGH mountain peaks are subject climatically both to local weather influences brought about by variations of temperature and humidity and to general weather influences. It has been said with truth that " mountains make their own weather," and it is difficult to generalise on Himalayan weather, owing to the number of local influences at work. Generally speaking, however, it may be said that the greater the distance a peak is from the plains of India, the more reliable is the weather. The exception to this rule occurs when peaks rise close to deep valleys that cut into the Himalaya from the plains. The fickleness of the weather obtaining on Everest is due to the fact that it stands so near to the great Arun Valley, which forms not only a natural channel for bad weather, but, owing to its own heat and humidity, manufactures local bad weather and high winds. Kangchenjunga is another example of a great peak constantly subjected to local influences, for there are valleys within but a few miles of it cloaked in dense tropical vegetation, the steamy floors of which are only 2,000 or 3,000 ft. above sea-level.

As regards local influences, Kamet is more happily situated than most great peaks in the Central Himalaya. It does not stand so close to deep tropical valleys as does Everest or Kangchenjunga, but rises from the northern extremity of the Zaskar Range, a northern bifurcation of the Himalayan chain, and the rise in altitude per mile from the deep tropical valleys is comparatively gradual. Thus, the temperature range is graded gradually, and Kamet, despite its great elevation, is incapable of manufacturing bad weather to compare with that manufactured by Everest or Kangchenjunga, for it has not the material with which to do it.

Strong westerly winds are notorious in the Eastern Himalaya, resulting from convection air currents due to the inflow of cold air from the snows and the plains of Tibet to take the place of the hot air rising from the tropical valleys on the Indian side. Not once while we were on Kamet did we encounter winds to rival in velocity those that were experienced on Kangchenjunga in 1930; the same influences were at work, but in a lesser degree. As on Kangchenjunga, winds were always strongest at night, and this is due to the difference in temperature between the valleys on the Indian side of the Himalaya and the Tibetan plateaux being greater at night than in the daytime. During the day both are warmed by the sun. At night, however, radiation from the elevated plateaux of Tibet is much greater than it is from the deep valleys, which tend to retain their warmth.

It is interesting to observe on Kamet how, at about nine in the morning, what wind there was suddenly dropped, only to manifest itself again at sunset. As on Kangchenjunga and Everest, the general trend of the wind on Kamet is westerly or north-westerly during the day, but tending to veer in a more northerly direction at night. I have not been able to discover records of summer snowstorms on Kamet comparable to those that make Kangchenjunga and Everest such terrible adversaries to the mountaineer. The only snowstorms we experienced were desultory in character, and precipitated but a few inches of snow. The desultory nature of these storms was due largely to the dryness of the westerly Tibetan wind. During the monsoon season the difference in precipitation between Kamet and the main chain of the Himalaya to the south is marked. Owing to the fact that so many foothill ranges separate Kamet from the plains of India, and the intervention of the main range of Himalayan peaks which break the force of the monsoon and relieve it of much of its moisture, only the strongest bursts of the monsoon penetrate to Kamet.

During the monsoon season it was interesting to observe the constant battle between the dry westerly Tibetan winds and the moisture-charged clouds from the south that had survived the foothills and the main range. Mass after mass of great cumuli would flood up the valleys of the Alaknanda and Dhaoli, only to meet annihilation from the westerly wind, which sheared them off as though it was a knife. So abrupt is this line of sheer between the two weather systems that in some valleys it is responsible for a difference of scenery between one side of the valley and the other. The difference between the northern and southern sides of the Arwa Valley is so marked that the only explanation is that the Arwa Valley is a natural funnel for the westerly wind, and forms the boundary of the two weather systems. This is borne out by the fact that the peaks bounding the southern side of the valley are of a snowy nature, and send down large glaciers to a low level, whilst those bounding the northern side have had much less snow precipitated on them, and their glaciers are correspondingly smaller.

At Mana, we were told by the villagers that only a week or ten days of bad weather was experienced as a rule during the monsoon season, and a few miles farther north the bad weather period is of less duration. Thus, a mountaineer might climb and experience fair weather throughout the monsoon season by keeping near to the Tibetan frontier in northern Garhwal, which it would be impossible to do with success and enjoyment in the neighbourhood of Trisul and Nanda Devi or on the ranges south of Badrinath.

Climbing during the monsoon season can be accomplished with the minimum of discomfort, for the weather is extraordinarily warm, and it is possible to sit on the summit of peaks over 20,000 ft. in the thinnest of clothing basking in a warm sun, or at the worst surrounded by sluggish mists. There is no doubt that the siege tactics which we had planned for Kamet would have enabled us to have climbed it during the monsoon season, for although the weather then was unsettled as compared with the weather before the monsoon, little precipitation took place on the upper part of the mountain. Had we climbed Kamet then, it is hardly likely that we should have suffered so severely from the cold. On the other hand, snow conditions might have been much worse, owing to the warmth, and under monsoon conditions it is possible that the final slopes might be dangerously avalanchy.

Those mountaineers who are not concerned with trying to climb the greatest peaks in the Himalaya, and who find their happiest hours on mountains of a lesser magnitude, can scarcely do better than outwit the monsoon and climb throughout the summer in the magnificent district north and north-west of Badrinath.

No doubt I am prejudiced in favour of the climate of Garhwal, and it is only fair to state that the season during which we climbed Kamet and explored the Badrinath Range was from all accounts an exceptionally fine one, and not for many years has such dry weather been experienced at Ranikhet and other hill stations on the foothills prior to the monsoon. Yet, if the experiences of former expeditions in this district are to be taken as indicative of the weather prevailing there, the foregoing details are applicable to an average season.

APPENDIX V

FOOD

THE IMPORTANCE of being provided with the right foodstuffs in Himalayan mountaineering can scarcely be over-estimated. Happiness or unhappiness, even success or failure, are determined by the inner autocrat of man. It may be an excellent thing on some obscure grounds of self-immolation to subsist in acute discomfort on a Spartan diet, but a Spartan diet is not going to get a man to the highest summits of the world. Mentally as well as physically the mountaineer requires the best and most varied foods that can be provided. Variety is as essential as quality, for lack of it inevitably induces boredom, and boredom on a mountain is tantamount to a defeatist attitude of mind. Something new is always to be learnt about food, and it is for this reason that I propose to deal in some detail with this all-important question, in the hope that the lessons learnt from the expedition may be of value to future expeditions.

An expedition must be fed first of all on its journey to its Base Camp, and then above its Base Camp on the mountain. It is well known that travellers who pass along the lower valleys and over the foothills of the Himalaya are often afflicted by stomach disorders which manifest themselves in mild forms of colic, constipation, and diarrhœa. Occasional bouts of this may result in no harm being done, but anyone afflicted continuously is liable to have his strength impaired for the exacting work of high climbing, whilst his whole mental outlook may be changed and he may become soured, disappointed and "fed up" with the expedition. How is this to be avoided? I believe that the cause of it is mainly due to extraneous matter in the food and water, coupled to poorly cooked food. Thus, the stomach disorders that are so commonly experienced at Ranikhet, and which are known locally as "Ranikhetitis," are mainly due to particles of mica in the local drinking-water and to dust, including mica, in the food, which sets up a local bowel irritation. The same trouble is probably experienced in all those parts of the Himalaya where mica schist exists and dust is blown about by the wind. It goes without saying that all water passing near houses or through cultivated land should be boiled if cholera, dysentery, typhoid and other diseases are to be avoided, particularly during the monsoon season when filth of all kinds is washed into the streams, but such boiling does not remove extraneous matter. I would strongly urge future expeditions to filter their water whenever possible, and this might be very easily accomplished by taking a small portable filter, or, failing that, filtration through linen cloths would remove much extraneous matter. Had we done this, our own slight internal ailments might have been further reduced.

Local flour should be avoided. It is coarse, and invariably contains much dust and grit which cannot be removed from it. Local rice should always be sifted. Another cause of stomach trouble is due to eating improperly cooked chupatties. I know of no more indigestible dish than the improperly cooked chupatti. If these are to be eaten, though they are best avoided altogether, they should be as thin and crisp as a wafer biscuit. They should break, not bend, for it is their uncooked doughy centre that is responsible for the trouble. Those hardened to Himalayan and Indian conditions by virtue of long residence may scoff at the foregoing, but those who come out from England will do well to mark it well.

The fact that we suffered for the most part from only minor disorders is, I believe, due to our avoiding local food so far as possible with the exception of fresh meat, which is unlikely to contain extraneous matter. We ate a certain number of chupatties during our journey to our Base Camp, but they were made from our own pure flour brought from Ranikhet. Their indigestible quality, however, forced those of us with the most susceptible stomachs to abandon them in favour of biscuits. The special " Expedition " biscuits kindly supplied by Messrs. Huntley & Palmer are the ideal campaigning substitute for bread, whilst other varieties such as " Krispbread " and " Oaten " were equally palatable.

Another important consideration, and one that is liable to be neglected, is the adequate provision of food containing the vital anti-scorbutic vitamin C. How much so-called " altitude deterioration " is due to lack of this essential vitamin is difficult to determine, but there is a strong probability that the deterioration, both mental and physical, experienced by some Himalayan expeditions in the past was partly due to lack of it. Polar explorers say that it is possible to go without fresh food of any kind for a considerable time. This may be possible at low altitudes, or at a few thousand feet above sea-level, where the evil effects of deterioration are not so obvious, but over 20,000 ft. the slightest ailment is magnified many times. Failing fresh fruit, vegetables and meat, pure lime-juice is probably the best and most easily assimilated anti-scorbutic. I venture to question whether raisins or any other forms of dried fruit or vegetables possess any beneficial anti-scorbutic property.

We took with us a quantity of lime-juice, and this was taken regularly by all members of the expedition. We were also able to obtain, up to about 12,000 ft., wild rhubarb, bracken-shoots, and on one or two occasions small wild onions. There seems no reason, however, why a supply of apples, green bananas, and lemons should not be taken by an expedition. Assuming these were eaten during an expedition of three months, and that six each of these fruits go to 1 lb. weight, this would mean a total weight of but 42 lbs. per man if each man was to eat one apple, banana, and lemon per day. Fruit might also prove useful as supplying acid to the body as compensation for the lack of bodily acidity which results from oxygen lack at high altitudes. If, in addition to fresh fruit, lime-juice was also taken, it is certain that the health of the mountaineer would be well cared for in regard to the anti-scorbutic vitamin.

As regards cooking, we were unlucky in having a bad cook, and most of the slight stomach troubles experienced must be laid at his door. Owing to high blood-pressure he was relegated to the Base Camp, and on Kamet what cooking was necessary was skilfully done by two of our other men. Our stomachs remained remarkably healthy taking into account the effects of altitude, which tend to upset the digestion. After two Himalayan expeditions I can only say that the importance of having a good cook cannot be over-estimated.

There is probably no more active or hard-working animal than the Garhwali sheep, for it is used as a beast of burden, and carries loads of grain, etc., over the passes into Tibet. For this reason it is lean and sinewy, and its flesh would test the teeth of a mastodon and the digestion of an ostrich. Thus, a mincing machine is an essential item of culinary equipment.

The dirtiness of native cooks is proverbial, and utensils, particularly aluminium pans, should be periodically inspected, including the mincing machine, which should be frequently cleaned to rid it of pieces of putrifying meat.

Actually, we reckoned on keeping most of our tinned meats for use above the Base Camp on Kamet and relying upon obtaining local mutton, chicken and eggs from the villages and pastures through which we passed, and on shooting bharhal (wild sheep). In this we were not disappointed, and our foodstuffs, with one or two exceptions, lasted out so well that we arrived back at Ranikhet with a supply in hand.

So far as the Base Camp, food, provided it is wholesome, well cooked and free from impurities, need not be carefully studied, but above the Base Camp its importance cannot be over-estimated.

At high altitudes the body resembles an engine that must be constantly supplied with fuel for heating and running—not fuel in large quantities at a time, tending to choke it, but small quantities at short intervals. This fuel is sugar. An excellent idea on a mountain is to carry a pocketful of lump sugar or sweets that do not induce thirst.

When planning an expedition, the leader will do well to estimate for the amount of sugar he thinks will be required and then double his estimate. I made the mistake of not estimating for enough sugar, but fortunately there is plenty of goa (native sugar) to be obtained in the upper valleys of Garhwal. I suspect, however, that the shortage of sugar was not entirely due to the voraciousness of the Europeans in the party, and future expeditions will do well to keep their sugar in sealed and numbered 1lb. bags which can easily be checked.

The most valuable alcoholic drink is rum, because of the sugar it contains. During a climb, alcohol is more dangerous than useful, but as a night-cap I know of nothing to equal a drink of hot rum. Unlike other alcoholic stimulants, it keeps the body in a warm glow for the remainder of the night, and best of all it induces sleep.[1] Other stimulants such as whisky and brandy should be kept purely as luxuries or for emergencies.

Fresh meat was taken up to Camp Three, 20,600 ft., and buried in the snow there, but above that point it was not easy to digest meats with the exception of tinned sausages, tongues, sardines, etc., and the craving for sugary foods became more and more pronounced. Jam, sweetened condensed milk, chocolate, sweets, tinned fruits, etc., all satisfy this craving. Hot cups of " Ovaltine " or Horlick's " Malted Milk " are excellent at night. Bovril pemmican represents the easiest way of taking meat, but should be well diluted owing to its essential fattiness. It is one of the most concentrated foods known and is an excellent standby in case of emergency.

[1] See also page 211.

Porridge can be eaten at any altitude, and so also can eggs, which also supply any meat that the body may require.

Food on Kamet was carefully rationed and apportioned, and a final word is due to Shipton, whose task this was. As with cooking, the work of rationing is more likely to evoke blame than praise, and the fact that it worked without a hitch on Kamet goes to prove how efficient were the arrangements of Shipton.

FOOD LIST

This list is intended as a guide to those who may be contemplating similar expeditions. It is not an exhaustive list, but merely intended to give some indication of general requirements. It does not include fresh food obtained locally.

Special " Expedition " biscuits (Huntley & Palmer).
Assorted biscuits, sweetened and unsweetened.
White flour.
Quaker Oats.
Chocolate, milk and plain, tinned (Nestlé's).
Condensed milk, sweetened and unsweetened (Nestlé's).
Malted milk powder (Horlick's).
Malted milk tablets (Horlick's).
Ovaltine.
Pasteurised butter, tinned (Polson's).
Tea.
Coffee.
Cocoa.
Sugar, lump and granulated, in 1lb. sealed and numbered bags.

Salt.
Pepper.
Mustard.
Pemmican (Bovril).
Meats, sausages, and vegetables (tinned) (special self-heating tinned meats are excellent).
Fish (tinned).
Raisins (seedless).
Curry powder.
Herbs for flavouring.
Sauces (various).
Jams and marmalade (assorted, tinned, in both large and small 4oz. tins).
Nuts (shelled, assorted).
Golden syrup.
Baking powder.
Spaghetti.
Macaroni.
Sago.
Rice.
Tapioca.
Arrowroot (good when light diet after stomach trouble is necessary).
Ginger cubes.
Mint cake.
Bull's eyes (glass jars).
Fruit drops (assorted).
Other sweetmeats.
Various delicacies, such as *pâté de fois gras*, tinned cod roe, etc.
Cereals (to choice).

Dripping (tinned).
Lime-juice.
Fresh limes, apples, oranges, bananas, lemons.
Whisky, brandy and rum.
Pickles and chutney.
Dried fruits (assorted).
Dried vegetables.
Fruits (assorted, tinned).
Suet (tinned).
Custard powder.
Jelly powder.
Spices, cloves.
Essences for flavouring.
Soups (assorted).
Currants.
Fruit cake (tinned).

APPENDIX VI

EQUIPMENT[1]

These notes are not intended to be comprehensive, but to give information, to those who may be planning similar expeditions, on various important particulars.

As PREVIOUSLY explained, difficulties of transport in the Himalaya are directly proportional to the load carried. The weight of equipment, therefore, must be reduced to the absolute minimum. At the same time, warmth and comfort must never be sacrificed for lightness, for on these two factors rest the enjoyment and even the success of an expedition.

TENTS

Light tents are useless for prolonged high-altitude mountaineering. Fabric must be windproof and waterproof and able to stand up to hard wear. The best fabric is "Willesden" canvas. Tents supplied by Messrs. Edgington were of the Meade pattern. In shape they are book-form, with Λ supports at either end consisting of sectional ash-poles. They were fitted with eaves on either side, and from these run guy-ropes. Thus water can drain off the eaves without making contact with the lower portion of the tents, against which the occupants may be lying. Aluminium tent-pegs save many pounds' weight,

[1] Where equipment of merit has been supplied I have no hesitation in mentioning the firms concerned for the benefit of others.

but they must be long otherwise they will pull out of snow. At the inner end of the tent is a small square window covered in mosquito netting, with a large overlapping flap outside which can be raised or lowered from inside the tent. The entrance to the tent should be closed by flaps having a double overlap, to prevent the ingress of fine powdery snow, which when blown by the wind penetrates in considerable quantities through the most minute cracks. When it is necessary to travel through tropical valleys, an extra mosquito net should be taken which can be fitted over the entrance to the tent, as it is too hot to sleep with the ordinary flaps closed.

The floor of the tent should lap up at least 8 or 10 ins. at the entrance. Even with the aid of an extra flap sewn in, powdery snow was not entirely eliminated. At high altitudes, therefore, a circular entrance similar to those used for polar work would be better than an ordinary flap. The total weight of one tent was 23 lbs. Each member of the expedition had his own tent, but the tents were designed to accommodate two men, and as such were used above Camp Three on Kamet.

GROUND-SHEETS

I cannot recommend too strongly the spongy rubber ground-sheets which were first used by German expeditions in the Himalaya. They are light and can be rolled up. They render the climber immune from the sharpness of stones beneath his tent. They insulate him from the cold of the rocks or snow, and in the lower valleys from the dampness of the ground. It is only necessary that they should extend from the knee upwards.

MATTRESSES

Cork mattresses proved excellent.

SLEEPING-BAGS

These bags were specially made to my own design by Messrs. R. Burns, Manchester. They are wide enough for the climber to slip into without effort—an important point, both from the point of view of warmth and of effort, at great altitudes. They are long enough to overlap the length of the climber by at least 6 ins., and their weight is 8½ lbs. The complete sleeping-bag consists of three separate bags, the inner bag was lined with Jaeger wool fleece and stuffed with pure eiderdown. Next came a bag also of pure eiderdown but unlined with fleece. Over both bags was a bag of light jaconet weighing but a few ounces. The advantage of these bags lies both in their warmth (no member of the expedition experienced a cold night), due to layers and plenty of air space, which is warmer than one thick layer and a tight bag, and to the variation possible in that warmth. In the lower tropical valleys, the unlined eiderdown bag only was employed. In moderate temperatures, the inner bag lined with Jaeger fleece was sufficient. Higher still, the two eiderdown bags were employed, and when maximum warmth was required the jaconet bag was added. It is interesting to note that the outer jaconet covering cannot be used in conjunction with only one eiderdown bag, owing to condensation, but when both eiderdown bags are employed condensation is eliminated by the extra air space between the two eiderdown bags. Having used these bags both for the Kangchenjunga and Kamet expeditions, I am in a position to state that not even the coldest weather or most violent winds were able to chill me at night.

MESS TENT

A small mess tent adds much to the social amenities of an expedition.

PORTERS' TENTS

These should be of the same design as the Meade tent, only larger and capable of accommodating four to six men.

CLOTHING

Clothing both for tropical valleys and high altitudes is largely a matter of personal choice. I venture, however, to give a few notes on what I have found best. It is not yet generally realised how immense is the advantage that several layers of light clothing have over one heavy layer. Clothing should never be tight, as this retards circulation and does not allow of a layer of warm air round the body which is so essential to maintain warmth. The body should not be divided into two separate departments by a waist-belt, and even the pessimist who wears a belt as well as braces would do better to risk only braces at high altitudes. Thus, combinations are preferable to separate vests and pants, which grip the waist, and trousers to breeches, which retard the flow of warm air down the leg. On no account should clothing be tight under the armpits ; frost-bitten fingers may easily result from this. On Kamet I wore a total of four Shetland wool jumpers weighing 6 ozs. each, supplied by Messrs. Bill of Portland Street, London. Over these was a light windproof jacket, also weighing but a few ounces, with a hood that could be pulled over the head, which was supplied by Messrs. Felbermayer of Neuer Markt, Vienna. The sleeves of this jacket were fitted with an inner elastic sleeve to prevent cold and wind entering, but I question the advisability of this, as it tends to retard circulation. Trousers should be made of smooth, closely woven material, to which snow cannot adhere.

Many mountaineers are not believers in puttees, and there is no doubt that these retard circulation to a slight extent, especially if put on tightly, but the Kashmir puttees recommended by General Bruce are in a different category. These puttees are much longer than ordinary puttees, and are made of a rough material that has the knack of staying " put " and not slipping down, even when wound very loosely. These puttees are wonderfully warm, and the fact that I was not frostbitten on Kamet and was the only one to wear them speaks for itself.

Head-gear should consist of a woollen Balaclava helmet as a protection from cold, and a double wideawake wide-brimmed planter's hat, known as a " Terai," as a protection against the sun. In this connection it is interesting to note that it is easily possible to have sunstroke and frostbite at the same time in the Himalaya. The disadvantage of having to put a hat over a Balaclava helmet is such that I suggest a combination of the two which will eliminate the crown of the Balaclava helmet. If the lower part is then attached to the hat, the hat cannot be blown off. A warm and long woollen muffler one end of which is shaped into a helmet was an excellent item of equipment brought by Shipton.

BOOTS

Boots are of vital importance. On Kangchenjunga and the Jonsong Peaks in 1930 I was able to keep warm in ordinary climbing-boots with two pairs of socks. On Kamet, therefore, I allowed for three pairs of socks. Despite my entreaties, however, my bootmaker supplied boots only large enough for two pairs of thick socks. They would take three—at a pinch—but a pinch over 23,000 ft. means frostbite. The boots supplied to the porters were the same as those supplied to the porters on Everest, but for a snow-mountain such as Kamet they are not warm enough. The same applies to the ordinary Alpine boots, with which the Europeans were equipped. The ideal Himalayan boot, when designed, will probably be of felt in its uppers and an equally cold-resisting material for its sole. Nails should be used which penetrate as small a distance as possible into the sole and thus conduct the minimum of cold to the foot. Plenty of spare bootnails should be taken, and a last and a hammer with which to knock them in. A new nail should be put in when wet, as it then rusts firmly into the sole.

PORTERS' CLOTHING

A complete outfit of warm porters' clothing—under-clothing, Balaclava helmets, gloves, etc.—may be obtained from the Cawnpore Woollen Mills.

CRAMPONS

For most Himalayan work these are more dangerous than useful. At high altitudes their weight is tiring. The snow conditions met with are seldom favourable for their use. Worst of all, they conduct cold through the feet, and, even though they do not retard circulation, frostbite is likely to result from their use.

SKI

Holdsworth enjoyed some excellent ski-ing on certain sections of Kamet, and on the glaciers at the head of the Arwa Valley. The ideal ski have not yet been designed for Himalayan mountaineering. They must be light, require no skill to use and must not slip backwards or slide downhill. A ski-raquette is the obvious compromise.

RAQUETTE

A good raquette has yet to be designed for Himalayan mountaineering. Any appliance that is to be useful to an expedition must be easy to use and very light and portable, as otherwise the effort saved by it on places where it can be used is eliminated by the effort expended of carrying it up places where it cannot be used. Possibly a raquette in the form of a ski might be useful. Had I supplied sufficient pairs of raquettes for all the porters above Camp Four on Kamet, Shipton and I would have been spared a very arduous day making tracks for them. The thing to be remembered is that anything that saves labour must be common to all members of an expedition, otherwise that essential team spirit on which success in climbing the highest peaks in the world rests ceases to exist.

GOGGLES

The glass that best protects the eyes from the glare of the sun at high altitudes without destroying colour values is Crooke's, which eliminates the ultra-violet from the sun's rays and glare from the snow. Thanks to the courtesy of Messrs. Melson Wingate, we were equipped with goggles similar to those used on the Everest expeditions. These goggles were fitted into a special mask, designed to protect the upper part of the face and the nose from wind and sun-burn. These masks are, however, quite unnecessary for high-altitude mountaineering. They result in condensation, which clouds the goggles, and which cannot be prevented even by boring numerous holes in the eye-shield. Sunburn need not occur if a good glacier cream is used and applied properly. None of those who were assiduous in applying the glacier cream supplied by Messrs. Bjornstadt of Bern suffered from sunburn. By removing the Crooke's glasses from my goggles and placing them in an ordinary one-franc pair of Swiss goggle-frames, I had all the protection necessary for my eyes, and they were never affected.

GLOVES

The best gloves I have yet discovered for mountaineering are those made by Messrs. Schuster of Munich. They are leather, with separate thumbs and forefinger, the remaining fingers being together, and are lined with thick wool fleece. Woollen gloves long enough to overlap the sleeve of the jacket should also be taken.

VACUUM FLASKS

It is better to take a large number of ordinary breakable vacuum flasks rather than rely on extra strong or unbreakable ones. It is a pity, in these days of unsplinterable glass, that a vacuum flask cannot be designed that *is* unbreakable. Its value in Himalayan mountaineering would be great.

ROPE AND PITONS

The rope supplied by Messrs. J. & J. Jones of Liverpool proved excellent. About 75 per cent. rope and 25 per cent. of ordinary Alpine rope is a good proportion. Pitons for use on rock or ice should always be taken, for apart from their usefulness in climbing they may be useful in other directions, such as rigging a rope bridge across a torrent, or even for camping purposes, where ordinary tent-pegs cannot be inserted into rocky ground.

RUCKSACKS

As regard rucksacks, it is extraordinary how weighty many of these are, especially those sold on the Continent. Thick leather straps, heavy steel buckles, and ridiculously thick and heavy material are often to be seen, to say nothing of frame-work monstrosities weighing pounds. One rucksack of this nature carried up Kamet weighed, I believe, over 5lbs. Such a weight may easily turn victory into defeat when a man is drawing on his reserves of energy. Frame rucksacks are totally unnecessary in high-altitude mountaineering. They are, I believe, anywhere, but I may be prejudiced by never having worn them, or found any need to wear them. Recently, a well-known expert on climbing equipment for guideless mountaineering, Mr. W. T. Kirkpatrick, showed me a rucksack with which he had climbed in the Alps. It weighs but a few ounces. Its shoulder-straps are a pair of ordinary webbing braces. Its material is waterproof mackintosh, and, best of all, it has as a substitute for a steel frame two or three loofahs which keep the rucksack well clear of the back, and thus provide the same ventilation as does the metal frame at a minute fraction of the weight. Such a rucksack is not intended to carry huge loads, but should be kept for the final assault. As a medium-weight rucksack I can recommend those supplied by Messrs. R. Burns. They weigh but 1lb., and will carry 50lbs.

COOKING EQUIPMENT

The importance of a mincing machine has already been mentioned. Where it is intended to use a Primus stove over 20,000 ft. a 50 per cent. mixture of petrol and paraffin should be used, for paraffin alone may not vaporise. Meta solid fuel is excellent where a Primus stove cannot be employed. It is a false economy to use little at a time, for the heat lost is then almost as great as the heat gained. Aluminium utensils should be used where possible, for a very careful eye must be kept on the cook to see that he cleans these or trouble may result. The same applies to the mincing machine, which should be kept scrupulously clean. A pressure boiler was used on the Kangchenjunga expedition with great success. Where plenty of fuel is obtainable it is unnecessary, but expeditions venturing into districts, such as Tibet, where fuel must be economised, should take one.

INSTRUMENTS

Even if an expedition has not avowed scientific objects, it should be equipped with boiling-point thermometers, maximum and minimum thermometers, a hygrometer and aneroid barometers. At least one prismatic compass should be taken. A X8 prism monocular is lighter and almost as efficient as an ordinary pair of binoculars.

MEDICAL

There are one or two points worthy of mention. In marching along tropical valleys, never allow the body to become chilled. Change sweat-soaked clothing immediately on arriving at camp. Carry the change of clothing in the rucksack, and thus there is no delay while it is being unpacked or waiting for it to arrive on the back of a laggard porter. I have always found silk bush shirts admirable. When I get soaked with perspiration, I merely hang the wet shirt on the back of my rucksack and change into the other one. It takes but a few minutes to dry. Each member of the expedition should carry with him his own private store of medicine, most important in which are laxatives. The best laxatives are not irritant vegetable preparations, but salts. Not more than twenty-four hours should ever be allowed to elapse without a dose. Much of the internal troubles experienced by those unused to tropical latitudes who pay a first visit to the Himalaya is due to ignorance. How is anyone fresh from England to know, for instance, that it is exceedingly dangerous to eat over-ripe fruit, or the skin of fruit, in the tropics? Never sit in the shade of a tree during the heat of the day without adequate head protection, for it is possible to get sunstroke by so doing, while even a minute or two unprotected in the sun may mean sunstroke. There are some who sneer at such precautions; they are thick-headed in more senses than one.

APPENDIX VII

PHOTOGRAPHY AND CINEMATOGRAPHY

THESE notes, based on two Himalayan expeditions, are intended to give some idea of the special difficulties of photography and cinematography in the Himalaya.

Before leaving for the Himalaya I was especially warned as to the peculiar lighting conditions. In the Himalayan valleys sunlight appears brilliant, and the photographer is tempted to "stop down" his lens to a small aperture. Assuming that an ordinary orthochromatic plate or film is being used, this temptation must be resisted. Owing to the presence of water vapour in the air in addition to the cutting down of the light by towering valley sides, exposures in the lower Himalayan valleys must be much longer than appears necessary. A good average, using ordinary Kodak film, is an exposure of 1/25 second at F.8, or, in more open situations, F.11. The higher the climber proceeds, the quicker is the exposure required, until at 20,000 ft. at mid-day he will find it difficult to under-expose. Many of my best exposed photographs on Kamet were made at 1/50 second at F.22, and I often "stopped down" as low as F.32, using the same exposure. Above 10,000 ft. it is safer never to use a shutter speed of less than 1/50 second owing to rapid breathing and consequent shaking of the camera.

The roll films and film packs used on Kamet were Kodak, and, while excellent results were obtained under all conditions, no signs of deterioration were observed, although the films were sent back to England undeveloped and had to pass through India during the height of the monsoon and the heat of the Red Sea. Used in conjunction with yellow filters of moderate density (i.e. K1 and K2), results almost equal to panchromatic were obtained on this film.

The plates employed were Ilford panchromatic, and some very fine results were obtained. In some cases however, spotting occurred, for which again climate must be blamed. Panchromatic plates are difficult to change during an expedition owing to their extreme sensitiveness, and I would recommend other explorers and mountaineers to use plates of a lower speed than 600 H. and D., and preferably not panchromatic, as by the judicious use of filters the difference in results obtained between panchromatic and orthochromatic is negligible.

Owing to the courtesy of Mr. Olaf Bloch, of Messrs. Ilford Ltd., I was supplied with a set of red filters for use with my cameras and cinematograph cameras. Of these I cannot speak too highly. Used in conjunction with panchromatic plates and panchromatic cine-film, the results obtained were singularly beautiful. By slightly emphasising blues they brought out to the full the delicate texture of the snow even in the fierce glare of mid-day at great altitudes, and the cloud effects produced were equally beautiful. At the same time rocks, snow and human figures were not rendered blank white and jet black, as is the case of 90 per cent. of snow photographs, but were in proper tone relationship to one another. These filters supply an essential need in mountain photography, and no photographer anxious to get effective photographs should be without them.

As regards cinematograph film, only Kodak panchromatic film was employed, and 15,000 ft. of this was taken. Like other photographic materials, it had to pass through temperatures varying between 115° F. and −20° F., yet it exhibited no sign of deterioration, and "shots" taken and developed recently, a year after purchase, showed it to be in perfect condition. Its advantages over ordinary orthochromatic film are too obvious to need mentioning, and, used in conjunction with Mr. Bloch's filters, the results obtained, especially of snow scenes, were as perfect as could be desired. This film was packed in air-tight tins.

The cameras used included a Leitz Leica, which was generously presented by the makers to Captain Birnie. This little camera takes pictures on full-size cinema film, but pictures that occupy two frames of film. Owing to the fine grain of cinema film, enlargements up to a considerable size can be made from the negatives without loss of definition. Also the telephoto lens is of fixed focus and easily attachable. But the most valuable point about this camera lies in its ability to take as many as thirty-six photographs on one spool of film. Those who have had to change a film pack, much less a spool of film, in a freezing wind, even on an Alpine peak, will appreciate the value of this, whilst the Leica's lightness and pocket portability are other valuable points in its favour. Unfortunately, this camera came to a watery end in a torrent when descending from the Base Camp on Kamet.

My own cameras were two "Etui" cameras, 6 × 9 cms. and 9 × 12 cms. in size, supplied by Messrs. Sands Hunter Ltd. The advantage of these lies in their compactness and consequent portability and lightness, for they are very thin and are easily slipped into the pocket. The results obtained with film packs were excellent. Good telephoto results were also obtained by using an "Adon" long-focus lens, but I strongly recommend the use of a fixed focus telephoto lens and special outside view-finder, as the time necessary to fix and focus the camera made telephoto work seldom possible. In spite of their capacity for folding into such a small space, these cameras are very rigid, and will stand up to hard wear and knocking about.

Two cinema cameras were taken, a Bell Howell full-size "Eyemo" camera, taking 100 ft. reels of film, supplied by the Autotype Co. Ltd., and a de Vry camera also taking 100 ft. reels.

The most important work was done with the "Eyemo" outfit, which included a spare lens on mount and a fixed focus 6 in. telephoto lens. Excellent results were obtained, and there was a complete absence of static electrical effects which are liable to affect cinema films at great altitudes. Like most if not all film cameras, this camera was sensitive to cold and after a hard frost would refuse to work until warmed, although specially thin oil was used. Warming it sometimes involved my taking it into my sleeping-bag and tenderly nursing it.

One disadvantage of this camera was the strength required to wind up its clockwork mechanism, and the key supplied is certainly not a satisfactory one for high altitudes where strength must be conserved.

This camera accomplished excellent work on Kamet, and the results obtained were fully equal to those of a more elaborate apparatus. Unfortunately, however, it broke after the descent of Kamet, a cam in the shutter mechanism sheering so badly that no repair or replacement was possible. Thenceforward, the de Vry camera was used, and though this only ran at sixteen frames per second as against twenty-four frames a second of the "Eyemo," which is the best speed for subsequent synchronisation of a film, it worked perfectly for the remainder of the expedition.

It is interesting to note that the "Eyemo" camera accompanied the expedition to the summit of Kamet, where the highest "shots" ever taken on the earth's surface were made. A light "Thalhammer" tripod accompanied the "Eyemo," and this was also taken to the top of Kamet, as it weighed only a few pounds. Its horizontal and vertical tilting movements made it indispensable for panoramic "shots."

Obviously, it would have been impossible to have taken a heavier outfit to the summit of Kamet, but it was a mistake not to have taken a camera capable of "shooting" more than 100 ft. at a time, not only because less changing would have been necessary, but because of edge fogging, which is liable to become a serious disadvantage when using 100 ft. reels, although this was minimised to a large extent by shielding the camera from the brightest light by a dark cloth.

So much for the technicalities of Himalayan photography and cinematography. The physical difficulties are considerable. Cinematography at least is a "whole-time" job, and the difficulties of manipulating a camera at high altitudes are great. I do not remember taking some of the photographs and cinema "shots" on the upper part of Kamet, so dulled was my brain by altitude. The explorer who would take a record of his work should remember that unless he has something really thrilling to offer the film magnates and the public his film will not prove acceptable; he must concentrate on "human interest." He must remember that his photographs of toil and difficulty on the "Roof of the World," which meant so much to him, count for nothing when the "accidents," "blizzards" and "avalanches" can be faked in the studio by the judicious use of "sets," salt, and aeroplane propellers. His miserable efforts at the authentic, his pictures of scenery, count for naught against the sensational products of Elstree and Hollywood. The public has been so soaked in sensational make-believe that the unvarnished truth is no longer anything but boring. Truth has been prostituted on the altars of "art." The cinema audience of to-day would hardly be content to see the conquest of Everest without the introduction of a fatality. The cleverness of the faker has encompassed the death of truth, and those who sit breathing the disinfected air of a cinema are incapable of realising the effort of the cinematographer who fumbles with frozen fingers at his apparatus on the snows of the Poles or the Himalaya; they will turn with relief from the sobriety of truth and enterprise to the insobriety of the cabaret and the murderous antics of the gunman. Truth is dead, and those explorers who contemplate an unfaked film record of their expeditions will do well to mark the fact.

INDEX

Aas, Monrad, 2
Abruzzi, Duke of the, 2
Acclimatisation, definition of, 338
Achung, cook, 44, 58, 82, 94, 98, 124, 261, 262, 292, 311
Alaknanda River, 259
  crossing of, 308
Alaknanda Valley, 262, 308
  flora in, 366
Alam Singh, porter, 90, 105, 111, 120, 228, 233, 245, 266, 273
Alpine mountaineering compared with Himalayan, 6
  plants in Himalaya, 281, 350 *et seq.*
  snow, 301
Alps, conquest of, 1
Altitude deterioration, 333, 341
Altitudes, acclimatisation in, 338
  blunting of senses in, 336
  breathlessness at high, 334
  dreams in high, 134, 175
  diminution of body acidity in, 180
  evil effects of, 333
  frostbite in, 338
  lassitude in, 129, 130, 131, 144, 335
  mental effects of, 336, 343
  sleeping attire for high, 193
Ang Nerbu, 147, 284
Arun Valley, 381
Arwa Valley, 271
  camping in, 275
  flora in, 363, 365
  prospecting in, 281
Avalanche Peak, 285, 291
  glissading on, 298
  members who climbed, 378
Avalanches, dangers from, 301
Badrinath, Expedition reaches, 263
  flora at, 365
  pass between Kedarnath and, 317
  people, poverty of, 321
    request for a cart road, 322
  pilgrim route to, 258, 319, 363
  pilgrimage to, 26, 326
  sacred bathing-pool in, 327
  temple at, 325
Badrinath, Rawal of, 90, 265
  invites members of Expedition to lunch, 325
  letters from, 267, 319
Badrinath Range, altitude deterioration on, 341
Bagini Pass, 91
Baijnath, arrival at, 53
Baltoro Glacier, 4
Bampa post-office, 95
Banke Glacier, 242, 244, 246, 247
Barcroft's expedition, 341, 342
Base Camp, food for, 390
  flora found near, 357
  is pitched, 114
  journey to, 105, 228
  return to, 357
Beauman, Wing-Commander E. B., 78, 79, 240, 249, 250, 277, 315
  acclimatisation of, 180
  arrival at Camp Two, 135
  arrival at Ranikhet, 48
  ascends Glacier 5, 284
  at Camp Five, 213
  climbing experience of, 34
  incident with yaks, 109
  returns to Mana, 315

Beauman, Wing-Comdr.—*contd.*
superintends transport of Lewa, 225
Benham, Miss Gertrude, 97, 234
Beynon, General Sir William, 45
Bhagat Kharak Glacier, 22, 29, 268, 271, 307, 314
Bharhal shooting, 97, 100
Bhotia people, 88, 111, 239, 252
porters, 105
Bhyundar Kanta Pass, 14, 22, 237
flora on, 359
journey over, 247
Bhyundar Valley, flora in, 250, 252, 358, 362
Birnie, Captain E. St. J., 32, 63, 84, 98, 107, 169, 241, 249, 250
account of last stage of climb, 217
arrives at Camp Two, 135
arrives at Camp Three, 149
arrives at Ranikhet, 48
as transport officer, 34
ascends Glacier 5, 284
descent to Base Camp, 226
frostbitten toes, 219
goes shooting, 80
lectures in Badrinath, 324
mauled by a tiger, 56
on Avalanche Peak, 298
on final stage of climb, 215
on Glacier 6, 289
on Glaciers 9, 10 and 11, 316
prospects for Camp Four, 151, 154
reaches summit of Kamet, 218
returns to Mana, 317
superintends stores, 45, 270
visits col between Glaciers 4 and 10, 296
Blanc, Justin, 20
Blanc, Pierre, 20, 22
Boots for mountaineering, 400
Bradford, Captain, 45, 52
Bread, campaigning substitutes for, 388
Breathlessness at high altitudes, 334
Bridge building, 232, 264
Brocherel, Alexis, 20
Brown, Mrs., 45
Bruce, General C. G., 2, 13, 95, 98
Buddhist religion, tenets of, 47
Budhibal Gurung, Lance-Corporal, 52, 62, 63, 81, 84, 180, 245, 266
leaves Base Camp, 120
pluck of, 186
returns to Camp One, 131
self-imposed penance, 224
shooting bharhal, 103, 110, 234
superintends Lewa's removal to lower camps, 212
Burns' rucksacks, 404
sleeping-bags, 397

Cameras for mountaineering, 408
Camp Five evacuated, 220
journey from, to summit, 195
journey to, 182
pitched, 187
Camp Four, choosing site for, 150
cold at, 174
evacuated, 221
is pitched, 173
journey to, 162
return to, 221
site found for, 160
Camp One is pitched, 124
journey to, 120
Camp Three, breathing conditions at, 335
is evacuated, 223, 226
is pitched, 145
journey to, 139
return to, 222
site chosen for, 141
Camp Two is pitched, 131
journey to, 127
moved higher up, 135
return to, 224
Campbell, J. Argyll, 335, 342, 343
Camps, distribution of personnel at, 379
Carr, Lieutenant, 66
Chettan, "Satan," death of, 77, 129

Cheyne Stokes breathing, 175, 334
Cinematography in the Himalaya, 407
Clarke, Captain J., 44, 237
Clothing for mountaineering, 398
  changes of, 405
Conway, Lord, 2
Cooking equipment, 404
  need for good, 390
Cowan, Dr. John, 343
Crampons for mountaineering, 400
Crooke's glass for goggles, 402

Darjeeling porters, 44, 96
Debal, arrival in, 60
  War Memorial, 62
de Crespigny, Colonel H. Ch., 15
Dhaoli River, 232, 235
Dhaoli Valley, 36, 89, 95, 96, 237, 238
Dorje, porter, 213, 288, 289, 290, 302
  keenness of, 162
  on Avalanche Peak, 298
Dotial porters, 48, 53, 72, 82, 105
Dunagiri Peak, 91, 104
Dutt, Pandit Nerian, 329, 330

East Kamet Glacier, 13, 14, 121, 207, 224
Eastern Ibi Gamin, 11, 12, 139, 183, 184, 216
Edelweiss, 281, 365, 368
Edgington tents, 395
Egg-wallah, 304, 305
  accident to, 309
Eri Udiar, camp at, 244
"Etui" camera, 408
Everest, weather on, 381
"Eyemo" camera, 409, 410

Food question in mountaineering, 37, 38, 343, 387
  taken on Expedition, 392
Forests, tropical, 55, 76
Freshfield, E. W., 2
Frostbite at high altitudes, 225, 338

Gamsali, porters from, 238, 273
  return to, 238
Ganges, Hindu reverence for, 26
  sources of the, 307, 317
Gangotri Glacier, 22, 28, 29, 30, 287
Garhwal, population of, 11
  scenery of, 10
  season for climbing in, 35
  weather in, 381
Garhwali natives, 65, 66
Gastern Thal, 95
Gauri Parbat, 252, 253
Gian Singh, porter, 316
Glacier cream, 402
  lassitude, 129, 130, 131, 144, 335
Glacier 4, 296
Glacier 5, 282, 284
Glacier 6, 282, 288, 290, 305
Glacier 8, 283
Glacier 10, 296
Glacier 11, 288
Gloves for mountaineering, 402
Goggles for mountaineering, 401
Gohna Fakir, 75
Gosain pilgrims, 326
Goting, camp at, 234
Gourlay, G. B., 45
Graham, W. W., 2
Greene, Dr. C. R., 64, 70, 71, 88, 89, 234, 235, 284, 292
  arrives at Camp Two, 131
  arrives at Ranikhet, 48
  ascends the Alaknanda Valley, 307
  at Camp One, 124
  crossing the Alaknanda River, 308
  descent to Base Camp, 226
  experimental treatment for altitude deterioration, 180, 340
  extracts Smythe's tooth, 245
  first view of Kamet, 73
  frostbitten fingers, 219
  has fever, 106
  joins the Expedition, 34
  kept busy at Debal, 60
  leaves Base Camp, 120

Greene, Dr. C. R.—*contd.*
leaves Camp One, 127
Camp Two, 140
makes blood-pressure tests, 68
march to Base Camp, 337
on East Kamet Glacier, 337
on final stage of climb, 215
on medical aspects of high climbing, 333
pitches Camp Three, 145
prospects for Camp Four, 151, 154
reaches summit of Kamet, 218
visits source of Alaknanda River, 313
Ground-sheets for mountaineering, 396
Gurla Mandhata, 191, 196, 206, 302
Gwaldam dak bungalow, 57, 58

Haidar, Mirza, 340
Hailey, Lady, 45
Hailey, Sir Malcolm, 45, 73
Hanuman Chatti, 237, 256, 261
Harris, P. Wynn, 35
Himalaya, alpine plants in, 350
danger of sunstroke in, 106
dangers in, 5
forbidden territory in, 3
last night in, 328
last view of, 331
plants in Eastern, 349, 367
political difficulties of exploring, 3
weather in Eastern, 382
Himalayan avalanches, 125
boots, 400
climate, 2
expeditions, size of, 32
exploration, 2
ice, 5
moraines, 114
mountaineering, compared with Alpine, 6
enjoyment in, 283
equipment for, 395
food question in, 37, 386
good cooking essential in, 389
Himalayan—*contd.*
mounteering, luck in, 31, 178
medical equipment for, 344
mincing machine essential in, 98
porterage in, 36
team work in, 31
use of ski in, 127
mythology of snows, 28
oaks, 350
peaks, deceptive angles of slopes, 148, 151
photography, difficulties of, 406
racial characteristics, 3
snow, 301
tea, 325
valleys, insect pests in, 329
weather, 6, 381
Hingston, Major, 345
Holdsworth, R. L., 84, 98, 104, 141, 142, 158, 256, 284, 288
ascends Glacier 5, 284
at Camp One, 124
at Camp Two, 131
at Camp Three, 145
at Camp Four, 173
at Camp Five, 187
at Ranikhet, 48
attempt on peak above Banke Glacier, 245
crossing Bhyundar Kanta Pass, 359
descends from Camp Five on ski, 221
first view of Kamet, 73
frostbitten toes, 211
goes shooting, 80
goes to Meade's Col, 216
is indisposed, 162
joins the Expedition, 34, 35
leaves Base Camp, 120
Camp One, 127
Camp Two, 140
on final stage of climb, 195
on Glacier 11, 288
on the flora of Kamet and Badrinath, 348
prospects for Camp Four, 151, 154

Holdsworth, R. L.—*contd.*
reaches summit of Kamet, 205
returns to Camp Five, 210
ski-ing, 138, 216, 401
smoking at 25,447 ft., 206
Hooker, Sir Joseph, 2
Hukam Singh, Assistant Commissioner, 67, 79, 105

Ilford photographic plates, 407
India, power of religion in, 260
Indian Posts and Telegraphs, 259

Jonsong Peak, 171
Joshimath hospital, 330
Juma, 89, 90

K2 Peak, height of, 4
Kailas, 191, 240
Kamet, attempt on, in 1920, 23
climate of, 9
eastern precipice of, 167
expeditions to, 26, 27
flora on, compared with Kashmir, 350
ice on, 164
members of Expedition who climbed, 378, 379
names for, 9
plans for final stage of, 189
situation of, 9, 11
snow at summit of, 195, 197
summit reached by first party, 205 ; by second party, 218
survey of, 12, 13
view from summit of, 206
weather on, 381
winds on, 382
Kamet Expedition of 1931, address of congratulation from Rawal of Badrinath, 319
altitude deterioration of, slight, 341
at Badrinath, 263, 319
at Baijnath, 53
at Debal, 60
at Gamsali, 238
at Goting, 234
at Gwaldam, 57

Kamet Expedition of 1931—*contd.*
at Joshimath, 330
at Khaliaghat, 79
at Malari, 92
at Mana, 266
at Niti, 97
at Ranikhet, 44
at Surai Thota, 87
at Thur Udiar, 243
Base Camp reached, 114
evacuated, 231
begin the descent, 220
Camp One pitched, 124
Camp Two pitched, 131
moved higher up, 135
Camp Three pitched, 145
evacuated, 223, 226
Camp Four pitched, 173, 179
evacuated, 221
Camp Five pitched, 187
evacuated, 221
crossing East Kamet Glacier, 127
danger from falling rocks, 88, 89
final stage of climb, 188
first mail arrives, 85
first party reach summit of Kamet, 205
first view of Kamet, 73
flowers met with, 250, 255, 348
food difficulties of, 93
food taken, 392
grow beards, 68
in the Arwa Valley, 275
in the Nandakna Valley, 70
journey over the Bhyundar Kanta Pass, 247
last night in the Himalaya, 328
leave Mana, 273
lunch with Rawal of Badrinath, 325
mail arrives at Camp Five, 212
march to Base Camp, 107
to Wan, 64
mascot of, 81, 88
members of, 34
objects of, 9
on the Khanta Khal Pass, 254
on the Kuari Pass, 82

Kamet Expedition of 1931—*contd.*
on the watershed of Alaknanda and Gangotri rivers, 288
peaks climbed by, 378
plans for camps, 117, 180
plants collected on, 369
porters of, 105
preparations for, 35, 45
prospecting for Camp Four, 149, 151
rapid acclimatisation of, 170
reach the summit of Kamet, 205, 218
return to Base Camp, 229
to Camp Two, 224
to Camp Three, 222
to Camp Four, 221
to Mana, 306
to Ranikhet, 331
second journey to Camp Three, 144
second party reach summit of Kamet, 218
site found for Camp Three, 143
start out from Ranikhet, 50
summary of, 373
Kangchenjunga, height of, 4
lessons learnt from, 178
weather on, 381
winds on, 382
Kanphata Yogis, 327
Karbir, 87
Kedarnath, 260
pass between Badrinath and, 317
pilgrimages to, 26
Kedarnath Valley system, 315
Kellas, Dr. A. M., 2, 23, 124, 165
Kesar Singh, porter, 112, 212
reaches summit of Kamet, 48
volunteers to climb summit, 214
Khaiam Glacier, 14, 15, 20
Khaliaghat camp, 79
Khanta Khal Pass, 14, 254, 358
flora on, 362
Kingdon Ward, Captain, 351, 367
Kirkpatrick, W. T., 403
"Kodak" films, 406
Kuari Pass, 82, 352, 354, 355

Lassitude in high altitudes, 129, 130, 131, 144, 335
Laxatives, 405
Lewa, sirdar, 44, 53, 63, 72, 109, 180, 181
as climber, 197
at Camp Four, 173
attitude towards porters, 105
character of, 90
depression of, 235
double work of, 131, 186
ill with frostbitten feet, 210, 212, 225, 266
in hospital, 330, 338
indisposed on summit, 208
leaves Base Camp, 120
on final stage of climb, 195
porters' opinion of, 214
reaches Camp Five, 187
reaches summit of Kamet, 205
returns to Camp One, 131
to Camp Five, 210
Lochmatter, Franz, 20
Lohajang camp, 62
flowers at, 351
Longstaff, Dr. T. G., 2, 13, 14, 22, 36, 87, 237, 242, 256, 302, 345

Mackinder, Sir Halford, 35
Maithana Mountain, landslip on, 73
Malari, 91, 92, 93, 95
Mana Pass, 272
Mana Peak, 14, 122, 191, 238, 247
Mana Valley, flora in, 358
Mana Village, 266
Mattresses for mountaineering, 397
Meade, C. F., 2, 318
attempt on Kamet, 20, 22
exploration in Garhwal Range, 29, 271
Meade's Col, 23, 24, 186, 196
Medical equipment for mountaineering, 344

Medical—*contd.*
hints for mountaineering, 405
supplies taken and used, 346
survey of the Expedition, 333
Morshead, Lieutenant-Colonel H. T., attempt on Kamet, 23
death of, 137
Mountain sickness, 333, 334, 335
among porters, 170
Mountaineering, alcoholic stimulants in, 391
best age for, 33
boots for, 400
breathing exercises as training for, 305
clothing for, 399
dangers of too quick descent, 207
diet, vitamins in, 38, 343, 388
gloves for, 402
goggles for, 401
ground sheets for, 396
head-gear for, 106, 399
instruments for, 404
loss of weight in, 335
mattresses for, 397
medical aspects of, 333
hints for, 405
need for sugar in, 240, 391
pitons for, 403
raquettes for, 401
rhythm in, 147, 195
ropes for, 403
rucksacks for, 403
sleeping-bags for, 397
tents for, 395
track-making in, 294
vacuum flasks for, 403
Mumm, A. L., 13, 238, 247

Naini Thal, 349
Nanda Devi, 4, 191, 192
Nanda Kot, 46
Nandakna Valley, 70
Nanga Parbat, 2, 7
Natar Singh, porter, 111, 233, 251, 273
Nilkanta Peak, 68, 83, 311, 312
Nima, porter, 147, 229, 246, 270
on Avalanche Peak, 291, 293, 300, 301
Nima Dorje, porter, 65, 77, 91, 146, 147, 151, 153, 181, 190, 197, 230, 270, 281
as cook, 124, 311
at Camp Four, 173, 174
at Camp Five, 187
on final stage of climb, 195, 201
returns to Camp Five, 212
Nima Tendrup, porter, 44, 47, 59, 112, 125, 147, 224, 236, 271
crossing the Alaknanda River, 308, 311, 313
indisposed, 162
superintends transport from Camp Three, 226
Niti, camping at, 97
return to, 234
Niti Valley, flora in, 356

Odell, N. E., 340
Ondi, porter, 96, 147, 290
turns cook, 124
Oxygen, lack of, 334
value of, 39

Panchromatic plates, 407
Pandukeswar, 329
Passang, porter, 313
character of, 132
crossing the glacier torrent, 284
Perrin, Jean, 20
Photography in the Himalaya, 406
Pigott, Mr., 277
Pilgrim route to Badrinath, 319, 363
Pillar Rock, 157
Pitons for mountaineering, 403
Pocock, I. S., 13
Pomo, porter, 112, 117
Porters, availability of, 37
Bhotia, 44, 105
clothing for, 400
disputes among, 136, 236
Dotial, 48, 53, 72, 82, 105

Porters—*contd.*
feeding of, 37, 45
Gamsali, 238, 273
Garhwali, 53
mountain sickness among, 170
on the Bhyundar Kanta Pass, 251
peace offerings of, 290
religious differences among, 136
Sherpa, 44
superstition of, 214
tents for, 398
Puttees for mountaineering, 399

Raikana Glacier, 22, 114, 115, 121
Raikana Valley, flora in, 357
Ram Singh, Assistant Commissioner, 67
Ramni camp, 72
Randhoj Kan, Lance-Corporal, 52, 62, 224, 245, 266
Ranikhet, arrival at, 44
climate of, 45
flowers at, 350
return to, 331
" Ranikhetitis," 387
Raquettes for mountaineering, 401
Rataban Peak, 247
Robinson, Heath, 264
Ropes for mountaineering, 403
Rubenson, Mr., 2
Rucksacks, 403
Ruttledge, Hugh, 36
Ryall, E. C., 12

Sanyasis pilgrims, 326
Sarsuti River, 273, 317
Sarsuti Valley, 271, 274
Satopanth Glacier, 22, 29, 271, 314, 315
Sattu as food, 94
Schlagintweit Brothers, 2, 9, 12
Scientific instruments for mountaineering, 404
Shackleton Expedition, 342
Shipton, E. E., 67, 88, 142, 158, 164, 240, 254, 288
as climber, 197
at Camp One, 124
at Camp Two, 131
at Camp Three, 145
at Camp Four, 173
at Camp Five, 187
at Ranikhet, 45
attempt on peak above Banke Glacier, 245
climbing experience of, 35
glissading on Avalanche Peak, 299
frostbitten toes, 211
in charge of commissariat, 92, 392
indisposed, 71
leaves Base Camp, 120
Camp One, 127
Camp Two, 140
on Avalanche Peak, 291
on final stage of climb, 195
physical fitness of, 171
prospecting for Camp Four, 147, 151, 154
in Arwa Valley, 281
reaches summit of Kamet, 205
returns to Camp Five, 210
to Mana, 317
sets out for Camp Five, 182
step-cutting, 165
superintends transport of Lewa, 225
Ski for Himalaya, 401
Sleeping-bags for Himalaya, 397
Slingsby, Captain A. Morris, attempt on Kamet, 15
Slingsby's Col, 17, 20, 21
Smyth, Colonel Edmund, 237
Smythe, F. S., 357, 358
ascends the Alaknanda Valley, 307
at Camp One, 124
at Camp Two, 131
at Camp Three, 145
at Camp Four, 173
at Camp Five, 187
at Ranikhet, 45

Smythe, F. S.—*contd.*
breaks a rib, 302
caught in an avalanche, 299
crossing the Alaknanda River, 308
descent to Base Camp, 226
films the party at summit of Kamet, 205
glissading on Avalanche Peak, 298
has a tooth extracted, 244
high altitude dreams of, 134, 175
immunity from frostbite, 211, 399
incident with yaks, 109
last night in the Himalaya, 328
last view of the Himalaya, 331
leaves Base Camp, 120
Camp One, 127
Camp Two, 140
makes speech at Badrinath, 325
on Avalanche Peak, 291
on final stage of climb, 195
on receiving mail, 85
physical fitness of, 171
prospecting for Camp Four, 147, 151, 154
in Arwa Valley, 281
reaches summit of Kamet, 205
return to Camp Five, 210
sets out for Camp Five, 182
shooting bharhal, 100
step-cutting, 164, 203
suffers from shortage of oxygen, 304
visits source of the Alaknanda, 313
Somervell, T. Howard, paintings of, 113
Stiffe, N. C., 36, 45
Strachey, Richard, 12
Sunburn, cream to prevent, 402
Surai Thota, camping at, 87

Tapoban, 86
Tents for mountaineering, 395, 398
Thur Udiar, 243
Tibetan music, 77
valleys, 110
Tiger shooting, 55
Tikia, porter, 57
Tobin, Colonel H. W., 44
Trisul, 54
ascent of, 15
flora of, 352

Vacuum flasks for mountaineering, 402
Valley of Flowers, 250, 252, 362
Vitamins, need for, in mountaineering diet, 38, 343, 388

Wan, camping at, 66
Wordie, J. M., 342
Workman, Dr. and Mrs. Bullock, 2
Wright-Smith, Professor, 353

Yaks, 107, 232, 233
Yogi pilgrims, 326
Younghusband, Sir Francis, 2

Zaskar Range, 381

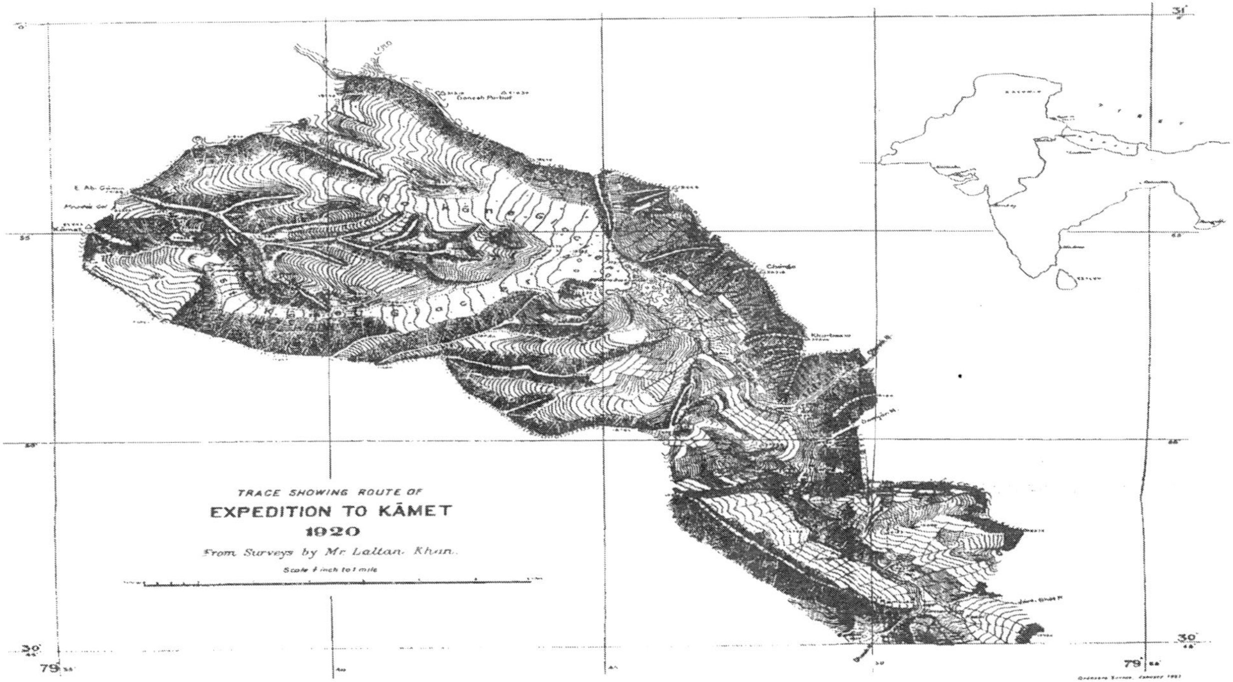

Reproduced by courtesy of the Royal Engineers' Journal and the Director-General of the Ordnance Survey.